PC Data Recovery
and Disaster Prevention

S Harris
S Nugus

NCC Blackwell

MANCHESTER · OXFORD

British Library Cataloguing in Publication Data

Harris, S. (Steve), *1966 –*
  PC Data Recovery and Disaster Prevention
  I. Title   II. Nugus, Sue
  658.478

ISBN 1-85554-162-9

First published in 1992 by:

NCC Blackwell Limited, 108 Cowley Road, Oxford OX4 1JF, England

Editorial Office, The National Computing Centre Limited, Oxford Road, Manchester M1 7ED, England.

NCC Blackwell Limited, 108 Cowley Road, Oxford OX4 1JF, England.

Typeset in 10pt Palatino by TechTrans Ltd, Kidmore End, Reading, RG4 9AY; and printed and bound in Gt. Britain by The Alden Press, Oxford

ISBN 1-85554-162-9

Contents

4

Introduction

WHY IS PC DATA RECOVERY AND DISASTER PREVENTION A MAJOR ISSUE?

Over the last ten years, personal computers have become a part of everyday life in the majority of organisations. They are encountered in many departments, from the shop floor to the managing director's office, and are used for a vast array of different tasks. The failure of a personal computer can cause a great deal of trouble, especially if the failure involved the loss of valuable data. However, despite this, few computer users make an effort to safeguard against such problems by making regular backups of their data. Therefore if disaster does strike, it is necessary to attempt to retrieve data from the damaged machine as quickly and efficiently as possible.

WHAT IS A DISASTER?

The definition of a disaster can vary greatly. According to the Oxford English Dictionary, a disaster is defined as:

Anything ruinous or distressing that befalls; a sudden or great misfortune, or mishap; a calamity.

When considering computer disasters this definition is somewhat vague. A slightly more concise definition could be:

Disaster; an unforeseen event resulting in loss of data or loss of system functionality for which no preventative action has been taken.

There are several key points within this definition.

- A disaster is an unforeseen event, implying that there is no prior warning of impending problems. If such warnings do occur, then it is pure foolishness to ignore them.

- A disaster results in loss of data or loss of system functionality. In either case it is necessary to remedy the problem in order to continue working normally.

- A disaster only occurs if no preventative action has been taken. For example, if a hard disk crashes with subsequent loss of data, then it is not a disaster if a backup is available. Similarly, if a PC that is used for mission-critical work is destroyed by fire, then it is not a disaster if steps have been taken to ensure that another PC can be used to continue the essential operations.

From this definition it can be seen that many of the potential problems can be prevented

7

altogether by taking a few common-sense steps. These include the process of taking regular backups, ensuring that warnings of future problems are heeded and acted upon, and also the creation of a comprehensive disaster recovery plan.

However, it is inevitable that problems will occur, and it is true to say that most computer disasters involve the loss of valuable data. This must be recovered quickly and efficiently, a task that can in some situations prove very difficult and time-consuming.

DATA RECOVERY

Until recently, data recovery operations were thought to be beyond the scope of all but highly skilled professionals. Fortunately, recent software developments have provided the tools and programs that are needed for such situations, and have made them usable by almost anyone who has a rudimentary knowledge of the personal computer. Even so, the issue of data recovery is a technological minefield, in which one false step could cause irrepairable damage to the data being recovered.

It is therefore essential that a good basic knowledge is attained by anyone who is likely to be involved with any form of data recovery. This book provides that basic knowledge, and additionally demonstrates through the use of examples and case studies how such data recovery problems should be approached if a successful solution is to be found.

SECURITY

Another subject that is becoming more and more important in the PC environment is personal computer security. As organisations become increasingly dependent upon their computer systems, the problem of unauthorised access to data becomes a serious one, especially if the accessing involves destroying or changing the data. To counter this threat, many companies are producing electronic security systems for the personal computer, some of which are excellent at protecting the system, whilst others offer little or no security at all.

The main issues surrounding the subject of personal computer security are discussed in detail in the latter section of the book, including an in depth examination of the features that should be present in any good PC security system.

TYPOGRAPHIC CONVENTIONS

Many of the examples shown in this book involve the execution of commands etc. To differentiate such commands from descriptive text they have been shown in **Bold** type. Many of the commands have optional parameters that may be specified, and these are shown enclosed in square brackets. For example,

CHKDSK [d:] [/F]

This implies that the command CHKDSK can be run with two optional parameters, the first of which is the drive identifier, and the second is the /F switch.

1   The Problems

1.1   WHAT CAN GO WRONG?

Modern computer systems are generally very reliable, giving hours of trouble-free service. However, it should be remembered that problems may still occur from time to time, especially with the components of the system which are of a mechanical nature.

The components in which such problems become most noticeable are of course the disk drives. These are precision-made devices, with a design life in excess of 10,000 hours. However, problems may still occur due to anomalies in the manufacturing process, careless handling of the system, or even due to software problems. In fact, it is true to say that every disk drive will fail at some point, and in the vast majority of situations this will be when the data on the disk is required urgently!

It is not only the disks which may fail – all the components of the computer have a limited lifespan and may fail at any time. However, the majority of these components are *non-critical*, ie whilst they may cause problems in the short term, they do not affect the long-term usage of the system. For example, the system can be connected to a different printer, monitor or keyboard if any of these components fail, or option boards can be changed in a few minutes if they show signs of a fault.

The most serious problems are encountered when a *critical* component fails. This may mean that either the entire system, or the data that was stored in the system, cannot be reinstated into a usable condition. Critical components include all forms of data storage media as well as the motherboard. In terms of data disasters, even the failure of the motherboard can be said to be non-critical, as the hard disk can be transferred to a working system with little or no loss of data at all.

The main difference between a disk failing and any of the non-critical components is that the disk usually contains reams of valuable data, and it is actually the data that is more important and valuable to the organisation than the media on which it is stored. Thus the majority of this book will deal with the problems of data safety, security and recovery, rather than those involving the other components of the system.

1.2   A CATEGORISATION OF PROBLEMS

There are three major categories of problems that must be dealt with:

–   Lost data

–   Corrupted data

–   Insecure data

1.2.1   LOST DATA

Data may be lost for various reasons, including the following:

- A program may crash before the user has had a chance to save their data
- A program may contain bugs which cause the data to seemingly be saved, although it is in an unintelligible format
- A program may overwrite information, without telling the user that it is doing so
- A disk may be physically damaged, such that all of the information that it contains is apparently destroyed
- Data may be erased from the disk by a user, either on purpose or by accident
- A disk may be reformatted, thus erasing any previous information
- Data may be misplaced, normally due to the user forgetting where it was stored

1.2.2   CORRUPTED DATA

Data becomes corrupted when it is altered, usually accidentally, but sometimes maliciously. Common sources of data corruption include:

- A program may crash midway through the saving process. Thus the file on the disk will be only partially complete
- A program may contain bugs which cause the data to be corrupted when it is written to disk
- A program may contain bugs which cause the data to be stored in the wrong area on the disk, thus overwriting an area that is already in use by the system, an application or other data
- A disk may be physically damaged such that some of the information that it contains is unreadable

1.2.3   INSECURE DATA

Many organisations rely on their data remaining confidential. Certain markets exist solely on the data that is owned, such as recruitment agencies, advertising agencies etc.

In such cases it is essential that unauthorised personnel are prevented from accessing the data, as any breach of this security may prove costly for the organisation. Threats come from many sources, but some of the more common include:

- Unauthorised use of a PC within the building to access confidential data
- Unauthorised access to the data from a remote location, usually by modem
- Theft of PC systems and data from the building

1.3   COMMON FAULTS

The following sections outline some of the most common faults that are encountered, together with comments on the likelihood of data recovery being successful:

1.3.1   PROGRAM CRASH

If a program ceases functioning before the user has had a chance to save their work then they will generally lose that data altogether. This is because the program will not normally terminate and return to DOS, but rather it will just seize up altogether. If however the system does return to DOS control, then it may be possible to recover the data that was in use. If the program happens to be a database or accounts system, then a great deal of information can become corrupted. However, generally speaking it is possible to recover the majority of this data, although it may take a considerable time.

1.3.2 LOSS OF END OF FILE MARKERS

Word processors and many other software packages denote the end of a file with a special end of file marker (EOF). If this is removed, the application may have difficulty in reading information from the disk. The EOF marker can be easily replaced, thus allowing the data to be recovered.

1.3.3 DISK CORRUPTION

Disks may be corrupted by software, malicious damage, mechanical failure, or simply by accident. In the majority of cases only a small area of disk is actually corrupt, and the data from the other sections can be recovered. Indeed in many cases it is also possible to at least partially recover the corrupt data.

1.3.4 PARTITION/BOOT/FILE ALLOCATION TABLE CORRUPTION

The corruption of the partition record, boot sector or file allocation table (FAT) is a special instance of disk corruption. These three areas are set aside for use by the system, and any data that is erroneously written to any of them will cause immense problems. However, given sufficient time and incentive, it is possible to recover most, if not all, of the data on the disk.

1.3.5 DISK CRASH

A disk crash is a mechanical failure of the disk hardware, caused when the read/write head of the disk touches the delicate disk surface. This normally destroys the magnetic surface of the area that was touched, and thus destroys the data. Whilst data from other areas of the disk can be salvaged, the area in which the crash occurred will be totally unusable.

1.3.6 SOFTWARE CONFLICTS

Certain application programs require that the system be set up in a particular way, usually through the use of the CONFIG.SYS and AUTOEXEC.BAT files. If two programs require different settings, it is quite possible that these settings will conflict, and only one program will execute correctly. By balancing the needs of one against the needs of another it is normally possible to allow both programs to execute satisfactorily. In many cases this compromise will cause the performance of one or both of the programs to be degraded. The extent of this performance loss is dependent on many factors, but can be quite significant for sophisticated applications such as desktop publishing (DTP) and computer aided design (CAD).

1.3.7 MISPLACED FILES

Misplaced files are extremely common, occurring mainly when the user is in a different subdirectory to the one they think they are in. Several proprietary utilities provide a facility for locating data according to its filename, date of creation, contents etc, regardless of its location on the disk.

1.3.8   MALICIOUS DAMAGE

Malicious damage, although relatively rare, is often the most difficult to recover from. The effects may vary from corrupted or lost data to mechanical failures and disk crashes. Generally speaking, if the person causing the damage has even a rudimentary knowledge of the PC then it will be very difficult to recover the lost information.

1.3.9   PHYSICAL DAMAGE

Physical damage is more common, and usually involves hard and floppy disk drive units. Severe shocks or rough treatment can cause disk crashes, as can excess heat, cold or humidity. It is often possible to recover all of the data from the hard disk, although it may be a time consuming process. It is inevitable that, in many instances, the actual disk drive itself will be have to be replaced.

Floppy disks are probe to damage, although the process of recovering the data is considerably simpler in this case mainly due to the smaller data area. Unfortunately the section of the disk that is physically damaged will often be totally unreadable, making it impossible for data to be retrieved from this area.

1.3.10   UNAUTHORISED ACCESS

Unauthorised access can be countered with a number of procedures including locking the room in which the computer is placed, locking the computer itself, as well as through the use of a security product. However, anyone with a good knowledge of DOS can bypass most security products that do not encrypt data in only a few minutes. Those products that do employ encryption routines, whilst offering a higher level of access control, introduce their own problems, as encrypted data is significantly more difficult to recover if the disk is corrupted than data in a standard format.

1.4   WHAT EFFECTS WILL THESE PROBLEMS HAVE?

The effect of losing data is dependent upon exactly what was lost, whether it was backed up, whether it can be recreated, and if so how much will the recreation cost. The following examples illustrate this point:

- Accidentally erasing two days' word-processed correspondence files may prove to be inconvenient (although in some professions, such as solicitors, it can be very serious), but the data is probably not essential for the continuation of the business.

- Losing an entire personnel database should also prove only inconvenient, as the files should be backed up. If, however, this is not the case, the situation is much more serious, and it may take days or even weeks to recreate the lost information.

- Corrupting the program file for an application that is used every day is not really a problem at all, as the software can be re-installed from the original disks.

- Corrupting a major financial plan by saving another worksheet under the same name will only be a problem if it is not backed up, when it will cause serious difficulties for the person assigned to rebuild it.

1.5 SUMMARY

This chapter has highlighted some of the most common faults that face the personal computer user. These are by no means all of the problems that may be encountered; some are dependent upon particular circumstances, while other difficulties may occur due to the way in which a particular system is being used.

However, from the above examples it can be seen that the key to avoiding difficulties is to ensure that data is properly backed up, a procedure that very few organisations follow properly. The process of producing a backup copy of the data is examined in greater detail in Chapter 3.

In the event that this has not been done correctly, it is still possible to recover most, if not all, lost data in the majority of situations. The remainder of this book deals with how this can be achieved.

2   Basic Techniques for Data Interpretation

2.1 INTRODUCTION

Computers, and the systems that run on them, use a range of notations for storing and manipulating information, including binary, bits, bytes, hexadecimal and decimal. This chapter explains how and where each of these are used.

2.2 BINARY NOTATION

Fundamentally, computers store and manipulate information as a series of electronic impulses which are either on or off. This is interpreted as 1 or 0, and is referred to as binary notation.

Using binary notation to represent even quite small numbers is complex. For example,

Decimal	Binary		Decimal	Binary
1	1		12	1010
2	10		.	.
3	11		.	.
4	100		16	10000
5	101		32	100000
6	110		64	1000000
7	111		128	10000000
8	1000		157	10011101
9	1001		223	11011111
10	1010		237	11101101
11	1011		255	11111111

In numbers such as these, individual digits are, in computer terminology, referred to as *BITs* (BInary digiTs). As a result of computer design factors, bits are traditionally grouped into eights, known as *bytes*. The byte has become the standard unit of computer storage and 1 byte can store values between 0 and 255. Furthermore, due to the complexity of manipulating binary numbers, computer designers developed a shorthand for referencing numeric values, known as hexadecimal notation.

2.3 HEXADECIMAL NOTATION

Throughout this textbook many of the examples and descriptions will make use of hexadecimal notation. This is simply base 16 mathematics, and provides a very convenient way of representing computer data.

In hexadecimal, the digits 0 to 9 are used conventionally, but the numbers 10 through 15 are represented as the letters A through F. The number 16 is then represented as 10. To differentiate hexadecimal numbers from decimals, they are suffixed with a small letter h, for example 1Ah, F4h or 13h. The following table shows how the number sequence progresses:

Hex.	Decimal		Hex.	Decimal
01h	1		11h	17
02h	2		12h	18
03h	3		13h	19
.			.	
09h	9		1Ah	26
0Ah	10		1Bh	27
0Bh	11		1Ch	28
0Ch	12			
0Dh	13		.	
0Eh	14		1Fh	31
0Fh	15		20h	32
10h	16		etc.	

It can be seen from the above that rather than having the numeric columns representing tens and units as in decimal, the hexadecimal columns represent 16s and units. Thus to convert from a two digit hexadecimal number to a decimal value, the left hand digit is multiplied by 16, and the value added to the right hand digit.

Referring back to computer terminology, any single hex digit (1–9, A–F) is equal to half a byte, sometimes referred to as a *nybble*.

The numbering scheme continues in exactly the same way for larger hexadecimal values. When dealing with larger hexadecimal values, the columns represent the following decimal values (Note that it is rare to encounter hexadecimal values that exceed 4 digits.):

$$65536 \quad 4096 \quad 256 \quad 16 \quad 1$$

Thus to convert a 4 digit hexadecimal number to its decimal equivalent the following procedure is adopted:

- Convert each digit in the number to its decimal equivalent.
- Multiply each of these values by the corresponding column value
- Add up the resulting products

For example, consider the hexadecimal value 2CE5h. This can be converted to decimal as follows:

- Convert each digit to decimal:

2	C	E	5	(hex)
2	12	14	5	(decimal)

- Multiply each by the column value:

$$2*4096 = 8192$$
$$12*256 = 3072$$
$$14*16 = 224$$
$$5*1 = 5$$

- Sum the resulting products: $8192+3072+224+5 = 11493$

The process of converting numbers from decimal to hexadecimal is only slightly more difficult. The number is repeatedly divided by each of the hexadecimal factors, noting down the result at each stage and then using the remainder for the next operation. For example, to convert 25673 to hexadecimal, the following procedure is used:

- First, divide the value by the highest hexadecimal factor that will fit, ie 4096 $25673 / 4096 = 6$ rem 1097

- Next, divide this remainder by the next highest factor, ie 256 $1097 / 256 = 4$ rem 73

- Repeat again with 16 $73 / 16 = 4$ rem 9

- And finally the units $9 / 1 = 9$ rem 0

Thus the hexadecimal equivalent is 6449h.

Unfortunately the human brain finds counting in hexadecimal somewhat awkward, at least initially. It is therefore recommended that anyone wishing to do more than just vaguely poke around inside a computer should purchase a hexadecimal calculator. These are available from many high street shops, and offer the ability to convert between decimal and hexadecimal, as well as perform hexadecimal arithmetic. They can be easily recognised as they will have the letters A through F on the keypad as well as the digits 0 to 9.

2.4 BIG ENDS AND LITTLE ENDS

Hexadecimal numbers always follow the conventional scheme for significance, ie they are written

Most significant digit, least significant digit

For example, consider the decimal value 28. The least significant digit is the number 8, ie the units, and the most significant is the number 2, ie the tens. A hexadecimal value is considered in the same way. For example, the value 8Ah has a least significant digit of A to represent 10 units, and a most significant digit of 8, representing 8 lots of 16. This is referred to as *big endian* format.

However, when the Intel 8086 processor was created, the designers took it upon themselves to alter this system a little. When dealing with a number consisting of two or more bytes, (or 4 or more hex digits), the least significant byte is stored first, followed by the most significant byte. This is known as *little endian* format.

For example, to store the value F4A8h (62632 decimal), the first byte stored would be A8h and the second would be F4h. Note that the digits within a byte are never reversed, but are always kept together,. ie, F4A2 would not be interpreted as 2A4F.

It is essential to note this anomaly, as it becomes very common when dealing with addresses and other similar numbers. Throughout this book, the use of little endian numbers will be highlighted wherever possible.

2.5   TOOLS REQUIRED

Data disasters are, by their very nature, software based. Thus the tools required to deal with such problems are also software based. Only in very rare circumstances is it necessary to use a hardware based approach to solving data disaster problems.

To ensure that the task of data recovery is as simple and effective as possible, it is essential to have a selection of basic utilities and programs. The following list outlines some typical requirements, although this may of course be considerably enhanced in certain organisations:

2.5.1   DOS

An original copy of every version of DOS used in the organisation is essential. The disk must be bootable, and must be in an appropriate format to allow it to be used on any machine. Thus it may be necessary to have both 5 ¼" and 3 ½" disks for each version.

Throughout this book the term DOS will be used to refer to MS-DOS, PC-DOS and any other versions that have been licensed to specific manufacturers. Where there are differences between the versions these will be noted and explained. All DOS based facilities and utility programs will, unless otherwise stated, refer to version 2.X or above.

2.5.2   DIAGNOSTIC DISKS

Some kind of diagnostic software is usually supplied with computer systems at the time of purchase. Very rarely do users ever need to run these diagnostics, so they tend to be stored away and forgotten about. When a problem occurs at a later stage, the trouble-shooter is unable to locate the appropriate disks.

To ensure that this situation does not arise it is essential for all diagnostics diskettes to be kept at a central location, typically in the office of the troubleshooter. They should be labelled to show which machine they come from, so that the appropriate disks can be found if problems occur. This has the added advantage of keeping these utilities away from the users, who may have a tendency to use them, either incorrectly, or at inappropriate times.

2.5.3   INTEGRATED UTILITIES

An integrated, general-purpose, utility package such as Norton Utilities, PC Tools, Mace Utilities or Baker's Dozen is absolutely essential. Such packages are excellent for run of the mill data recovery operations, as they provide a wide range of disk examination and modification facilities, as well as other functions including disk analysis and automated data recovery tools.

In larger organisations it may be necessary to have more than one package, as certain products deal more effectively with particular situations than others.

2.5.4 SPECIALISED UTILITIES

A variety of specialised utilities are available, either in the form of commercial programs, or as shareware. These utilities cater for specific situations, and in some situations allow data to be recovered more easily than with the integrated utilities. The following products are typical of such utilities (Appendix 6 gives full details of all products mentioned in this book):

- TestDrive – a general purpose floppy disk drive testing program. Available in the form of shareware, it requires the use of a special diskette if maximum use is to be made of its features.

- Disk Explorer – a product designed to allow floppy disk based problems to be easily and quickly diagnosed and remedied. It is much more flexible when working with floppies than any other utility available.

- Rescue – a special product designed to allow damaged Lotus 1-2-3 files to be quickly and easily repaired and recovered.

2.5.5 PROGRAMMING LANGUAGES

A programming language is a useful tool to have available in situations where it is anticipated that there will be regular data recovery problems. The use of such a language will allow simple, highly specialised, utilities to be produced for particular data recovery problems. Appropriate programming languages include Pascal, BASIC and C.

2.5.6 MANUALS FOR ALL SOFTWARE

It is important to have available all of the manuals for any software product which is in use. This includes all manuals for DOS, the various utilities, and for any applications that are in use on machines that experience problems.

In many cases it is impractical for the troubleshooter to keep all of these manuals to hand. However, it is essential that if someone else keeps them, the location of the books is known to the person in charge of data recovery operations.

2.5.7 REFERENCE BOOKS

In addition to the original product manuals, it is advisable to have a number of additional reference books to hand. Such reference books may refer to applications programs, to utilities, or to DOS. They usually give information of a more technical nature than the standard manual; information which becomes of great value when problems are encountered. The reading list in Appendix 3 suggests some relevant titles.

All of the software tools outlined above are discussed in later sections of the book. The use of several of these tools in typical data disaster scenarios is shown in Chapter 7.

2.6 SUMMARY

The fact that personal computer systems perform all internal operations and calculations using binary can make it difficult for the human user to understand exactly what is happening. These difficulties can be overcome largely through the use of a more conventional numbering system, such as hexadecimal, which effectively acts as a form of shorthand for communicating data between the computer and the user. However, there are other anomalies in the storage techniques employed by the PC, in particular the distinction between little-endian and big-endian storage, which make the task of mastering these basic techniques for data interpretation a challenging one.

Fortunately there are many software products available which considerably simplify this process, and which are essential as the basis of any data recovery toolkit. In addition to these general utilities, it will be necessary to acquire a number of more specialised utilities which can be selected to cater for problems that are specific to the particular environment. The toolkit can be further enhanced by the provision of a suitable programming language, which will allow utilities to be created on an ad-hoc basis, thereby aiding the data recovery process in situations not covered by commercial products.

Finally, it is very important that the user has a clear understanding of exactly how the computer operates, and in particular exactly how data is stored on disks. This subject is examined in detail in Chapter 3, although it will be advantageous if other background material is available in the form of reference books or technical manuals.

3   How Data is Stored

3.1   THE HARDWARE

There are many different devices and media available for data storage, offering a range of different capacities, speeds and other characteristics. Such devices include:

-   Hard disks, the most popular form of data storage media on PCs, ranging in capacity from 20MBytes to over 600MBytes.

-   Floppy and mini disks. The 5¼" and 3½" disks are still the major media for transferring software onto a computer, and are widely used as backup media.

-   Magnetic tape, often used for backup purposes but rarely for everyday data storage. It has the advantage of being relatively inexpensive, but is slow and often subject to mechanical failure.

-   Demountable hard disks, such as the Bernoulli box, Tandon DataPac etc. These devices have only recently become freely available at a realistic price, and offer high capacity, high speed, efficient data storage. They are still relatively expensive however.

-   WORM drives (Write Once Read Many times), such as CD ROMs. These devices offer immense capacities, but are still quite expensive. Original products could only be written to once, although more recent developments have produced devices capable of being used again and again.

3.1.1   HARD DISKS

Hard disks, also known as Winchester disks, have been used on computer systems for many years. The original devices were physically very large, around 18 inches in diameter, capable of storing between 5 and 20MBytes of data, and were very expensive. However, the development of the hard disk has kept pace with technology, meaning that they are now physically much smaller, less expensive, faster, and able to contain a greater amount of data than their predecessors. The hard disk has now become so much a part of the personal computer that it is a recognised part of a standard configuration.

Hard disks are generally reliable, providing trouble-free service for many thousands of hours. However, this fact alone means that many users place implicit trust in their machines, and do not make regular backup copies of their data. Thus when a problem occurs it is normally essential that as much data as possible is recovered from the original disk, as this is the only source.

The hard disk unit, as shown in Figure 3.1, is made up of one or more *platters* revolving around a central spindle. Each platter has its own read/write head, although all of the individual heads move in unison. The layout of the information on the disk is discussed below. The hard disk platters and read/write heads are enclosed in a sealed, airtight box, in order that dust and other contaminants cannot affect the operation.

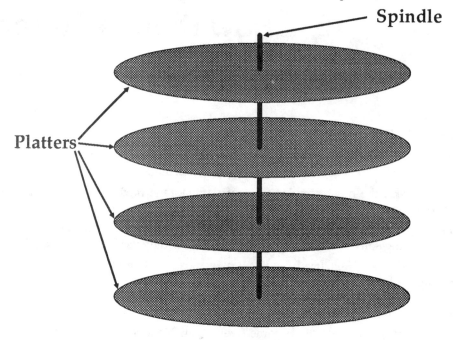

Figure 3.1   Construction of a hard disk unit

Each platter of a disk has two sides, usually referred to as heads, one or both of which will be coated with ferrous oxide to allow it to store information. In the case of hard disks it will often be found that the underside of the bottom platter cannot store information, although the user is not aware of this. Floppy disks may have just one side coated (in which case they are known as single sided), or both (double sided).

Heads are sometimes referred to as sides, and are numbered sequentially from the top down, starting with 0.

3.1.2   FLOPPY DISKS

Floppy disks were actually developed after hard disks, as the technology required for the reliable operation of such a device took longer to develop. The first floppy disks were 8 inches in diameter, although these have been abandoned in favour of more modern designs such as the 5 ¼, 3 ½, and 3 inch sizes.

Floppy disks are much more vulnerable than hard disks, as the magnetic surface is open to the environment. Thus they have a more limited lifespan, often of 2 to 3 years. Note that this applies even if the disk is used only on an infrequent basis, as the magnetic surface will deteriorate whilst the disk is in storage.

Floppy disks are made of a single piece of *Mylar*, a thin flexible plastic, and coated with a very thin layer of ferrous oxide. 5 ¼" disks are contained in a flexible plastic envelope, whilst 3" and 3 ½" disks are housed in a more rigid plastic case, giving rise to their nickname of *stiffies*. A small hole punched in the surface of the disk informs the hardware how the data should be positioned, and where it can expect to find the start of the disk. Figure 3.2 shows the construction of floppy disks.

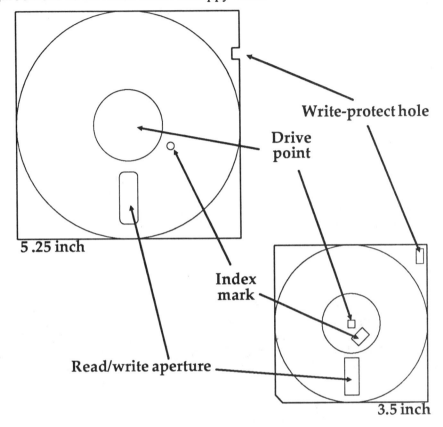

Figure 3.2   Construction of floppy disks

3.2   HOW A DISK IS USED

Before a disk can be used to store data it has to be *formatted*. In the case of hard disks the first procedure that must be performed is a low level format. It is this procedure that divides the disk into the fundamental sub-sections of tracks and sectors that are used by DOS. Hard disks should have been low level formatted before shipment, and floppy disks have tracks and sectors assigned with the normal DOS FORMAT command.

3.2.1   CYLINDERS/TRACKS

Each side of the disk surface is divided into a number of concentric circles, known as cylinders or tracks. Tracks are numbered from the outside, starting with 0.

The number of tracks on a hard disk platter will vary greatly, but it can be over 1000. Floppy disks on the other hand tend to have either 40 or 80 usable tracks. The number of tracks stated on floppies will typically be 48tpi (Tracks Per Inch) or 96tpi. However, the area of disk actually used for data storage is less than an inch, 40 or 80 tracks being common.

The radius of potentially usable disk on a 5¼" floppy is the length of the read/write aperture (about 1.4 inches). However, due to the magnetic nature in which data is stored on the surface of the disk, there is a limit as to how close together the pieces of information can be before they become corrupted. Therefore tracks having small circumferences (those nearer the centre) cannot be used. Hence the maximum number of tracks that can be put on a low density 5¼" floppy is 42.

3.2.2   SECTORS

There are three types of sectors - disk, physical and logical.

3.2.2.1   Disk Sectors

Each track is divided radially into a number of sections, which are known as disk sectors, as shown in Figure 3.3. These are numbered from 1 upwards. Floppy disks have either 8, 9, 15 or 18 sectors. Hard disks vary greatly, although 17 sectors per track is quite common. Each sector contains a predetermined number of bytes, dependent upon the media and DOS version in use. The most common is 512 bytes, and this is used on floppies and most hard disks.

3.2.2.2   Physical Sectors

A physical sector, as can be seen from Figure 3.3, is a sub-section of a disk sector, and a different numbering system is used. Physical sectors are numbered from 0 upwards, with physical sector 0 being cylinder or track 0, head or side 0, disk sector 1. The numbering continues with physical sector 2 being cylinder 0, head 0, disk sector 2 etc, until physical sector 16 is cylinder 0, head 0, disk sector 17. On a disk with 17 disk sectors per track, physical sector 17 is cylinder 0, head 1, disk sector 1. Thereafter the numbering scheme continues along the same lines, with the disk sector being the least significant value, the head number next, and the cylinder number as the most significant value.

The term physical sector number is often abbreviated to PSN. Thus the PSN for any location on the disk can be calculated by:

$$PSN = (S-1)+(H*Max\_Sectors)+(C*Max\_Heads*Max\_Sectors)$$

S is the disk sector number
H is the head number
C is the cylinder number
Max_Sectors is the number of sectors per track
Max_Heads is the number of heads or sides

For example, when working with a 17 sectors/track disk that has 9 usable sides, the PSN of the physical sector at disk sector 6, head 3, cylinder 33 can be calculated:

$$PSN = (6-1)+(3*17)+(33*9*17) = 5105$$

3.2.2.3   Logical Sectors

Logical sectors are the areas of disk storage that are seen by DOS. In many cases, as can be seen in Figure 3.3, the logical sectors are exactly the same as the physical sectors.

However, due to the limitations inherent in MS- DOS versions up to and including 3.3, only hard disks of up to 32MB capacity are supported directly. To overcome this problem, many vendors (including Compaq and Tandon) have slightly modified DOS to use what are known as *Large Logical Sectors (LLS)*. In such versions two, four or even eight physical sectors are linked together to form each logical sector, giving logical sector sizes of 1024, 2048 or even 4096 bytes. MS-DOS version 4 uses a similar system, although it has been more economically designed to allow more efficient use to be made of the storage area.

The numbering system for logical sectors is slightly different to that of physical sectors as there may be more than one *partition* present on a disk. A partition is a theoretical division which allows more than one operating system to use a disk. Whilst each partition uses a different area of the disk, the logical sector numbers in each one always start at 0. More detail about partitions is given below. The term logical sector number is often shortened to LSN.

3.2.3   THE GEOMETRY OF THE DISK

The specification of the number of heads, cylinders and sectors is known as the geometry of the disk. It is important to have this information available, as it is often essential to the success of data recovery operations. For floppies it is easy to determine the geometry of the disk (see diskette density below). The geometry of a hard disk can usually be found in the manual, or it may be printed on the actual case. Figure 3.3 below shows diagrammatically the layout of a disk.

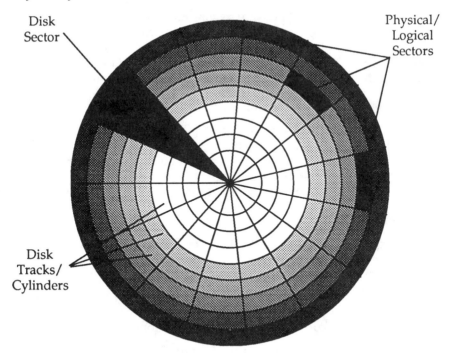

Figure 3.3   The layout (or format) of a disk

Figure 3.4 shows the numbering schemes used for physical and logical sectors on a disk.

The diagram assumes that the device has two platters, the underside of the bottom platter is unused, and that there are 15 disk sectors.

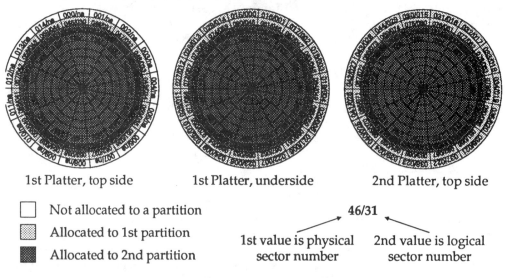

1st Platter, top side   1st Platter, underside   2nd Platter, top side

☐ Not allocated to a partition

▨ Allocated to 1st partition

■ Allocated to 2nd partition

46/31

1st value is physical   2nd value is logical
sector number   sector number

Figure 3.4   Cluster and sector numbering for multiple platters

As can be seen from Figure 3.4, physical sector 0 occupies the first disk sector of track 0 (the outermost track) on the top of platter 1. The sector numbers increase around the disk, until physical sector 14 occupies the last sector on track 0. The numbering continues with physical sectors 15 through 29 being situated on track 0 of the underside of the 1st platter. Track 0 of the top of 2nd platter is used for the next 15 physical sectors, numbers 30 through 44. The underside of the 2nd platter is not used , so the numbering continues with track 1 on the top of the 1st platter again.

As can be seen, the logical sectors are numbered slightly differently, as they start from 0 for each partition on the disk. Partitions typically start on disk sector 1 of a given track, and therefore the first partition usually starts on head 0, disk sector 1, track 1. This will be logical sector 0. The logical sectors then follow the physical sector numbering scheme until they reach the end of the partition, when they begin at 0 again for the next partition.

3.2.4   DISKETTE DENSITY

Floppy disks are quoted as being either double or high density. This refers to the amount of information that can be accommodated on the disk, and is linked directly to the number of sectors and tracks that the disk can contain.

– Double density disks store either 360K of data (5 ¼" size) or 720K (3 ½"). This is derived from the fact that a 5 ¼" disk will contain 40 tracks of 9 disk sectors each, and a 3 ½" disk will contain 80 tracks of 9 disk sectors each.

– High density disks store either 1.2M or 1.44M of data for 5 ¼" and 3 ½" sizes respectively. These both contain 80 tracks, but the 5 ¼" will have 15 disk sectors and the 3 ½" will have 18 disk sectors.

All of the above figures are based on each sector containing the standard 512 bytes, and assume that the disk is double sided. It is now very rare to find computer systems that use disks that do not obey these standards.

A commonly held belief is that high density disks are made of the same material (but of a higher quality) as double density disks. This is in fact untrue, as the chemical composition of the ferric oxide coating on the disks is slightly different. Because of this physical difference, it is extremely unwise to format a double density disk as a high density one, or vice versa. Whilst such a disk may appear to work reliably it is possible that the data will become corrupt over a period of time. This can be as short as a few weeks, or in some cases it can be as long as two or more years; it is dependent upon many factors including the composition of the disk, the condition of the drive, the frequency of use of the disk, and the way in which the disk is stored.

Thus unless there are exceptional circumstances, it is recommended that the two disk types are never interchanged. A good way to differentiate between the two types, and thus avoid problems with accidental mix-ups, is to use standard (black) disks for double density disks, and coloured ones for high density disks. Appropriate coloured disks can be obtained at little or no extra cost from most suppliers.

3.2.5   CLUSTERS

After dividing the surface of the disk, it can be calculated that there are over 700 storage areas (logical sectors) even on the smallest capacity floppy. This number can increase to over 150,000 for a hard disk. Thus the task of maintaining all of these areas is an immense one and, rather than face it head on, DOS adopts a method whereby it groups adjacent logical sectors into *clusters*.

The exact number of sectors in each cluster varies between disks and DOS versions, although it is common to find 1 or 2 sectors per cluster for floppies, and anything up to 16 sectors per cluster for hard disks. DOS then uses a cluster as the smallest amount of storage that it will allocate for any use, thus simplifying the task of storing information. Therefore the cluster size determines the minimum amount of space that DOS will allocate to any file, irrespective of how little space the actual data requires. Naturally, disks that use the LLS technique will have abnormally large clusters due to the size of the logical sector, and thus are quite inefficient in their use of the storage space. In fact it is not uncommon to find such systems allocating 8K of disk space for even the smallest batch file, thereby wasting over 90% of the available storage area.

Clusters are numbered sequentially from 2 upwards, and encompass the remainder of the partition. The cluster numbering sequence follows the logical sector numbers, and so the cluster number proceeds in the same way as the logical sector numbering scheme. Figure 3.5 shows how the numbering system is most often continued over several sides, in this case the two sides of a high-density 5¼" floppy disk.

As can be seen from Figure 3.5, the cluster numbers follow a very similar scheme to the logical sector numbers, starting at 2 within each partition. The first track on each side, ie the first 30 logical sectors, is used by the system for the Boot sector, FAT and directory (See section 3.3). Therefore, assuming that 2 logical sectors are used for each cluster, cluster 2 occupies the first two logical sectors of the data area, ie track 1, head 0, disk sectors 1 & 2. Cluster 2 occupies the next two logical sectors, ie track 1, head 0, disk sectors 3 & 4. This scheme continues for the remainder of the disk.

A similar scheme is used when there are multiple platters and/or multiple partitions.

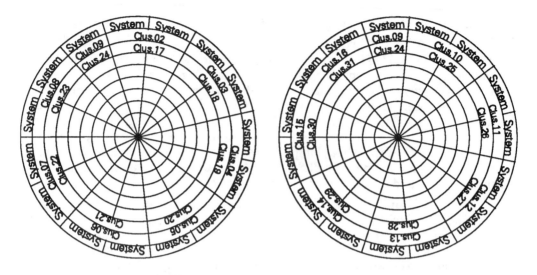

Figure 3.5   Cluster numbering for a floppy disk

3.3   THE SOFTWARE

The previous sections have explained how the disk surface is prepared and sectionalised, making it ready to receive information. However, before the disk can be used to store data or programs, the operating system must be correctly installed. This is achieved during the format process, or alternatively with the SYS command from DOS. These processes perform a number of tasks, including the creation of the partition record, the boot sector, the file allocation table and the directory area.

3.4   PARTITION RECORD

The partition record, sometimes called the *master boot record (MBR)*, is the section of the disk that informs the computer of what it should do to boot up and how the disk is organised. The partition record is created with FDISK, and may be removed by low-level formatting the disk. The partition record is situated at PSN 0 (C:0 H:0 S:1), and will be 1 physical sector long. Figure 3.6 shows the bytes from a typical partition record on a Tandon system displayed using Norton Utilities. The left hand side of the screen shows the hexadecimal values, and the right hand side shows the ASCII text equivalents.

It can be seen that the first section of the partition record consists of some seemingly unreadable characters. This is the assembly language program that tells the system how it should boot up, and occupies around a third of the sector. This is followed by some readable text which represents the messages that will be displayed if errors are encountered or if the partition record is corrupted. Typically the messages will read *Invalid partition table, Error loading operating system* or similar., although partition records created with some licensed versions of DOS may be different. These messages are followed by a large number of 00h values, which represent space that is unused. The last section of the partition record contains some detailed information that tells the system where the separate partitions are located, how large they are, and what data they contain. This is known as the *partition table*.

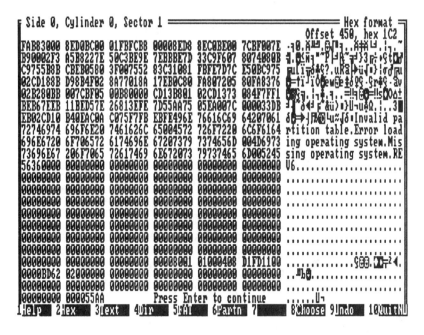

Figure 3.6   The first bytes of a partition record

The partition table is a key area of the disk which is required for the system to operate. If it is damaged, then it is very likely that the system will not be able to be booted from the hard drive, nor will it be able to access data stored on the disk.

3.4.1 PARTITION TABLE FORMAT

The partition table contains four records of identical format. Figure 3.7 shows diagrammatically how the partition table records fit into the overall partition record.

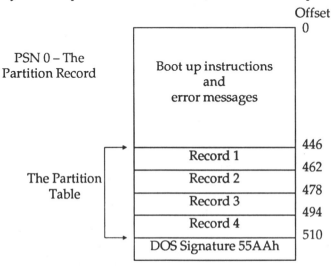

Figure 3.7   The partition record layout

As can be seen, the four partition table records are located within the partition record as follows:

Offset	Table
446	Partition #1 (16 bytes)
462	Partition #2 (16 bytes)
478	Partition #3 (16 bytes)
492	Partition #4 (16 bytes)

Additionally, at offset 510, there is a special signature character sequence to identify this area of the disk as a DOS area. This sequence is AA55h.

The information held in each partition table record is as follows:

Offset	Value	Description
0	00h	Non-bootable partition
	80h	Bootable partition
1..3		Start address for partition, (Encoded specially – see Appendix C on interrupts)
4	00h	Unknown system
	01h	MS-DOS with a 12 bit FAT
	04h	MS-DOS with a 16 bit FAT
	05h	MS-DOS extended partition
5..7		End address of partition, Head, Sector, Cylinder, encoded in the same way as the start address.
8..11		Number of sectors from the physical start of the disk (little endian format)
12..15		Number of sectors in this partition (little endian format)

Offset is the number of bytes from the start of the record. Therefore in the case of the first partition table record, offset 0 is byte 446 in the overall partition record, offset 1 is byte 447 and so on.

3.4.2   FURTHER DEFINITIONS

3.4.2.1   Bootable/Non-bootable partitions

If a partition is bootable, then it contains the appropriate operating system data to allow the computer to be booted up. In DOS terms, this means that the partition contains the two hidden system files, usually named IBMIO.COM and IBMDOS.COM or similar, and the corresponding COMMAND.COM file. If the partition is specified as being bootable but does not contain these files then errors will be produced. Additionally, there should be only one bootable partition on any system.

A disk may be made non-bootable by altering this attribute for the partition. Thereafter, the system will have to be booted up from a floppy disk, as any attempt to boot from the hard disk will produce *Non System Disk or Disk Error* messages.

3.4.2.2 Partition Type

The attribute that defines the partition type may have any value, although only four are recognised by DOS; 00h, 01h, 04h, or 05h. Some operating systems, such as Novell, use additional values for their own purposes, but these will not be recognised by DOS.

The first DOS value, 00h, specifies that the partition is being used by a non-DOS operating system. It is not usually possible to use DOS to access data stored in these 'unknown' partitions.

The second and third values, 01h and 04h, indicate that the partition is what is known as a *Primary DOS Partition*, ie it is in use by DOS, and should be treated as a normal drive. One of the partitions on a disk must be a primary partition, and unless the non-bootable attribute is set, DOS expects to be able to boot the system from this partition.

The final value, 05h, specifies that the partition is what is known as an *Extended DOS Partition*. The extended partition was created with MS-DOS 3.3 in order to allow large physical drives to be used with DOS. Unlike a primary partition, which may only contain one logical drive, an extended partition may contain several logical drives, each of which is considered as a separate unit. Each of the logical drives within an extended partition may be up to 32MB, thus allowing extremely large hard disks to be used.

With recent versions of DOS, notably the licensed versions of DOS 3.3 and all versions of DOS 4, the need for extended partitions has been removed, as the operating system is now able to access the entire hard drive as a single logical unit.

3.4.3 DECODING A PARTITION RECORD

In certain situations it may be necessary to manually decode the data stored in the partition record. This is most often required when a hard disk crashes or becomes corrupted, or when a suitable utility such as Norton cannot correctly interpret the data. The following is a step by step breakdown showing exactly how the partition record data shown in Figure 3.6 can be decoded. Note that although it may not be possible to interpret or rebuild the contents of all or part of a disk using the automatic utilities provided by Norton, PCTools etc, it should be possible to at least view the required sectors in order that they may be manually decoded.

The start of the partition table is known to be at offset 446, and so it can be decoded from this point onwards. As the first partition table record often represents the bootable partition, searching for the 80h indicator can help locate the beginning of the partition table. As it is known that each record contains 16 bytes, they can be listed. Thus for the first entry in the table shown in Figure 3.6 the values are:

80h 01h 01h 00h 04h 08h D1h FDh 11h 00h 00h 00h BDh 62h 02h 00h

- The first byte, 80h, indicates that the partition is bootable.
- The next three bytes, 01h 01h 00h, denote the start position of the partition. These are encoded by DOS, in order to minimise the amount of space they occupy. The first byte represents the starting head number. The second and third bytes need to be decoded more carefully: The least significant six bits of the second byte represent the sector number. This byte translates to 00000001 in binary, so the least significant bits are 000001. The remaining bits of this byte and the entire third byte represent the starting cylinder number, which in binary is 0000000000. Thus the address of the start position is Head 1, Cylinder 0, Sector 1.

- The next byte, 04h, specifies that the partition is used by DOS, and that it has a 16-bit FAT (See section 3.6 for more details).

- The next three bytes, 08h D1h FDh, denote the end address of the partition. They are also encoded by DOS, in the same way as the start position. Thus 08h represents the head number, 010001 is the sector number, and 1111111101 is the cylinder number. These values translate to Head 8, Cylinder 1021, Sector 17.

- The next four bytes, 11h 00h 00h 00h, specify the number of physical sectors between the start of the disk and the start of the partition. This is in little endian format, so represents the decimal value 17, ie the partition starts in the 18th physical sector on the disk.

- The last four bytes, BDh 62h 02h 00h, specify how many physical sectors the partition contains. This is also in little endian format, so it translates to the decimal value 156349, ie the partition contains 156349 physical sectors, each of which is 512 bytes. Thus the entire partition is 156349*512 bytes, or approximately 80MB.

As the remaining records are all empty (ie they contain 00h values) there is no need to decode them. However, when working with a disk containing several partitions it is necessary to decode each of them separately. Once this information has been decoded, it can be checked against the actual locations of each of the partitions.

If there are any differences, or if for some reason the partition record has become corrupted and contains meaningless data, then it is most likely that the system will not boot up, or if it does then it will not operate correctly. In such cases it will be necessary to reverse the decoding procedure to reinstate the correct values.

3.5   BOOT SECTOR

The boot sector contains more information about the disk layout as well as the code to actually get the machine up and running. This code firstly checks for the presence of the two hidden system files, and executes them if it finds them. They in turn execute CONFIG.SYS, COMMAND.COM and AUTOEXEC.BAT. All of these DOS programs rely on the data stored in the first part of the boot sector (see below) to provide details on the size and usage of the disk space. If it is corrupted it is very likely that DOS will begin to destroy data on the disk if it is used.

There will be one boot sector in each partition on the disk, which should be located at LSN 0. Figure 3.8 shows a typical boot record from a Tandon system. This is from a disk formatted with MS-DOS 3.3, and can be seen to contain not only the executable code and data, but also a number of readable error messages as well as the names of the two hidden files.

The area of most interest in the boot sector is the first 30 bytes. These contain a variety of information about the usage of the partition, including many details that are dependent on the DOS version used to format the drive. The information is as follows:

Offset	Description
0..2	Near jump to boot code (machine code instructions)
3..10	OEM Name and version number (ASCII). This is a textual representation of the name of the operating system that created the boot record.

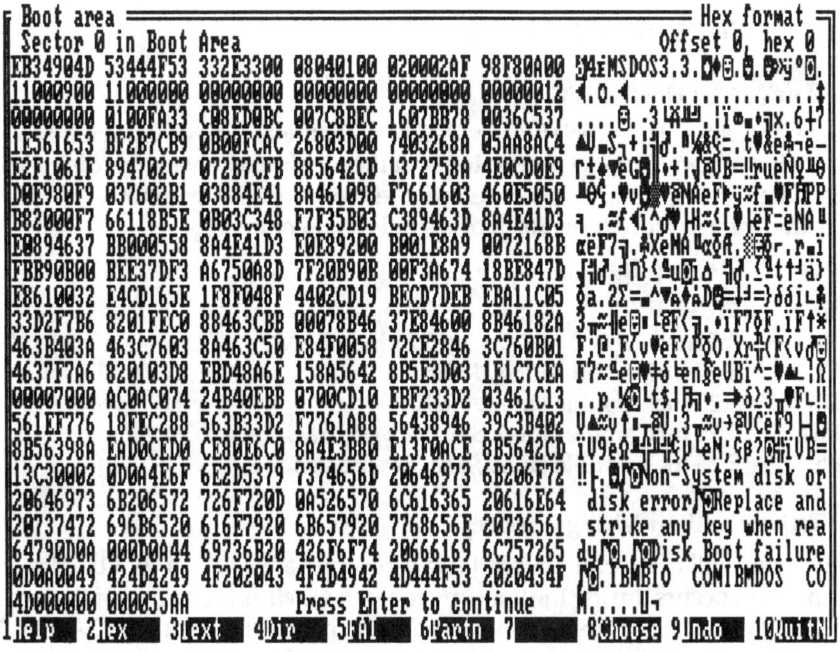

Figure 3.8   The boot sector displayed with Norton Utilities

Bytes 11..23 are known as the *BIOS Parameter Block (BPB)*, and give detailed information on how disk space is to be allocated. All data in the BPB is stored in little endian format:

Offset	Description
11..12	Bytes per sector
13	Sectors per cluster
14..15	Number of reserved sectors (including the boot sector)
16	Number of FAT copies (usually two)
17..18	Maximum number of root directory entries
19..20	Number of sectors in DOS partition
21	Media descriptor byte (see below)
22..23	Number of sectors in each copy of the FAT

The final section of this area contains data that helps in defining the geometry of the drive. As with the BPB, all of this data is stored in little endian format.

24..25	Number of sectors per track
26..27	Number of heads on the drive
28..29	Number of hidden sectors

The remainder of the boot sector contains the code to load and transfer control to the two system files as well as some readable error messages. The final 2 bytes in the boot sector are the hexadecimal 55AAh signature.

The information in the boot sector is sufficient to allow the system to determine exactly how it should allocate space to files, how much space it should reserve for DOS etc. Indeed it is essential for these tasks, and if the boot sector is damaged then it is quite likely that the system will be unable to access the data stored in the partition.

3.5.1   FURTHER DEFINITIONS

3.5.1.1   The Media Descriptor

The media descriptor is a specially encoded byte that tells the system what type of disk is in use. This allows DOS to determine whether it should check for disk swaps (for example when using floppies), as well as the capacity and geometry of the disk. It provides this information in the form of a single byte code:

Code	Description
F8h	Fixed disk
F9h	3.5 inch 720K or 1.44M, or 5.25 inch 1.2M
FCh	5.25 inch single sided, 180K
FDh	5.25 inch double sided, 360K
FEh	5.25 inch single sided, 8 sectors per track
FFh	5.25 inch double sided, 8 sectors per track

3.5.1.2   Other Distinguishing Features

The boot sector will often contain readable error messages which will be displayed on screen if an error occurs during the bootup process, as well as the names of the two system files (IBM.COM and IO.SYS or similar). It will also have a signature of 55AA at the end.

3.5.2   DECODING THE BOOT SECTOR

Just as it may be necessary to manually decode a partition record, it is also possible that it will be necessary to manually decode the data supplied by the boot sector. The following breakdown shows how the boot sector shown in Figure 3.8 can be decoded.

The area of most interest is the 30 or so bytes that specify the BPB and the disk geometry. It is known that this area starts at offset 3, so the values can be easily located. As explained above these bytes represent three distinct sections of data:

3.5.2.1   OEM Name

The first 8 bytes give the OEM name.

> 4Dh 53h 44h 4Fh 53h 33h 2Eh 33h

It is the ASCII values which are of greater importance, and in this case they represent the text 'MSDOS3.3'.

3.5.2.2   BIOS Parameter Block

The next 13 bytes form the BPB. Their values are:

> 00h 08h 04h 01h 00h 02h 00h 02h AFh 98h F8h 0Ah 00h

When translating these values, it is essential to remember that they are in little endian format.

- The first two bytes, 00h 08h, give the number of bytes per (logical) sector. This decodes to 2048 decimal, as this system uses large logical sectors.
- The next byte, 04h, gives the number of sectors per cluster. From these values it can be calculated that the cluster size is 2048*4 , or 8192 bytes.

- The next two bytes, 01h 00h, give the number of reserved sectors. This decodes to 1, showing that only the boot sector is reserved in this case.

- The next byte, 02h, gives the number of FAT copies.

- The next two bytes, 00h 02h, specify the maximum number of root directory entries. In this case, it can be seen that the size of the root directory is limited to 512 entries.

- The next two bytes, AFh 98h, give the number of sectors in the current DOS partition. This translates to 39087, showing that there are 39087 logical sectors in the current partition. As each of these is 4 physical sectors, the number of physical sectors in the partition is 39087*4, or 156348. This corresponds to the partition record value of 156349 when the additional reserved sector is taken into account.

- The next byte, F8h, is the media descriptor byte. The F8h value specifies that this is a boot sector from a fixed disk system.

- The last two bytes of the BPB, 0Ah 00h, define the number of sectors that are used for each copy of the FAT. Thus it can be seen that each FAT occupies 10 logical sectors, which equates to 20K.

3.5.2.3 Disk Geometry

Bytes 25–30 define the disk geometry. For the example in Figure 3.8 their values are:

> 11h 00h 09h 00h 11h 00h

Again it must be remembered when translating these values that they are stored in little endian format.

- The first two values, 11h 00h, specify the number of sectors per track. This translates to 17.

- The next two values, 09h 00h, specify the number of heads on the drive.

- The last two values, 11h 00h, define the number of hidden sectors. These are sectors that DOS cannot access. In this case the values specify that there are 17 hidden sectors.

3.6 FILE ALLOCATION TABLE

The File Allocation Table, or FAT, is perhaps the most essential single area of the disk. So essential in fact that DOS keeps two copies of it just in case one is corrupted. The FAT is an indexing system that tells DOS where the separate parts of a file are located. The FAT is located immediately after the boot sector, the second copy following immediately after the original.

The first byte of the FAT is the media descriptor, as encoded in the boot sector (see above), and the second is always FFh. Thus the first two bytes of a FAT on a hard disk are F8FFh. The remainder of the FAT consists of a series of 2 byte values (in little endian format), which indicate how and where the data files and programs are stored. Additionally the FAT records any bad sectors, so that they are not used for data storage. The operation of the FAT is discussed in detail in section 3.10.

3.7   DIRECTORY AREA (ROOT DIRECTORY)

The directory area keeps track of file names, attributes, creation dates and times, starting positions and lengths. It is positioned in the cluster immediately following the second copy of the FAT, and contains a number of entries (as determined in the boot sector). Each entry is 32 bytes long and contains the following information:

Offset	Description
0..7	Filename, padded with spaces (see below)
8..10	Extension, padded with spaces
11	Attributes (see below)
12..21	Unused - a hangover from CP/M days
22..23	Time of creation/last change
24..25	Date of creation/last change
26..27	First cluster of file (little endian format)
28..31	File size in bytes (little endian format)

The first byte of the filename may contain one of two special values:

00h implies that the directory entry has never been used
E5h indicates that the file has been deleted.

3.7.1   ATTRIBUTES

The attribute is a single byte that indicates what status the file has. It may have any combination of the following values:

01h	Read only	10h	Subdirectory
02h	Hidden	20h	Archive
04h	System	40h	Not used
08h	Volume label	80h	Not used

3.7.1.1   Read-only

The read-only attribute denotes that the file cannot be altered or deleted. It can only be read.

3.7.1.2   Hidden

The hidden attribute specifies that the file does not appear when a DIR command is issued, and cannot be accessed in the normal way.

3.7.1.3   System

The system attribute means that the file is a DOS system file. It should only be applied to the two DOS files called IBMDOS.COM and IBMIO.COM or similar.

3.7.1.4   Volume Label

The volume label attribute implies that this entry is not to be treated as a file, but rather the text used for the filename should actually be used to represent the label for the current disk. The entry with this attribute should only occur once on any logical drive, and should be situated in the root directory.

3.7.1.5 Subdirectory

The subdirectory attribute specifies that the data referenced by the entry is not to be treated as a normal data file, but should be interpreted as a subdirectory. The actual subdirectory entries are stored on the disk in the cluster that is pointed to.

3.7.1.6 Archive

The archive attribute indicates whether a file has been backed up since it was last changed.

3.7.1.7 Assigning Attribute Values

To assign a combination of these values to a file, the attribute values are added together. Thus a read-only hidden system file would have an attribute value of 01h+02h+04h, ie 07h.

3.7.2 DECODING A DIRECTORY ENTRY

The following is a typical root directory entry (all values in hex):

    4D 4F 55 53 45 20 20 20 43 4F 4D 20 00 00 00 00

    00 00 00 00 00 00 5C 61 30 0D FD 04 46 2E 00 00

This can be decoded as follows:

– The first eight bytes, 4D 4F 55 53 45 20 20 20, give the name of the file. In this case they represent the name MOUSE, which is suffixed with three spaces to complete the entry.

– The next three bytes, 43 4F 4D, represent the extension, specified as COM in this case.

– The next byte represents the file attributes, the value of 20 specifying that the Archive attribute is set.

– The next 10 bytes are unused by DOS. They all contain 00h values.

– The next two bytes, 5C 61, give the time the file was last modified or created. This value represents the 16th September 1986

– The next two bytes, 300D represent the time of the last change. These values represent the time 12:10 pm.

– The next two bytes, FD 04, give the address of the first cluster containing the file's data. As this is in little endian format, it translates to the value 1277. Thus cluster 1277 contains the first section of the file.

– The last four bytes, 46 2E 00 00, give the file size in bytes. These again are in little endian format, so represent the value 11846.

Directory entries for program and data files are of exactly the same format; it is the file extension that tells DOS what the data represents. Directory entries for subdirectories are also very similar, differing only in the fact that the size will be specified as 0, and the subdirectory attribute will be set. In all other respects they are the same as other directory entries, and may have extensions, varying cluster numbers, and other attributes.

3.8 FILES

Most PC users are familiar with files – they are the units in which programs and data are stored. Their names appear on the display when DIR is entered. More importantly, as far as the user is concerned, they appear to be comprised of exactly the right number of contiguous bytes.

All data in a file is actually stored in the form of bytes, each of which can represent a value between 0 and 255. It is up to the application program, or DOS, to interpret this data correctly and convert it into a meaningful form. In most cases the data falls into a particular pattern, known as the *file format*, which is often very distinctive. There are many different file formats, some of which are more meaningful when the data is viewed in hexadecimal format, whilst others are more meaningful when the data is viewed in terms of its ASCII character equivalents. Some common file formats are outlined in the Appendix 5, and their importance in practical situations is illustrated in Chapter 7.

3.9 SUBDIRECTORIES

A subdirectory is actually just a special form of data file, but rather than contain user's data or programs, it contains a directory structure in the same format as the root directory. It is denoted as being a subdirectory with a special attribute in its directory entry.

The first two entries in a subdirectory are special. They represent the . and .. entries that appear on every subdirectory listing. The . entry represents the current directory whilst .. represents the parent directory. The length of subdirectory entries in a directory should always be 0 bytes, and the starting position will be the cluster containing the subdirectory data. Thus the starting position for the . entry should be the current cluster whilst the starting position for the .. entry should be the cluster containing the parent directory.

The . and .. entries cannot be altered or deleted using DOS commands, as this would cause untold problems when next DOS tries to access the directory data. However, they can be accidentally altered when a program crashes.

3.10 HOW DOS MANAGES THE DISK

A file is not necessarily stored in a single area of the disk, and may not be contiguous. It is possible that a file may be spread widely over a disk, and it is common to find this when a disk is quite full. It is the job of the FAT to keep track of all the separate parts of a file, so that they can be brought together when the user wants to read the data.

The operation of the FAT is somewhat complex, and is best illustrated as follows:

The disk surface may be thought of as a series of contiguous storage areas – these are the clusters. The clusters are numbered sequentially, an example of which can be seen in Figure 3.9. Notice that the numbering of clusters is in hex. Although they could be referenced with decimal numbering – where cluster 20h would be cluster number 32 – most utility software counts clusters in hex and thus it is useful to practice using this numbering technique.

Files may be stored in these clusters, either in contiguous or non-contiguous areas, as shown in Figure 3.10. Assuming a 512 byte cluster size, the directory entries for these files would appear as shown in Figure 3.11.

02h // 20h	21h	22h	23h	24h	25h

26h	27h	28h	29h	2Ah	2Bh

2Ch	2Dh	2Eh	2Fh	30h	31h

Figure 3.9   Sequential nature of clusters

02h // 20h	21h – File A	22h – File A	23h – File A	24h – File B	25h – File B

26h – File C	27h – File B	28h – File B	29h – File D	2Ah – File D	2Bh

2Ch	2Dh	2Eh	2Fh	30h	31h

Figure 3.10   Allocation of clusters for file storage

File Name	First Cluster No. (Little Endian)	File Size
File A	2100h	9C05h = 1436 bytes
File B	2400h	5007h = 1872 bytes
File C	2600h	B601h = 438 bytes
File D	2900h	5D03h = 861 bytes

Figure 3.11   Directory entries for the files

It can be seen from Figure 3.11 that the file size in the directory for File A is 1436 bytes. Looking at Figure 3.10, File A occupies 3 clusters which, at 512 bytes each, equates to 5136 bytes. On typing DIR at the DOS prompt, the file size for File A would be listed as 1436 bytes, as DOS reads this information from the directory entry. It would NOT display the amount of disk space used, which is actually 1536 bytes. If the directory entry for File A is viewed in hexadecimal, it will appear as:

46 49 4C 45 4A 20 20 20 20 20 20 20 00 00 00 00
00 00 00 00 00 00 11 5C D3 16 21 00 9C 05 00 00

Figure 3.12 shows how the FAT entries would appear for the files illustrated in Figure 3.10 and 3.11 above. Note that all data in the FAT is stored in little endian format, and is illustrated in hexadecimal format.

FAT Entries

Entry #	Offset	Value	Entry #	Offset	Value
0	0	F8FF	25	4A	2700
1	2	FFFF	26	4C	FFFF
.	.		27	4E	2800
.	.		28	50	FFFF
21	42	2200	29	52	2A00
22	44	2300	2A	54	FFFF
23	46	FFFF	2B	56	
24	48	2500	2C	58	

Figure 3.12 FAT entries for the files

3.10.1 HANDLING FILES

The procedures followed by DOS when reading, writing and deleting files are relatively simple and straightforward, and illustrate exactly how DOS makes use of the FAT and directory structures when controlling disk usage.

Thus each of these processes are examined below, with emphasis being placed on when the directory, FAT and data area are referenced, and for what purpose.

3.10.2 READING FILES

When DOS reads a file, it obtains the number of the first cluster containing the file from the directory entry together with a note of the file size. Thus to read file A it would start at cluster 0021h. DOS goes to this cluster on the disk and reads the data into memory. As the file is greater than 1 cluster in size, DOS needs to know where to continue. It gets this information from the FAT by looking at the FAT entry for the current cluster, which in this case is cluster number 0021h. Therefore DOS looks at FAT entry number 21h, which gives a value of 2200h (little endian format), ie the file continues in cluster 0022h.

Once DOS has read the data from cluster 0022h, it repeats the process of looking in the FAT, and is directed to cluster 0023h. Once DOS has read 412 bytes from this sector, it knows that the file is complete, as the total of 1536 bytes have been read. Therefore, DOS reads no more data and returns control to the application program that requested the file. Note that it does not read the FAT entry for cluster 0023h, and therefore will not encounter the FFFFh entry.

As can be seen from this example, the FAT is effectively a form of index system for the files, allowing DOS to keep a record of where different sections of a file are stored. There is actually a FAT entry for every cluster on the disk, even those that are unused, and these entries are listed sequentially. Figure 3.13 shows a hexadecimal listing of the FAT data shown in Figure 3.12. Note that the offset value shown in Figure 3.12 is not stored in the table at all, nor is it even used by the computer; it is provided in these diagrams for clarity and allows the reader to locate each of the FAT entries according to their physical position. Thus the first byte in Figure 3.13 is at offset 0, the second at offset 1 etc.

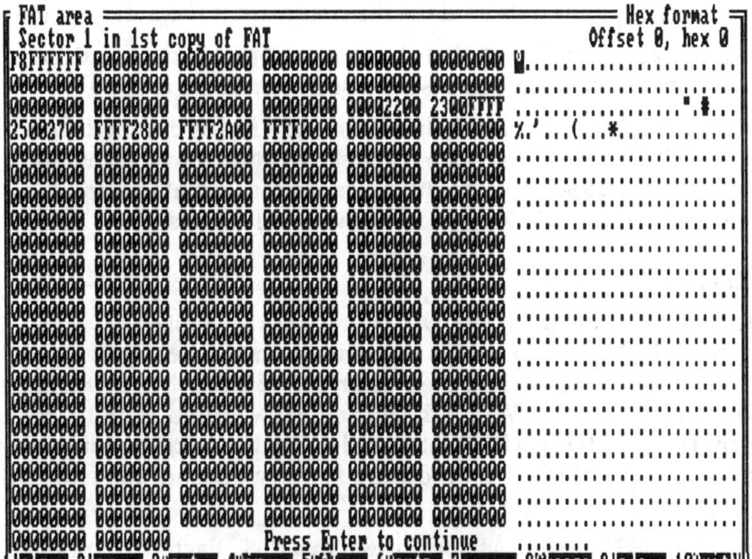

Figure 3.13   FAT data in hexadecimal format

The use of the FAT becomes even more essential when considering a file which is stored in non-contiguous clusters. The following illustrates the procedure necessary to read file B:

The starting cluster for File B is obtained from the directory entry as cluster 0024h. DOS reads the data from this cluster, and obtains the number of the next section from the FAT, which is cluster 0025h. Again DOS reads the data from this cluster and looks to the FAT for the next cluster, which returns 0027h, ie cluster 0026h is skipped. The process continues with DOS reading clusters 0027h and 0028h.

Single cluster files, as illustrated in the above example with File C, are even easier to access. The starting cluster number of 0026h is obtained from the directory area as before, and DOS reads the data. However, before it reaches the end of the sector it realises it has read the total number of required bytes (438) so returns control.

Note that in all of these processes DOS does not encounter the FFFFh indicator in the FAT. If it does, then this implies that there is a difference between the file size specified in the directory, and the actual amount of disk space allocated. In this situation DOS will report an error. The DOS utility CHKDSK performs this check, and cross-references every file's directory entry with the actual amount of space allocated, returning error messages if it encounters any anomalies.

3.10.3 HOW DOS ALLOCATES DISK SPACE

The FAT can contain four different types of values:

-   0000h indicates that the cluster is available for use, ie it is not currently allocated to a file

-   FFF7h indicates that the area of disk contained within this cluster is unusable, ie it contains one or more bad sectors

-   A value between 0001h and the maximum cluster number, eg A057h, indicates that the area contains data, and the file continues at the indicated cluster

-   A value of FFFFh indicates that the cluster contains data, but the file does not continue anywhere else, ie this is the last cluster in the chain.

When the disk has been formatted, and before any files are copied onto it, the FAT is largely full of 0000h values, apart from the first two entries which should be F8FF FFFF or similar. If any bad sectors were identified during the format process, then the clusters using these areas will have FFF7h values for their FAT entries.

3.10.4 WRITING FILES

The first file that is written to the disk will be stored in the first empty cluster, invariably cluster number 2. DOS recognises this as it will be the first entry of 0000h in the FAT. DOS writes the data for the file into the cluster, and if it requires no further space, DOS writes an entry of FFFFh in the FAT for the cluster that was used. If the file requires further space, DOS finds the next 0000h FAT entry, and writes the corresponding cluster number in the original FAT position. This procedure is repeated until the entire file has been written.

For example, a 1986 byte file is to be written to a disk. Each cluster on the disk is one logical sector, and thus each cluster holds 512 bytes. Therefore 4 clusters are required. Figure 3.14 shows how the FAT will appear before the data is written.

FAT Entries

Entry #	Offset	Value	Entry #	Offset	Value
0	0	F8FF	8	10	0000
1	2	FFFF	9	12	0000
2	4	0000	A	14	0000
3	6	0000	B	16	0000
4	8	0000	C	18	0000
5	A	0000	D	1A	0000
6	C	0000	.	.	.
7	E	0000	.	.	.

Figure 3.14   FAT entries for a blank disk

To write the file, DOS looks for the first entry of 0000h in the FAT, which is the entry for cluster 2. Therefore cluster 2 is available and is used to store the first part of the file. DOS knows that it requires more space for the file, and searches for the next entry of 0000h, which it finds at position 3, indicating that cluster 3 is available. It writes this cluster number as the FAT entry for cluster 2, at which point the FAT will appear as shown in Figure 3.15.

FAT Entries

Entry #	Offset	Value	Entry #	Offset	Value
0	0	F8FF	4	8	0000
1	2	FFFF	5	A	0000
2	4	0300	6	C	0000
3	6	0000	7	E	0000

Figure 3.15   FAT entries after the first cluster has been written

The process is repeated until all of the file has been written, using clusters 2, 3, 4 and 5. The FAT entry for cluster 5 will be FFFFh as it is the last one in the chain. Figure 3.16 shows the FAT at this stage.

FAT Entries

Entry #	Offset	Value	Entry #	Offset	Value
0	0	F8FF	4	8	0500
1	2	FFFF	5	A	FFFF
2	4	0300	6	C	0000
3	6	0400	7	E	0000

Figure 3.16   FAT entries after the entire file has been written

The next file that is written will be stored in exactly the same way, and will use clusters 6 onwards, as necessary. For example, Figure 3.17 shows the FAT after a 783 byte file has been written.

FAT Entries

Entry #	Offset	Value	Entry #	Offset	Value
0	0	F8FF	4	8	0500
1	2	FFFF	5	A	FFFF
2	4	0300	6	C	0700
3	6	0400	7	E	FFFF

Figure 3.17   FAT entries after the 783 byte file has been written

3.10.5   DELETING FILES

The above illustrates how files are written to disk. Deleting files is actually a similar process, consisting of 2 steps.

- Firstly, DOS replaces the first character of the filename in the directory table with a value of E5, indicating that the file has been deleted. This allows the directory entry to be re-used by DOS.

- Secondly, DOS replaces all of the FAT entries for the file with values of 0000h, indicating that the space is available for use.

Thus, deleting the first file written in the above example will alter the directory entry and leave the FAT as shown in Figure 3.18.

FAT Entries

Entry #	Offset	Value	Entry #	Offset	Value
0	0	F8FF	4	8	0000
1	2	FFFF	5	A	0000
2	4	0000	6	C	0700
3	6	0000	7	E	FFFF

Figure 3.18   FAT entries after the file has been deleted

3.10.6   FRAGMENTATION

Fragmentation is the situation that occurs when a file is written into non-contiguous clusters. Fragmentation is caused when a file is deleted, and then another, larger file written to the disk. As the second file is larger than the first, it cannot fit into the space vacated when the original file was deleted, so it is continued at the next available location.

For example, if a 6 cluster file is written to the disk used in the previous example, the FAT will appear as shown in Figure 3.19.

FAT Entries

Entry #	Offset	Value	Entry #	Offset	Value
0	0	F8FF	6	C	0700
1	2	FFFF	7	E	FFFF
2	4	0300	8	10	0900
3	6	0400	9	12	FFFF
4	8	0500	A	14	0000
5	A	0800	B	16	0000

Figure 3.19   FAT entries after the entire file has been written

It can be seen from this diagram that the file now occupies clusters 2, 3, 4, 5, 8 and 9. As the process of erasing and adding files is repeated again and again, fragmentation occurs more and more.

Many people feel that excess fragmentation leads to a degradation in performance. However, this is not necessarily the case, although the vendors of defragmentation products may wish the public to believe otherwise.

3.10.7 FAT FORMATS

There is one final problem associated with the FAT; it is sometimes represented in different forms, depending on the media, capacity and DOS version that is being used.

- The first form for the FAT, uses 16-bit numbers, ie two bytes comprise each FAT entry. This is exactly the same as in the above examples.
- The second form of FAT uses 12-bit numbers, ie 1½ bytes are used for each FAT entry. This form of FAT is much more difficult to decode, especially as it is stored in a special, rather convoluted, way.

12-bit FATs are used when there are less than 4094 clusters, or DOS version 2.0 or below is in use. 16-bit FATs are used in all other cases.

3.10.7.1 Decoding a 12-Bit FAT

The twelve bit FAT is stored in a special format so that it occupies the minimum amount of disk space possible. This was considered to be essential when DOS was developed, as most PCs were using relatively low capacity floppy disks, and so as many space saving techniques as possible were used.

The data in a typical twelve bit FAT may appear as follows:

    03 40 00 05 60 00 07 80 00

This is known as Roman form, and is the precise way in which the data is stored on disk. These values can be decoded to produce more readable FAT entries as follows:

- Swap the most and least significant digits of each byte:
  30 04 00 50 06 00 70 08 00
- Divide the resulting series of digits into triples:
  300   400   500   600   700   800
- Swap the order of the first and last digits in each triple:
  003   004   005   006   007   008

To encode entries for a 12-bit FAT, simply reverse the above procedure. For example, the entries:

    057   058   059   05A   05B   05C

can be encoded into the following FAT data:

    57 80 05 59 A0 05 5B C0 05

It is important to determine whether a 12- or 16-bit FAT is in use before attempting to make any modifications to the entries.

3.11 SUMMARY

This chapter has dealt with the techniques and methods that DOS uses to control the storage of data on a disk. It is essential to have a firm grasp of this knowledge before attempting any form of data recovery or direct modification of the disk.

No attempt has been made to explain how the data can be examined, or how it can be modified, as this is entirely dependent upon the software tool in use. These issues will be covered in later chapters.

4   Avoiding Problems

4.1   THE IMPORTANCE OF PREVENTATIVE ACTION

'Prevention is better than cure' is a much used phrase, and is as applicable in terms of computer and data disasters as anywhere else. The preventative steps that can be taken to reduce the number of data disasters are simple, and should be an everyday part of using the computer. However, when no action is taken and a problem occurs, it can be very time consuming to remedy the fault and recover the information.

Preventative steps range from the physical stability of the computer system in terms of its location and configuration through to ensuring that users are trained in the basic operation of the systems, at least to a level that enables them to understand what should never be changed, what can be adjusted to optimise performance, where their data is stored etc. All too often it seems that the users are trained in the software applications that they need to work with, and left to their own devices when it comes to general housekeeping routines. This chapter looks at general issues that users should be made aware of, which will prevent time-consuming actions being required to find or recover lost files. These issues include the SETUP program supplied with many systems, the use of directories, the CONFIG.SYS and AUTOEXEC.BAT files, and the importance of knowing what version of DOS is in use and why this should be standardised wherever possible. Finally, when and how to backup data is addressed.

4.2   SETUP

Systems based around the 80286, 80386 and 80486 processors usually have a special routine built into them. This is known as the SETUP routine, and controls the way in which the computer accesses peripherals, memory, and more importantly, storage devices. The display from a typical setup procedure is shown in Figure 4.1.

It can be seen from this display that the system allows the user to specify a wide range of settings regarding the computer system, and how it has been configured. Information about the international configuration of the system is often specified in SETUP, and if changed by a user can cause erratic problems such as keys on the keyboard being seemingly incorrect.

The SETUP screen in Figure 4.1 has an option to specify how the system files are loaded. This setting can be changed to fixed disk only or floppy disk only, which can help impose security procedures.

Of particular interest are the settings for the disk units. In this case, it can be seen that there are two floppy disk drives, one of which is high capacity and one is low. It is

```
┌──────────────────────────────────────────────────────────────────────────┐
│ SETUP SCREEN                                              REV 3.13.11.89   │
│ ========================================================================= │
│ Date  (MM/DD/YY)    11/08/90                   Time (HH:MM:SS)  16:47:12   │
│ ------------------------------------------------------------------------- │
│ Language    = English              Keyboard    = UK                       │
│ Country     = 044                  Security    = No locks                 │
│ Cache       = Enabled              Display     = Monochrome               │
│ Processor   = 20MHz                System Load = Diskette/Fixed           │
│ ------------------------------------------------------------------------- │
│ Set Diskette Unit 0 = Diskette Drive (5.25")      High Capacity          │
│ Set Diskette Unit 1 = Diskette Drive (5.25")      Low Capacity           │
│                                                                           │
│ Set Disk Unit 80 = Fixed disk (Standard MFM, Device 0)    Type 42        │
│ Set Disk Unit 81 = Not installed                                          │
│ Set Disk Unit 82 = Not installed                                          │
│ Set Disk Unit 83 = Not installed                                          │
│ ------------------------------------------------------------------------- │
│ Memory     Base: 640KB        Extended: 384KB        Next Extd: 1408KB    │
└──────────────────────────────────────────────────────────────────────────┘
```

Figure 4.1   A typical SETUP screen display

important that these settings are not inadvertently changed as data may be lost if the wrong combination of disk, drive and density specifications are used. The hard disk type has been specified as 42, which the system interprets as being a fixed disk that uses MFM encoding. The code also indicates the *geometry* of the disk, ie how many platters, sectors and cylinders it has. If this value is incorrectly specified, then it is highly likely that any data on the disk will be destroyed when the system tries to write any information.

The correct code number for any particular disk should be supplied in the manual that accompanies the product. Alternatively it may be provided by the software that installs the disk and formats it ready for use. This setting should only need changing if the setup information is for some reason lost, or if a new disk drive is installed into the system. The setting should not change at all during normal use, but if it is suspected that for any reason there is some problem with the code specification, it is wise to check.

The setup procedure is accessed in different ways on different machine. For example, some machines supply it on floppy disk in which case it is executed as if it were a normal program, while others supply it in the form of a ROM. In the latter case it is usually invoked by pressing a special key combination at the time of bootup, such as [Ctrl] [Alt] [Esc] or [Ctrl] [Alt] [S].

It is advisable to keep a written or printed copy of the data shown on the setup screen, so that it can be reinstated if necessary. Some systems will allow a hard copy to be produced by pressing the [Print Screen] key, whilst others disable the action of this key until DOS is up and running.

4.3 USING DIRECTORIES

Many personal computer users do not make full or proper use of DOS sub-directories. Subdirectories provide a means of sub-dividing the contents of the hard disk into manageable sections, in much the same way that office paper is filed in cabinets. A subdirectory is actually held on disk in the same form as a file, and contains a list of the names of the files in the directory. Thus it can be damaged or corrupted in much the same way as any other data file. However, more fundamentally, problems occur with subdirectories in 2 other key ways,

- over-use
- under-use

4.3.1 OVER-USE

If too many subdirectories are created, particularly if they are nested, the system will often have to search repeatedly through several to find a file. This can cause severe delays in accessing data, especially with disk-intensive applications such as databases etc. There is also an increased risk of data loss with these multiple layer directories, as the occurrence of a bad sector or data error in one of the directory files will mean that the files in that directory, and often files in directories further down the structure, cannot be accessed.

A less damaging, but equally time consuming problem, that may also occur is the misplacement of data files. It is surprisingly common to find that the location of a file has been forgotten, leaving the user to hunt through the different subdirectories to find it. An alternative solution to this problem is to use a file finding program such as Norton's FINDFILE.

4.3.2 UNDER-USE

If subdirectories are not used sufficiently, a whole range of problems will be encountered, including:

- The number of entries in the root directory is limited, often to 512. If the system attempts to exceed this value when saving a file then an error will occur and the file will not be saved.
- Certain software packages use similar names for parts of their programs; a typical example is INSTALL.EXE. Thus it will not be possible to store two different files with the same name on the same machine if sub-directories are not employed. This in turn may lead to compatibility problems.
- The use of wildcards when deleting files from a large directory can be devastating, as the command that is issued may remove more files than was planned for. This fact may not be immediately obvious, making recovery of such data difficult or even impossible.

Thus a balanced approach to using directories is required. Figure 4.2 shows a directory structure that has been designed with the above problems in mind, and has adequate scope for expansion and modification.

One of the issues relating to use of directories is which files should be stored in the root directory. Obviously certain DOS files such as COMMAND.COM, AUTOEXEC.BAT and CONFIG.SYS will need to be resident there, as may some other device drivers etc. However, it is advisable to restrict the use of the root directory to only storing these essential files. All applications, utilities and data, should be stored in subdirectories arranged in a suitable structure.

Files that need to be stored in the root directory can be protected from accidental corruption or deletion by setting the read-only attribute for each one.

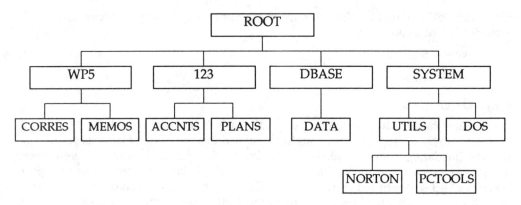

Figure 4.2   A well designed directory structure

4.4   CONFIG.SYS

The correct specification of device drivers etc in the CONFIG.SYS file will go far towards remedying and preventing problems. Two of the most common faults that are encountered are the incorrect use of the FILES and BUFFERS commands.

The line *FILES = XX* in the CONFIG.SYS file controls the maximum number of files that DOS will allow to be open at any one time. This number includes not only applications and data files, but also DOS files such as COMMAND.COM, the two hidden system files, any special device drivers etc, as well as any temporary files that may be created. Setting this value too low may cause certain applications to crash if they are executed. Setting the value too high will waste memory space. The correct setting for the FILES = line may vary between different applications, and will usually be found in the program documentation.

The line *BUFFERS = XX* controls the number of DOS buffers that are used. A buffer is an area of memory in which DOS temporarily stores data before it is written to disk. When a buffer is full, DOS *flushes* it by writing its contents to the disk. This process means that the number of disk writes can be kept to a minimum, thus enhancing the speed of the system. However, as each buffer is 512 bytes, they consume a relatively large amount of memory. Therefore, setting the value for the BUFFERS command too high will waste valuable space, whilst setting it too low will degrade system performance, or even cause applications to crash.

Additional problems may be encountered with other statements in CONFIG.SYS, which typically exhibit themselves in the form of one or more components of the system not working correctly, if at all. Many of these problems are due to conflicts in the software drivers that are used to interface the peripheral to the computer system. Quite often, the problem can be resolved by changing the order in which the drivers are specified within CONFIG.SYS, but it may be necessary to remove one or more of them in order to reach a satisfactory solution. It is this area that may require the CONFIG.SYS file to be edited when new software is introduced on the system. Whilst not all users should be encouraged to change this file themselves, they should at least be aware that it is a potential problem area.

From the above it can be seen that the contents of the CONFIG.SYS file play an important part in the operation of the system. If the values specified for FILES or BUFFERS are too low then program crashes can result, with consequential loss of data. If they are too high then system performance can suffer. Similarly the other statements within CONFIG.SYS can cause their own problems, some of which can be very serious and may involve considerable data loss.

Figure 4.3 shows a typical CONFIG.SYS file, with a brief description of each statement.

BUFFERS=15	Specifies the number of DOS buffers to be 15.
FILES=25	Specifies that a maximum of 25 files may be simultaneously open.
LASTDRIVE=F	Denotes that drives A through F are valid.
DEVICE=GMOUSE.SYS	Loads a third-party mouse driver
DEVICE=VDISK.SYS 348 512 64 /E	Sets up a virtual disk of 384KB size, each sector being 512 bytes, with a limit of 64 root directory entries. /E specifies that extended memory is to be used.
COUNTRY=044	Specifies that United Kingdom time and date styles are to be used
BREAK=ON	Enables break key action

Figure 4.3   A typical CONFIG.SYS file

4.5 AUTOEXEC.BAT

The AUTOEXEC.BAT file is executed every time the computer is booted, and allows a pre-determined sequence of DOS commands to be executed. From the point of view of preventing problems, two of the most important statements in an AUTOEXEC.BAT file are PATH and PROMPT.

4.5.1 PATH

The PATH command specifies the list of directories that the computer will search if it cannot find a program file in the current directory. The use of PATH allows users to run programs in different directories, for example the wordprocessor can be executed from within the spreadsheet directory, but it is also very important from the point of view of the applications themselves. Many products use a programming technique known as overlays, which allows large programs to be broken up into smaller units. This technique requires the system to regularly load different overlays depending on the actions of the user, and therefore the system needs access to the directory that they are held in. The most efficient way of providing this access is through the path command.

The directories specified in the command must be separated by semicolons, and should ideally be prefixed with the drive identifier. Thus a typical PATH statement may be

PATH C:\;C:\DOS;C:\123;C:\WS6

Thus if a program is executed, and DOS cannot find it in the current directory, it searches through the specified list. If it still cannot find it, it will produce a *Bad Command or file name* error.

4.5.2 PROMPT

Whenever DOS is waiting for input from the user it displays the DOS prompt on the screen. By default, this takes the form of the current drive letter. However, it is more useful to be prompted with the name of the current directory as well, thus allowing the user to see exactly where they are in the directory structure.

The PROMPT command allows this to be easily controlled. For example, PROMPT $P causes the current drive and directory to be displayed. Sometimes this can prove confusing, as there is no space allowed between the directory that is displayed by DOS, and the command entered by the user. This can be improved by specifying PROMPT PG, which displays and additional right arrow character (>). Thus using the PG option, the prompt would typically appear as:

C:\123\DATA>

Many users take advantage of AUTOEXEC.BAT to automatically execute certain memory-resident programs such as SideKick etc. Whilst such programs can occasionally help and simplify the day-to-day work for the user, they can, from a DOS point of view, cause unnecessary problems. This is due to the fact that they are TSR (Terminate-Stay-Resident) programs, and may not be fully compatible with other applications that are run. It is therefore recommended that all unnecessary TSR programs are removed from the AUTOEXEC.BAT file, and only executed if expressly required for a particular purpose.

Just as the order of statements in CONFIG.SYS is important, so too is the order of the commands in AUTOEXEC.BAT. Similar problems may well be encountered if the order of commands that install TSRs and device handlers is incorrect. There is unfortunately no hard and fast set of rules that can be used to determine the order of execution, so in many cases it is necessary to adopt a trial and error technique.

Figure 4.4 shows a typical AUTOEXEC.BAT file, with a brief description of each command.

4.6 DOS VERSIONS

DOS was originally designed by MicroSoft in the late 70s and early 80s. The first versions were very primitive by modern standards, and only offered a limited subset of the current commands. They were also designed to work with floppy disks, and provided very restricted facilities for handling hard disks. If such a version of DOS is in use on a hard disk system, then all manner of problems will be encountered.

It is therefore essential that a more modern version of DOS is used. However, this is not as simple as it seems. DOS has had a chequered history, and has passed through many transitions. The main releases are as follows:

1.0	Very rare nowadays, offered very restricted functionality
1.1	Produced from 1981–1983, and was a major upgrade on 1.0
1.25	Exactly the same as 1.1 but licensed to companies other than IBM

CLS	Clear the screen.
DATE	Display/modify system date.
TIME	Display/modify system time.
PROMPT PG	Set the prompt style to show current drive & directory.
PATH C:\;C:\DOS;C:\123;C:\WP5	Specify a search path.
MODE COM1:9600,N,8,2,P	Set up the communications port (the serial port) ready for use by a printer.
MODE LPT1:=COM1:	Redirect standard printer to use the serial port.
CLS	Clear the screen again.
ECHO OFF	Suppress screen display.
CD \BATCH	Change into the BATCH directory.
TYPE MENU	Display a text file listing the available application programs

Figure 4.4   A typical AUTOEXEC.BAT file

2.0   A major upgrade. This versions handles device drivers, sub-directories etc, as well as providing a much larger command set

2.1   Similar to 2.0, but contains a number of bug fixes to remove the errors that were present

2.11   As 2.1, but licensed to non-IBM companies

3.0   Produced for the AT class machine. Handles 1.2MB floppy disk drives

3.1   Another major upgrade – offers Network support

3.2   Similar to 3.1 but contains a number of bug fixes

3.3   Supports 3.5" diskettes. Fixes a few bugs from 3.2, but introduces many of its own. Some manufacturers, namely Apricot, Tandon and Research Machines adapted this version to allow for large volumes, ie hard disks of greater than 32MB

3.31   Version licensed to Compaq. Adapted to support large hard disks

4.0   A major upgrade supporting disks in excess of 32MB directly. It also offered a WIMPs type environment.

4.1   Similar to 4.0 but fixes many of the bugs present in the original. It can be difficult to differentiate between the two.

It can be seen that there have been a large number of different versions of DOS, each of which has its good and bad points. The problems lie not only in the bugs within DOS itself, but also the fact that some DOS versions cannot always read disks created by other versions. This is normally encountered when attempting to read a disk created with a later version of DOS. It is therefore highly recommended that all computer systems in an organisation use the same version of DOS. It is generally recommended that either DOS

3.2 or 4.1 is chosen, depending on whether the advanced facilities of the latter product are required. These two versions have the least number of known problems whilst still offering a high level of functionality.

4.6.1 UPGRADING DOS VERSIONS

At some time or other it is inevitable that the troubleshooter will be called upon to upgrade the version of DOS used on a machine, either due to a company-wide stand-ardisation programme, or because the user needs the extra features of the later release. This operation is viewed by many as a source of untold problems, as DOS offers little or no help in achieving the desired results.

Unfortunately it is true to say that upgrading DOS is not as simple as upgrading an application program; it is not possible to simply delete the existing program files and copy the new ones onto the system in their place. The reason for this is that the operation of DOS is ultimately dependent upon the two hidden system files, IO.SYS and IBM-DOS.COM or similar. These two programs are executed during the boot-up process and effectively determine the way in which DOS functions and what facilities it provides. Therefore in order to upgrade DOS it is necessary to upgrade these two files, and there are some quite stringent rules enforcing their placement on the disk.

- Firstly, they should be the first two files on the disk, ie they should be the first two entries in the root directory.

- More importantly, the data for IO.SYS (or its equivalent) must be at the start of the data area on the disk and must be stored in contiguous clusters. Therefore it should start in cluster 2 and run contiguously from there on.

- IBMDOS.COM (or equivalent) should then follow, although its data needn't be in contiguous clusters. However its directory entry must be the second on the disk.

There are some exceptions to these rules, notably concerning the licensed versions of DOS. These are often more flexible in the placement of the hidden files. For example Tandon DOS 3.30 allows IO.SYS to be non-contiguous, and also allows the directory entry for IBMDOS.COM to be anywhere in root. A further exception is DOS 4, which allows both of the hidden system files to be placed anywhere in the root directory with no need for them to be in contiguous clusters. The process of converting to DOS 4 is made even easier by the fact that it actually provides an INSTALL command which does the majority of the work, rather than leaving it all to the user. Thus the task of changing to DOS 4 is actually far simpler than any other DOS upgrade.

To help with the upgrading process, DOS provides the SYS command. The aim of the this command is to copy the hidden files to the required part of the disk, overwriting any previous system files that may be there. However, SYS will quite often fail and reports *No room for system files*, due to the fact that the system files for later versions of DOS are noticeably larger than the earlier ones. Thus DOS cannot fit them into the previously used area, and therefore cannot obey the placement and allocation rules defined above.

To overcome this problem it is necessary to free some space at the start of the disk by moving the files that are located in the required area. This can be done most easily by a four step process:

- Identify which files are using the required area at the start of the disk, and which ones are using the first two root directory entries.

– Make copies of these files, preferably with new names. They needn't be moved from their respective directories if different names are used.

– Delete the original files once copies have been made.

– Rename the copied files back to their original names.

For obvious reasons it is essential to take a backup before commencing this operation. Once the process has been completed, it will be found that the required area at the start of the disk is now available for use by the system files, and therefore the SYS command can be successfully used. Alternatively a program such as Norton Utilities can be used to transfer the two files.

A final point to note is that in some situations it is impossible to change from one DOS version to another using the SYS command. This situation is most often encountered when a large jump is made from a very dated version of DOS, such as version 2.0, to a more recent version, such as 3.31. In such cases there may be great difference between the actual format of the data on the disk, and in particular the way in which the FAT is used. The only solution to this problem is to reformat the disk and then reinstall all software and data. This will also allow the use of the disk to be optimised to take advantage of an orderly subdirectory structure. Before commencing this operation it is essential to ensure that there are at least two copies of the data and programs on floppy disk, tape etc, in case a problem is encountered when restoring one of them.

4.7 BACKUPS

A backup is considered by many to be a *duplicate* copy of an *original* piece of data. For example, a file stored on a hard disk may be considered to be the original, and the copy stored on a floppy disk is considered to be the backup. If the file is removed from the hard disk, the floppy disk copy is no longer a backup as it is the only version in existence. Thus there is no longer a backup copy of the data, and if the floppy disk were to fail then all would be lost.

For this reason the above definition is not strictly true. In a situation in which a full backup is maintained, it should be possible to restore data following a disaster without having to use the only remaining copy. Thus a true backup requires a minimum of two copies, in addition to the original data, to be maintained at all times.

Many organisations only retain a single copy of their data, and this situation can lead to serious problems. The approach to backup that should be employed is a minimum of the Grandfather-Father-Son hierarchy:

– The *Son* is a set of backup disks or tapes, one of which is updated at the end of every working day with everything that has been altered that day. The Son backup media is reused every week.

– The *Father* is a set of backup media, one of which is updated at the end of every working week by copying all data on the original media. The Father backup is typically reused every month. Ideally a second copy of the Father backup should be maintained off-site.

– The *Grandfather* is a backup that is created monthly, by performing a full backup of all information on the computer system. The Grandfather must also be stored safely, with a second copy off-site. It should not be reused for at least 1 year.

Figure 4.5 illustrates this procedure, showing how 10 sets of backup media are used to maintain a 3 month backup cycle.

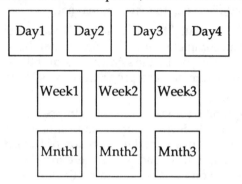

10 sets of media required, labelled as follows:

| Day1 | Day2 | Day3 | Day4 |

| Week1 | Week2 | Week3 |

| Mnth1 | Mnth2 | Mnth3 |

These are cycled over 12 weeks, backing up onto the disks as shown below

	Monday	Tuesday	Wednesday	Thursday	Friday
Week 1	Day1	Day2	Day3	Day4	Week1
Week 2	Day1	Day2	Day3	Day4	Week2
Week 3	Day1	Day2	Day3	Day4	Week3
Week 4	Day1	Day2	Day3	Day4	Month1
Week 5	Day1	Day2	Day3	Day4	Week1
Week 6	Day1	Day2	Day3	Day4	Week2
Week 7	Day1	Day2	Day3	Day4	Week3
Week 8	Day1	Day2	Day3	Day4	Month2
Week 9	Day1	Day2	Day3	Day4	Week1
Week 10	Day1	Day2	Day3	Day4	Week2
Week 11	Day1	Day2	Day3	Day4	Week3
Week 12	Day1	Day2	Day3	Day4	Month3

Figure 4.5   The backup cycle

Thus to restore the information following a disk failure, the most recent Father backup is first restored. This is followed by all of the Son backups that were taken since the Father was created. If the most recent father backup proves unreadable, then the second most recent one can be tried etc. If none of these are readable then the most recent Grandfather backup can be restored. The adoption of such a procedure means that the maximum amount of information that can possibly be lost is a single days work, although the amount of time that is required to create the backups is kept to a minimum.

This procedure must be accurately followed if it is to be at all effective. The off-site storage of a second copy of the backups is essential, as a single set can easily be damaged by fire, theft, flooding etc. There are many examples illustrating this point, one of the most notable being the entire destruction of the Open University computer department in Milton Keynes (UK), when the computer centre was engulfed in fire. They lost not only their hardware and working data, but also *all* of their backups as they were stored in the same building.

4.7.1 THE BACKUP PROCESS

Any backup procedure is ultimately dependent on the fact that the actual backing-up process is carried out correctly, and there are a number of problems that can occur in this area. There are many different ways of producing a backup of data, depending on the media, the data and the way in which it is to be stored:

4.7.1.1 Magnetic Tape

Standard magnetic tape (0.25"), otherwise referred to as QIC (Quarter Inch Cartridge), can be quite unreliable. The tape itself can stretch, break, or simply be magnetically damaged, the tape drive is subject to large mechanical stresses and strains and so can cease functioning, and the software is not always up to the required standard.

These factors may go unnoticed for months, or even years, if they are not monitored, especially if there is no need to restore the information from the tape. There have in fact been a number of instances where the magnetic tape backup has actually been blank due to failure of either the tape, drive or software. This leaves the system without a backup of any form whatsoever.

The only reliable way to test whether everything is working correctly is to actually restore a backup, and check that there are no problems. This obviously requires another machine to be available to restore the backup onto, so is not a cheap option.

A second, less obvious, problem involves the design of the tape drives themselves. In many cases a tape written by one device cannot be correctly read by another. Therefore if the original device fails, is damaged, or is stolen, it may prove difficult, or even impossible, to restore the backup using a different drive. If problems are encountered in attempting this operation it will be necessary to call in a hardware engineer to check and adjust the alignment of the tape heads etc.

4.7.1.2 Floppy Disks

Backing up to floppy disk is generally more reliable than backing up to magnetic tape, providing the correct method is employed. DOS supplies two appropriate commands, BACKUP and RESTORE. However, it has been noted that from time to time their operation is less than 100% reliable. Therefore, it is recommended that, where possible, the standard DOS COPY or XCOPY commands are used to transfer information to and from a floppy. This is not only a more reliable method, it also allows the contents of the floppy to be examined very easily, as the data is still in its standard format. Of course when files larger than a single floppy are being copied, the BACKUP command must be used as this allows files to be split over several disks. There are a number of other software utilities available that perform the backup process, one of the more popular being FASTBACK, and other general utilities such as PCTools include backup routines.

The problem with floppy disk based backups is that they can be very time consuming. For example, to backup an 80MB hard disk requires in excess of 225 360K floppy disks.

If each disk takes 1 minute to create, then the entire process takes over 3 hours. It is also an incredibly tedious process, which means that there is a high likelihood that errors will be made.

4.7.1.3 Other Media

A variety of other backup media are becoming available. In general the reliability of any new device cannot be proven until it has been in everyday use for a year or so, and even then the technology may still not have settled down.

Some of these devices, such as WORMs and demountable hard disks, offer immense advantages over current backup media in the form of very large storage capacities. There currently appear to be no negative aspects for these devices, except for the high price tags, and they do seem set to become more and more common as backup media.

Other backup media are being developed for PC applications from tried and tested mainframe technologies. One of the most notable in this class is half inch tape. This is physically stronger and more robust than its smaller counterpart, and the tape drives themselves are generally built to finer tolerances. These facts combine to mean that half inch tape is perhaps one of the best backup media available. Its major drawbacks are expense and the physical size of the tape drives. As they are developed from mainframe devices, they tend to be of a similar size, shape and cost. This may put them beyond the scope of many organisations, at least until they drop in price.

4.7.2 BACKUP TESTING

As previously noted, it is surprisingly common to find that the backup media are actually unusable for some reason, especially when QIC tape drives are used. A similar problem is that the software supplied with the backup system refuses to allow the data to be restored.

For these reasons it is essential to regularly test the backup, to ensure that the data can indeed be restored to a usable condition. The only way to do this is to actually restore the data onto a system. For obvious reasons this must not be done on the original system, as it may destroy the original data if it is unsuccessful. Thus it is necessary to have a second machine available, which can be used for such regular testing.

4.8 SUMMARY

This chapter has discussed a variety of preventative measures that can be taken to reduce the incidence of data loss or destruction. In many cases these are very minor things, such as double checking the CONFIG and AUTOEXEC files, using the SETUP procedure correctly, or allocating subdirectories sensibly. Taking these few simple steps may well negate the necessity of performing a full data recovery if something were to happen at a later stage.

5 Using DOS to Recover Data

5.1 DOS UTILITIES

A number of utilities are supplied with DOS for the maintenance and recovery of data on disk. These are supplied under a number of guises, and are mainly aimed at those users with a good understanding of how the disk stores data.

The following six DOS utilities have a role to play in data recovery:

- CHKDSK
- VERIFY
- RECOVER
- DEBUG
- EDLIN
- COPY CON:

Most are designed for specific situations, and using the wrong utility at the wrong time could produce disastrous consequences. Thus it is essential to gain a firm understanding about how these programs work, and what they actually do.

5.2 CHKDSK

CHKDSK, or 'check disk' as it is pronounced, is one of the most widely used, and least understood utilities available. It is supplied with almost every version of DOS, and will probably be executed by most users at some time.

The purpose of CHKDSK is to scan the disk and report any errors that it finds. Additionally, it returns information showing the size and usage of the storage area. In addition to this simple reporting facility, CHKDSK is able to try and repair any faults that it finds. The techniques that it uses for this remedial action are primitive, which means that the results may not be perfect, but in many cases it is one of the quickest and easiest way to perform a data recovery.

The format of the command is:

CHKDSK <Drive:> <Path> <Filename> /F /V

All of the arguments for the CHKDSK command are optional.

- <Drive:> determines which disk is scanned, and is specified as A: B: C: etc. Omitting this argument causes the current disk to be scanned.

59

- <Path> is the subdirectory path indicating the area that is to be scanned. For example, specifying the path as \123\DATA confines CHKDSK to only scanning the areas of disk used by the files in the \123\DATA directory. Omitting the argument causes the system to scan the current directory.

- <Filename> is the name of the file that CHKDSK is to scan. The extension must be specified for this to work. Omitting this argument causes all files to be scanned.

- The /F switch tells CHKDSK that it is to Fix any errors that it finds. This should be used judiciously (see below). Omitting this switch causes CHKDSK to just display a report, and take no further action.

- The /V switch tells CHKDSK that it should produce Verbose reports, ie fully detailed. Omitting this switch causes only summary reports to be produced.

5.2.1   USING CHKDSK

CHKDSK is ideal for *reporting* any errors that have occurred on the disk. It will give information on almost any problem that it finds, and will present it in a clear and concise way. However, it is far from ideal for *fixing* most errors, and thus it is essential to first run the command without the /F switch, even if it is expected that errors are present.

The reason for this is that the utility will have a go at fixing *any* error it finds, even if it is very serious. However, it only has the ability to correct a select few problems, and in attempting to remedy anything else it may cause absolute chaos with the information on the disk. Thus if the command (without the /F switch) is automatically invoked every time the machine is rebooted, the user is alerted to any problems and can them fix them in a more controlled manner.

One of the main problems CHKDSK can fix effectively is that of *lost clusters*. A lost cluster is a series of data sectors that are not referenced in the directory entries, and thus have no filename, attributes or other details. CHKDSK remedies the situation by assigning a new directory entry for the chain, with a filename of FILEXXXX.CHK. XXXX is replaced by a number from 0000 upwards, so that each file has a unique name. CHKDSK completes the remainder of the directory entry so that the data can be accessed normally. The problem then faced by the user is how to interpret this data. If it appears to be a text file, then it can almost certainly be read into a word processor. If however it is a program or special data file, then it may be more difficult to make sense of it.

5.2.2   A WORKED EXAMPLE

Consider the following situation: A user wishes to test their disk to determine whether or not there are any errors present; the CHKDSK command is used with no arguments:

CHKDSK

The system scans the current disk, which in this case is an 80MB hard disk, and produces the report shown in Figure 5.1.

Note that the user is reminded that the /F option has not been specified and that no changes will be made. From this report it can be seen that there are two errors on the disk. Firstly, the system has found a file in the C:\DATAREC directory called TESTFILE.PCX which has its file size incorrectly specified. By looking at the directory entry, it can be seen that TESTFILE.PCX is currently specified as:

```
TESTFILE.PCX     57032    1-11-90    1:00p
```

```
Volume TECHTRANS    created 27 Nov 1989 11:13a

Errors found, F parameter not specified.
Corrections will not be written to disk.

C:\DATAREC\TESTFILE.PCX
    Allocation error, size adjusted.

6 lost clusters found in 1 chains.
Convert lost chains to files   (Y/N)? n
    49152 bytes disk space
          would be freed.

 79986688 bytes total disk space
    73728 bytes in 5 hidden files
   761856 bytes in 93 directories
 74145792 bytes in 3538 user files
  4956160 bytes available on disk

   655360 bytes total memory
   568096 bytes free
```

Figure 5.1   The CHKDSK report

Also, the system has found a chain of lost clusters, and prompts the user to confirm that they want this converted to a file.

After considering the above, the user decides that they want CHKDSK to fix these two errors. The following command is then issued:

CHKDSK /F

The system scans the disk, and again prompts the user to confirm that the chain is to be converted into a file. On replying Y, the file is created. The display will appear as shown in Figure 5.2.

```
Volume TECHTRANS    created 27 Nov 1989 11:13a
C:\DATAREC\TESTFILE.PCX
    Allocation error, size adjusted.

6 lost clusters found in 1 chains.
Convert lost chains to files   (Y/N)? y

 79986688 bytes total disk space
    73728 bytes in 5 hidden files
   761856 bytes in 93 directories
 74153984 bytes in 3539 user files
    49152 bytes in 1 recovered files
  4947968 bytes available on disk

   655360 bytes total memory
   568096 bytes free
```

Figure 5.2   Report from CHKDSK /F

The file has now had its size truncated, and is listed in the directory as:

```
TESTFILE.PCX      8192    1-11-90    1:00p
```

The lost clusters are converted into a file, which is placed in the root directory. The directory entry for this file is:

```
FILE0000.CHK     49152    6-11-90    1:38p
```

Repeating the CHKDSK command with no arguments produces the display shown in Figure 5.3, indicating that there are no further errors present.

```
Volume TECHTRANS    created 27 Nov 1989 11:13a

79986688 bytes total disk space
   73728 bytes in 5 hidden files
  761856 bytes in 93 directories
74211328 bytes in 3541 user files
 4939776 bytes available on disk

  655360 bytes total memory
  568096 bytes free
```

Figure 5.3   CHKDSK report for corrected disk

At this point, the user is left with two amended files. The first is the original TESTFILE.PCX, which has had its size truncated from 57032 bytes to 8192 bytes. The second is the new file called FILE0000.CHK, which is 49152 bytes long. Performing a quick addition of these two sizes produces an answer of 57344, only a little more than the original size of TESTFILE.PCX. This indicates that it is highly likely that the following had happened:

A large section of the original TESTFILE.PCX file became detached, almost certainly because of an error in the FAT. Thus the directory entry for TESTFILE.PCX was incorrect, as it specified a size of 57032 when an insufficient number of logical sectors were referenced. The remainder of the file had no directory entry and became a chain of lost clusters. CHKDSK fixed both of these problems and recovered the data, albeit in the form of two separate files.

Unfortunately, if an attempt is made to load the files into an application program such as PC Paintbrush or Ventura Publisher it will be found that errors are produced. This is due to the fact that the file formats have not been preserved when the data was split into two separate files. Thus it is necessary to transform the data back into a usable format. The way in which this is accomplished is dependent upon the type of the original file:

–   If it was a simple ASCII file, such as from a word processor, then the two sections can probably be read into the application normally, and combined using the in-built facilities of the program.

–   If this does not work, or produces incorrect data, then it may be necessary to join the two halves of the file first. This can be achieved with the copy command:

```
COPY TESTFILE.TXT+\FILE0000.CHK NEWFILE
```

This concatenates the two parts of the original file to form a single file called NEWFILE.

- This technique is only valid for ASCII files, and will not work for more sophisticated data formats. In the above example, the file actually had an extension of .PCX, meaning that it is a PC-Paintbrush file and will therefore not be in ASCII format. Thus the concatenation process needs to be slightly different to take account of this fact. The required command is:

    COPY /B TESTFILE.PCX+\FILE0000.CHK NEWFILE.PCX

    The /B switch means that the files are to be treated as Binary files, and the entire contents should be copied. Omitting this switch will cause the copying process to terminate when it encounters an ASCII end-of-file character (hex value 2Ah). As this is a non-ASCII file these characters could appear anywhere, and therefore the copy process would not concatenate all of the data from the two files.

- After concatenating the file using either of the COPY commands above, it is still necessary to adjust the size, which is currently specified as 57344 bytes, to its correct value of 57032. This can be accomplished most easily with Norton Utilities, which are covered in detail in Chapter 6. After the size has been adjusted the file can be used in the normal way.

5.3 VERIFY

By default, the system does not verify that disk write operations are successfully completed. However, using the VERIFY ON command instructs DOS to check that there are no problems each time it writes something to the disk. Thus, any errors or faults that occur when the data is written to disk are made obvious at an early stage.

Unfortunately the verification process is not as thorough as many people believe. A true verification process means that the system would write the data to the disk, read it back from the disk, and compare this data with what it thought it was writing. Any differences between the two sets of data would indicate that there were errors.

The DOS verification process is much simpler, and uses the CRC (cyclic redundancy check) values to pinpoint any problems. The CRC is a special value that is written at the end of each sector whenever new data is stored on disk. This value is created by a special algorithm from the data in the sector, and will almost certainly be unique. To verify the data in a particular sector, DOS first reads the CRC value from disk, and then the data in the sector. Next, it performs the CRC calculation on the data and compares the value obtained with the value that it read from the disk; if they differ then there is an error.

This means that there is considerable scope for faults to slip through, and so the verification process must not be relied on to provide accurate results.

5.3.1 CRC ERRORS

A further problem surrounds the verification process and the use of CRCs. As the data is only verified when it is written, the system can take no account of any faults that develop while it is stored on disk. These may be due to disk crashes, software faults etc, and can cause the CRC to become incorrect. On attempting to access a sector of the disk, the system performs the verification process again (automatically), and if it finds a difference between the calculated and disk CRCs it produces a *Data Error*. At this point it will refuse to allow the user to access the data using any normal application program.

The remedy for this problem is to force the system to read the sector, and then write it back in the same place. The act of writing the data will cause the new, correct CRC value to be written to disk. This process can be accomplished in a number of ways, as will be seen in Chapter 6.

5.4   RECOVER

This is a rather dangerous command, and can easily destroy reams of data if used incorrectly. Its purpose, as defined in the DOS manuals, is to recover a file or a disk that contains bad sectors, by copying all readable data to unused areas. However, it does this in much the same way as CHKDSK, and allocates arbitrary filenames to the new data. These filenames are of the form FILEXXXX.REC, where XXXX is replaced by a sequential number from 0000 upwards. Furthermore, it abandons any directory structure that was in use on the disk and places all of the files in the root directory.

More problems occur when a part of a file is unreadable, usually because it occupies a bad sector. In this case RECOVER will just ignore the part it cannot read, and continue at the next area that it decides is readable. Thus many of the supposedly recovered files may have large chunks missing from them; if they are program files they will be unusable, if they are databases or worksheets they will be unreadable, and even if they are text files they will require a great deal of work to restore them to a useful condition.

This process of recovering data from bad sectors can be performed much more satisfactorily by other software, notably Norton Utilities, PC Tools or The Disk Explorer. These products exercise a greater degree of control over the data than RECOVER, and allow the user to determine which areas are deemed unusable etc. Thus the effects on the data are in no way as drastic.

Another problem that occurs with RECOVER is due to its name. It is a rather appealing name, especially to a user who thinks that they have accidentally lost a file. Therefore, in many cases they will type RECOVER C: in the belief that this may do some good and bring back their lost data. The command should never be used in this way, particularly as the C: drive is almost certainly a hard disk. When used in this way, the command will rename any file it finds on drive C: as FILEXXXX.REC as explained above, placing all files in the root directory. It will be virtually impossible to recover the original filenames and directory structure, and thus the hard disk will be left in an unusable condition.

For this reason it is recommended that the file RECOVER.COM is removed from the hard disk of any user who does not fully understand its implications. Indeed it is wise to remove it from all hard disks and just run the utility from floppy if it is required at a later date.

5.5   CREATING SMALL FILES

In many situations it is useful to be able to quickly and easily create a small file. This may be a batch file, text file, or simple data file. DOS offers two ways of accomplishing this.

5.5.1   COPY CON:

The COPY command can be used to copy all keyboard entries into a file. The format of the command is:

COPY CON: <filename>

CON: is the device name of the keyboard. Therefore copying from this device to a file replicates all keystrokes. After entering the command, the system will appear to pause. In fact it is waiting for the data to be entered from the keyboard. The information should be entered, using the Enter key to end each line. Note that no changes can be made to previously entered lines, so care must be taken to ensure that no typing mistakes are made. Once the data has been entered, the Ctrl+Z key combination is pressed to signify the end of file. ie press and hold the Ctrl key, then press the Z key. Finally, pressing Enter terminates the command.

5.5.2   EDLIN

Edlin is the built in line editor for DOS. It is used to create text files on a line by line basis. All functions are carried out through the use of single character commands, the most common of which are shown below:

D   Delete lines of text

E   End the editing session and save any changes that were made

I   Insert new lines of text

L   List the contents of the file on the screen

Q   Quit from Edlin without saving any changes that were made

To edit an existing line, the current line number is entered. The function keys F1 through F6 may then be used as follows:

[F1]   Copy and display one character from the retained line

[F2]   Copy all characters up to the specified one

[F3]   Copy all remaining characters from the retained line

[F4]   Skip all characters up to the specified one

[F5]   Re-edit the current retained line

[F6]   Used to exit insert mode

Either Edlin or COPY CON: may be used to create small ASCII files. These may be batch files, CONFIG.SYS files, or any other form of ASCII file that is required.

5.6   DEBUG

Debug is a special tool that allows the computers memory to be examined and, if required, altered. It also has a variety of other facilities: it can execute a program one step at a time, allowing the user to check that a system is operating correctly; it can trace the execution of a program, compare values before and after an instruction, and compare, move and fill sections of memory. Finally it can read and write disk files and sectors.

Many of these facilities will be of use only to assembly language programmers and those who wish to 'poke about' inside the system. However, Debug is a very powerful tool for data recovery purposes, and can be used for a wide variety of tasks, including:

– Patching program files

– Examining memory

– Exploring the contents of disks, including the boot sector, FAT and directory

- Altering directory entries, including file attributes, name, size
- Altering FAT entries
- Altering Boot sector data
- Creating short .COM files to perform simple tasks
- Examining program instructions
- Undeleting short files
- Recovering files that are stranded in memory
- Repairing damaged files

Some of these tasks will be more efficiently performed with proprietary software, particularly those involving writing directly to the disk. However, in many cases software may be unavailable, or it may not work with the particular hardware configuration in use. If this is the case then Debug is a safeguard against total disaster.

5.6.1 LIMITATIONS OF DEBUG

Whilst Debug is very powerful in what it allows the user to do, it does not supply much help. In particular Debug is unable to apply any interpretation to the data it handles, other than to display it in hexadecimal, ASCII, or assembly language. Because of this it is impractical in many cases to use Debug to work extensively with the FAT or directory structure. It is also impossible for Debug to reference the partition record data, as it is confined to working within the current DOS partition.

5.6.2 USING DEBUG

Before using Debug it is essential to have a good basic knowledge of how computer data is stored. Chapter 3 explained how data is stored by IBM PC and compatible machines. Another difficulty encountered with Debug is its exclusive use of hexadecimal notation. Thus it is again essential to be familiar with this notation, and appreciate the differences involved. Chapter 2 of this book discusses hexadecimal notation. As will become clear, Debug is a prime example of a situation in which a hexadecimal calculator is a necessity rather than a luxury.

There are some situations in which Debug displays data in both hexadecimal format and ASCII character format, provided that the value is between 32 and 126. This means that when Debug displays the data, the screen generally shows it as hexadecimal (in which the value of all bytes can be seen) and ASCII (in which the printable characters are displayed). Figure 5.4 is a listing of COMMAND.COM produced by Debug.

5.6.2.1 Debug Commands

There are 22 basic commands available within Debug, as shown below. They consist of one or two letters, and are entered at the keyboard in response to the prompt. Any command shown in several different formats indicates that any one may be used.

A
A [start-address]
> Assembles machine language assembler statements into memory as binary machine code

```
C:\>debug command.com
-d
251C:0100  E9 2D 0D BA DA 0A 3D 05-00 74 1B BA BF 0A 3D 02  .-....=..t....=.
251C:0110  00 74 13 BA 85 0A 3D 08-00 74 0B BA 71 0A 3D 0B  .t...=..t..q.=.
251C:0120  00 74 03 BA 62 0A 0E 1F-E8 6A 06 EB 0C CD 21 72  .t..b....j....!r
251C:0130  D2 B4 4D CD 21 2E A3 EA-0B E9 76 01 2E F6 06 59  ..M.!.....v....Y
251C:0140  0C 01 74 0C 2E F6 06 59-0C 02 74 03 E9 02 13 CF  ..t....Y..t.....
251C:0150  2E F6 06 59 0C 04 74 11-80 FC 01 72 F2 80 FC 0C  ...Y..t....r.....
251C:0160  77 ED 83 C4 06 F9 CA 02-00 2E 80 0E 59 0C 04 FB  w...........Y...
251C:0170  0E 1F A1 F3 0B 0B C0 75-06 50 B4 0D CD 21 58 F7  .......u.P...!X.
-d
251C:0180  06 97 0B FF FF 74 4B 0B-C0 75 47 E8 5F 02 E8 A8  .....tK..uG._...
251C:0190  03 73 39 53 8E 06 97 0B-26 8B 1E 04 00 83 FB 00  .s9S....&.......
251C:01A0  74 08 06 8E C3 B4 49 CD-21 07 26 8A 0E 01 00 26  t.....I.!.&....&
251C:01B0  8B 1E 02 00 B4 49 CD 21-89 1E 97 0B FF 0E FC 0B  .....I.!........
251C:01C0  75 D2 5B 88 0E ED 0B C6-06 5A 0C 00 E8 C3 05 E9  u.[......Z......
251C:01D0  40 02 33 C0 8B E8 A2 F8-0B A2 F9 0B E8 1C 00 39  @.3............9
251C:01E0  06 F3 0B 74 06 C7 06 F3-0B FF FF 80 26 59 0C FB  ...t........&Y..
251C:01F0  38 06 E9 0B 75 03 E9 25-01 F9 CB 50 33 C0 2E 86  8...u..%...P3...
-
```

Figure 5.4   The DEBUG display

C [start-address] [end-address] [start-address2]
C [start-address] L [length] [start-address2]
> Compares the contents of two blocks of memory

D
D [start-address]
D [start-address] [end-address]
D [start-address] L [length]
> Displays the contents of a specified area of memory

E [start-address] [data-list]
E [start-address]
> Enters a list of byte values or characters into memory. Second command causes each byte to be displayed separately, allowing it to be changed if required

F [start-address] [end-address] [data-list]
F [start-address] L [length] [data-list]
> Fills a block of memory with a list of byte values or characters. If the block is larger than the list then the list is repeated until the block is filled

G
G=[start-address]
G=[breakpoint(s)]
G=[start-address] [breakpoint(s)]
> Begins execution of a program in memory (Stands for Go)

H [number1] [number2]
> Adds and subtracts two hexadecimal numbers

I [port-address]
> Reads and displays a byte from one of the PC input/output ports

L
L [start-address]
> Loads a file into memory

L [drive] [sector-number] [sector-count]
L [start-address] [drive] [sector-number] [sector-count]
> Loads specified sectors from the disk into memory

M [start-address] [end-address] [start-address2]
M [start-address] L [length] [start-address2]
> Moves a block of data from one memory location to another

N [filespec]
> Names a file

N [parameter-list]
> Names a list of parameters that must be specified when the file is executed

O [port-address] [byte]
> Sends a byte value to an input/output port

Q
> Quits from Debug

R
R [register-name]
RF
> Displays the contents of the machine registers and status flags, allowing them to be changed if required

S [start-address] [end-address] [data-list]
S [start-address] L [length] [data-list]
> Searches a block of memory for a specified list of values

T
T=[start-address]
> Traces program operation, by executing one or more instructions

U
U [start-address]
U [start-address] [end-address]
U [start-address] L [length]
> Unassembles machine code into assembly language

W
W [start-address]
> Writes a file to disk

W [drive] [sector-number] [number-count]
W [start-address] [drive] [sector-number] [number-count]
> Writes one or more sectors to disk

XA
> Allocates EMS pages

XD

Deallocates EMS

XM

Maps an expanded memory page into the page frame

XS

Displays the status of expanded memory

Note that all data that is entered using any of the commands, and all data that is displayed, must be in either hexadecimal format or the ASCII equivalent character. To make matters worse, Debug does not suffix its hexadecimal values with 'h'

5.6.3 A WORKED EXAMPLE USING DEBUG

This book is not intended to be a tutorial on the full use of Debug, but rather it is intended to provide a range of examples showing how such tools can be used to recover data. It should always be remembered that no single tool will solve all problems, and therefore the user should appreciate just how far they can go in using Debug for data recovery.

Debug is one of the most user-unfriendly programs available, due mainly to its poor command set. As some are very complex, care should be taken to ensure that they are fully understood before modifying important files.

Generally speaking, it is unwise to attempt to modify important program files, and on no account should untrained staff use Debug unsupervised. Debug can easily be used for modifying Boot Sector, FAT, and Directory information, and also for exploring memory. It is even possible to change the SETUP information through the use of Debug, and to low-level format the entire hard disk. Thus Debug should be treated with a great deal of care.

5.6.3.1 Ground Rules

Before attempting to make any changes at all, it is essential that a copy is made of the data, and any work then carried out on the copy. If anything then goes wrong, it is a simple matter to make another copy from the original.

Whilst this is relatively simple with single files, it becomes noticeably more difficult when considering entire floppy disks, and almost impossible in the case of an entire hard disk. The following are some hints on the production of such a copy:

–   Single files can be copied using the DOS copy command, although it is more than likely that this will not copy any lost data as well.

–   Floppy disks can be copied using a product such as COPYIIPC. The DOS DISK-COPY command is not recommended as it can in some cases introduce unwanted problems of its own.

–   Entire hard disks can be copied across a network or by attaching a second hard disk to the computer. A special program will have to be written to accomplish the actual copying, and this can be most easily achieved with a language such as Turbo Pascal (see Chapter 6).

–   **Above all, the copy should always be made onto a different device to the original, ie, use a separate floppy or hard disk. Changes should NEVER be made to the original data.**

5.6.3.2 Patching a File

As explained above, Debug can be used to patch files on disk. This may be necessary due
to data loss or some other factor. This example considers the situation in which a memo
has been written in WordStar, to which it is necessary to attach a list of filenames from a
specific directory. The simplest way to obtain the list is to use the DOS redirection facility
which allows the output from any command to be diverted to a printer, or alternatively
a file. To redirect the output from the DIR command to a file, issue the command

DIR >[filename]

To append the output from the DIR command to the end of an existing file, issue the
command

DIR >>[filename]

Thus if WordStar is used to create a file called MEMO.TXT, the directory listing can be
appended to the file by entering:

DIR >>MEMO.TXT

It would be reasonable to assume that if the memo file was now loaded back into
WordStar, then the directory listing would be appended to it. However, this is not the
case, as WordStar uses a special character to indicate the end of the file. Although
MS-DOS has appended the list of files to the end of MEMO.TXT, it has not removed the
special characters, and so WordStar does not recognise that there is more data in the file.
Debug can be used to remove these special characters, and thus correct the file.

The memo should be created to read as follows:

```
John,
     Here's a floppy with the files for the newsletter that you
wanted. See the directory listing below:
```

The size of this file is 256 bytes, as can be seen from the directory listing. The DIR
command can then be used to list the files:

DIR >>MEMO.TXT

The size of the file will now have changed to reflect the additional data. This can be
verified by checking the value returned by the DIR command, which is 769 for the listing
of the files used here.

Debug is then invoked, specifying the name of the file so that it is automatically loaded:

DEBUG MEMO.TXT

The screen then displays the debug prompt, shown as a hyphen (-). Entering the D
(display) command causes the first few lines of the file to be displayed on the screen, as
shown in Figure 5.5. If D 100 L 120 is entered, then the subsequent lines are also displayed,
as shown in Figure 5.6.

It can be seen from this display that the memo does not actually begin until some way
into the file. In fact the first few bytes of the file contain special control characters and
information used by the WordStar program. However, it is easy to see where the memo
ends, and the list of file names begins. The space between the two sections is filled with
values of 1A. This is the hexadecimal value for the end-of-file characters used by
WordStar, and is the numeric equivalent of pressing [Ctrl]+[Z].

```
C:\NEWS>debug memo.txt
-d
2502:0100  1D 7D 00 00 55 48 50 00-00 00 00 00 00 00 00 00   .}..UHP.........
2502:0110  00 01 00 00 00 00 00 00-00 00 00 00 00 00 00 00   ................
2502:0120  00 00 00 00 00 00 00 00-00 00 00 00 00 00 00 00   ................
2502:0130  00 00 00 00 00 00 00 00-00 00 00 00 00 00 00 00   ................
2502:0140  00 00 00 00 00 00 00 00-00 00 00 00 00 00 00 00   ................
2502:0150  00 00 00 00 00 00 00 00-00 00 00 00 00 00 00 00   ................
2502:0160  00 00 00 00 00 00 00 00-00 00 00 00 00 00 00 00   ................
2502:0170  00 00 00 00 00 00 00 00-00 00 00 00 00 7D 00 1D   .............}..
-
```

Figure 5.5   The listing of the first 128 bytes of the file

```
2502:0130  00 00 00 00 00 00 00 00-00 00 00 00 00 00 00 00   ................
2502:0140  00 00 00 00 00 00 00 00-00 00 00 00 00 00 00 00   ................
2502:0150  00 00 00 00 00 00 00 00-00 00 00 00 00 00 00 00   ................
2502:0160  00 00 00 00 00 00 00 00-00 00 00 00 00 00 00 00   ................
2502:0170  00 00 00 00 00 00 00 00-00 00 00 00 00 7D 00 1D   .............}..
-d 100 l 120
2502:0100  1D 7D 00 00 55 48 50 00-00 00 00 00 00 00 00 00   .}..UHP.........
2502:0110  00 01 00 00 00 00 00 00-00 00 00 00 00 00 00 00   ................
2502:0120  00 00 00 00 00 00 00 00-00 00 00 00 00 00 00 00   ................
2502:0130  00 00 00 00 00 00 00 00-00 00 00 00 00 00 00 00   ................
2502:0140  00 00 00 00 00 00 00 00-00 00 00 00 00 00 00 00   ................
2502:0150  00 00 00 00 00 00 00 00-00 00 00 00 00 00 00 00   ................
2502:0160  00 00 00 00 00 00 00 00-00 00 00 00 00 00 00 00   ................
2502:0170  00 00 00 00 00 00 00 00-00 00 00 00 00 7D 00 1D   .............}..
2502:0180  4A 6F 68 6E 2C 0D 0A 20-20 20 20 20 48 65 72 65   John,...    Here
2502:0190  27 73 20 61 20 66 6C 6F-70 70 79 20 77 69 74 68   's a floppy with
2502:01A0  20 74 68 65 20 66 69 6C-65 73 20 66 6F 72 20 74    the files for t
2502:01B0  68 65 20 6E 65 77 73 6C-65 74 74 65 72 20 A0 74   he newsletter .t
2502:01C0  68 61 74 20 8D 0A 79 6F-75 20 77 61 6E 74 65 64   hat ..you wanted
2502:01D0  2E 20 53 65 65 20 74 68-65 20 64 69 72 65 63 74   . See the direct
2502:01E0  6F 72 79 20 6C 69 73 74-69 6E 67 20 62 65 6C 6F   ory listing belo
2502:01F0  77 3A 1A 1A 1A 1A 1A 1A-1A 1A 1A 1A 1A 1A 1A 1A   w:..............
2502:0200  0D 0A 20 56 6F 6C 75 6D-65 20 69 6E 20 64 72 69   .. Volume in dri
2502:0210  76 65 20 43 20 69 73 20-54 45 43 48 54 52 41 4E   ve C is TECHTRAN
-
```

Figure 5.6   The listing of the first 288 bytes of the file

To correct the file, these need to be replaced with spaces. The simplest way to do this is to use the F (fill) command. However, before this can be accomplished, it is necessary to establish the addresses of the locations containing the end-of-file markers. This is achieved by searching a section of the file for the 1A value. The S (search) command can be used for this by entering the following:

    S 100 L FF 1A

This translates into search the data, starting at location 100h and continuing until 256 bytes have been checked, noting any locations that contain the value 1Ah. When this command is executed, the display will appear as shown in Figure 5.7.

```
2502:01A0  20 74 68 65 20 66 69 6C-65 73 20 66 6F 72 20 74    the files for t
2502:01B0  68 65 20 6E 65 77 73 6C-65 74 74 65 72 20 A0 74    he newsletter .t
2502:01C0  68 61 74 20 8D 0A 79 6F-75 20 77 61 6E 74 65 64    hat ..you wanted
2502:01D0  2E 20 53 65 65 20 74 68-65 20 64 69 72 65 63 74    . See the direct
2502:01E0  6F 72 79 20 6C 69 73 74-69 6E 67 20 62 65 6C 6F    ory listing belo
2502:01F0  77 3A 1A 1A 1A 1A 1A 1A-1A 1A 1A 1A 1A 1A 1A 1A    w:..............
2502:0200  0D 0A 20 56 6F 6C 75 6D-65 20 69 6E 20 64 72 69    .. Volume in dri
2502:0210  76 65 20 43 20 69 73 20-54 45 43 48 54 52 41 4E    ve C is TECHTRAN
-
-s 100 l 256 1a
2502:01F2
2502:01F3
2502:01F4
2502:01F5
2502:01F6
2502:01F7
2502:01F8
2502:01F9
2502:01FA
2502:01FB
2502:01FC
2502:01FD
2502:01FE
2502:01FF
-
```

Figure 5.7 The results of the search command

The first and last addresses that are listed give the start and end of the range containing the end-of-file markers. The fill command can now be used as follows:

F 01F2 01FF 20

This means fill locations 01F2 to 01FF with the value 20, which is the hexadecimal equivalent of the space character. Thus all of the end-of-file characters are replaced with spaces. The write command is then issued to write the changes to the disk, and Debug may then be exited:

W
Q

If the memo is then loaded into WordStar, or displayed on the screen, it includes the directory listing, as shown in Figure 5.8.

Although this is only a simple example of the facilities offered by Debug, it does show how powerful the program can be. This form of patching and modification could not be accomplished in any other way, although the final result of the directory listing appended to the memo could perhaps have been achieved more easily by creating two files, then reading one into the other within WordStar.

Figure 5.8   The patched memo file

However, one area in which the file patching feature is particularly important is that of damaged file recovery. For example, if the power to the system is removed while a file is being saved, then the operation will not be completed, and this in turn will cause errors if the file is later read. The reason for this is that the end-of-file marker is not in place. Using the above method, the end-of-file marker can be inserted so that at least some of the file is recoverable.

5.7 SUMMARY

This Chapter has shown how some of the DOS utilities can be used in the process of data recovery. The useful, but fairly primitive, CHKDSK program will be of great use to many users as lost clusters are one of the most common occurrences of data loss on personal computer.

The techniques for creating small ASCII files will also be found to be of help to many users, not only for creating simple text files, but also for the initial creation of the AUTOEXEC.BAT and CONFIG.SYS files on new machines.

Finally, the brief examination of Debug has shown it to be a powerful and versatile utility, although the way in which commands are issued and data displayed tend to make it difficult for the inexperienced to come to terms with this program.

Debug is by far the most powerful DOS utility, and allows the user to do almost anything from examining and modifying the computers memory to writing directly to the disk. Thus it can be used for repairing damaged files, making alterations to data from proprietary software packages that could not be made in any other way, and creating small programs, to name only a few of its many applications.

It should always be remembered that some tasks are more efficiently performed with proprietary software such as The Norton utilities or PCTools. Chapter 6 will discuss such applications in detail, as well as provide a number of guidelines relating to which applications are suitable for which problems.

6   Utility Software

6.1   THE ADVANTAGES OF THIRD-PARTY UTILITY SOFTWARE

Whilst the DOS utilities provide the user with a number of disk editing facilities, it is still necessary in many cases to resort to using third-party utilities such as PCTools, Norton Utilities, Disk Explorer or any one of a number of others.

The main reason for this is because of the way in which DOS addresses the disk. As any DOS partition is held in a single area of the disk, the DOS utilities will not read areas beyond the partition limits. This means that DOS utilities cannot be used for accessing extended partitions, non-standard partitions, or more importantly the partition record itself which is situated at PSN 0.

Third-party utilities manage to overcome this barrier by using slightly different instructions in their programs, and are thus able to access the entire disk area, from physical sector 0 upwards. An additional bonus is that the majority offer a more user-friendly interface, allowing commands to be entered in a more meaningful way, and displaying the data in a much more readable format.

There are many different utilities available, some of which are excellent whilst others are terrible. However, due to space limitations, this publication cannot cover all, or even a large range of them. Therefore only the most relevant and functional have been covered:

- The two market leaders for general purpose utilities, Norton Utilities and PCTools.
- One of many specialised disk editors, Disk Explorer.
- Shareware utilities which provide good, simple, inexpensive programs.
- COPYIIPC, which may not immediately be thought of as a data recovery tool, but which is excellent for such tasks in many situations.
- Programming Languages, which allow specialised programs to be written.

No lengthy worked examples are included, as Chapter 7 will cover the detailed application of these systems.

6.2   NORTON UTILITIES

Norton Utilities has been available in some form or other for a number of years, and its name is well known. It is famous primarily for its undeleting facility, whereby deleted files may be recovered with extreme ease. However, the package offers a much greater range of facilities than this alone, including disk management programs, file finders, and also an excellent disk editor. Version 4.5 of the package was perhaps the most widely

75

distributed, and is the easiest to use for most data recovery operations. Therefore the examples shown in this section deal exclusively with this version. Later versions offer similar facilities, although they have a different front-end user interface.

The different utilitiess are supplied as separate files which must be executed from the DOS prompt. However, a special program called the Norton Integrator provides an easy-to-use front end for the other commands. The Norton Integrator is executed by typing NI from the DOS prompt, and produces the display shown in Figure 6.1.

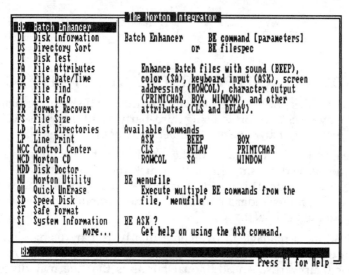

Figure 6.1   The Norton Integrator (NI)

The commands are listed down the left hand side of the screen, together with a short description. The right hand side of the screen provides much more detailed information

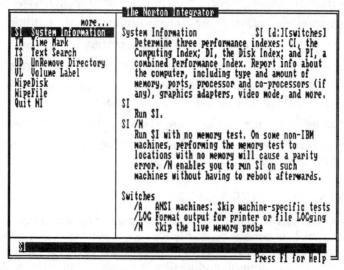

Figure 6.2   Remaining options for the Norton Integrator

on the currently highlighted command, in this case the BE command. The highlighting bar is moved using the cursor keys. Pressing PgDn moves the cursor onto the next page, and produces the display shown in Figure 6.2.

A number of the different programs are of interest in terms of data recovery, namely DI, DT, FA, FF, FR, NDD, NU, QU, SI, and UD. Each will be examined in greater detail. The majority of the remaining commands are concerned with disk management routines, and so are of more interest to the everyday users of the system rather than the trouble-shooter.

6.2.1 DI – DISK INFORMATION

The disk information program displays a variety of technical information about the chosen disk. This includes the number of sectors, the sector size, the cluster size, the FAT size, offsets to important areas etc.

This information is of a more technical nature than that provided by the NU program (see later section). This information is essential for further examination of the disk, as it allows the user to determine the positioning of all the important sections. The data is read from the boot sector of the disk directly, and also from DOS. The two values are shown side by side so that any anomalies or differences can be easily seen. However, if the boot sector of the disk has been corrupted or altered, then both of these checks may produce incorrect results, although they may still be identical. Thus it is important to take a subjective view of the information produced by DI if there is any chance that the boot sector has been corrupted.

The best way to ensure that this information is to hand is to print the screen display once the command has been executed. This can be achieved with a screen grabber such as *Pizzaz Plus*, or simply by pressing the [Print Screen] key. Figure 6.3 below shows a report produced by the DI command.

```
DI-Disk Information, Advanced Edition 4.50, (C) Copr 1987-88, Peter Norton

   Information from DOS          Drive C:        Information from the boot record
-----------------------------------------------------------------------------------
                              system id            'MSDOS3.3'
                         media descriptor (hex)         F8
            2               drive number
        2,048              bytes per sector          2,048
            4             sectors per cluster            4
            2               number of FATs              2
          512            root directory entries        512
           10              sectors per FAT              10
        9,764            number of clusters
                          number of sectors         39,087
            1               offset to FAT               1
           21             offset to directory
           29               offset to data
                          sectors per track            17
                                sides                   9
                             hidden sectors            17

Press any key to continue...
```

Figure 6.3   The Disk Information report

The DI command can be used with or without a drive specifier. Executing the command without specifying a drive will produce information on the current device.

6.2.2 DT – DISK TEST

The Disk Test program will test a disk for physical errors. It can then move any questionable clusters to good areas, marking the bad ones so that they are not used again.

DT can check the entire disk, just the data area (ie ignoring the system areas), or just a particular file. The format of the command is:

DT [drive:] [filespec] [switches]

- **[drive:]** specifies the drive to test. Omitting this causes the current drive to be tested.
- **[filespec]** determines which file(s) will be tested. Wildcards can be used as required. Omitting this parameter causes all files on the current drive to be tested.
- **[switches]** define the operation of the command:
  - /B   Perform both a disk and file test
  - /Cn   Mark Cluster n as bad
  - /Cn–   Mark Cluster b as good (opposite of /Cn)
  - /D   Test the entire disk
  - /F   Test file area only
  - /LOG   Format output for printer or file
  - /M   Move doubtful clusters to a safe location
  - /S   Test subdirectories also

Figure 6.4 shows the display produced by the DT command.

```
DT-Disk Test, Advanced Edition 4.50, (C) Copr 1987-88, Peter Norton

Select DISK test, FILE test, or BOTH
Press D, F, or B ... D

During the scan of the disk, you may press
BREAK (Control-C) to interrupt Disk Test

Test reading the entire disk C:, system area and data area
    The system area consists of boot, FAT, and directory
        No errors reading system area

    The data area consists of clusters numbered 2 - 9,765
        No errors reading data area


Press any key to continue...
```

Figure 6.4   The Disk Test report

As with CHKDSK and many of the other automated data recovery tools, it is generally recommended that the DT command is used without any switches, so that it only produces a report and does not attempt to rectify any faults that it finds. The user can then take the appropriate action to remedy any problems that are highlighted.

6.2.3 FA – FILE ATTRIBUTE

The FA command allows the attributes of files to be displayed, and optionally altered. The attributes of a file were discussed in Chapter 3, and control whether the file can be altered, displayed, executed etc.

The format for the command is

FA [filespec] [options] [switches]

- **[filespec]** determines which files are to be used. If no files are specified, then *.* is used instead to match all files in the current directory.

- **[options]** determines which attributes are altered. The possible alternatives are

  - /A   Archive
  - /HID   Hidden
  - /R   Read-only
  - /SYS   System

  Each option is followed by a + or - to set or reset the attribute. Specifying an option without a + or - causes it to be treated as another criterion that the files must match.

- **[switches]** further determines how the command acts:

  - /CLEAR   Clears all files attributes, ie resets them all
  - /P   Pause after each screenful of display
  - /S   Act on subdirectories also
  - /T   Produce a summary (total) report only
  - /U   Unusual files only, ie those with any attribute set.

The FA command is quite powerful, and provides a very quick and easy way to modify the attributes. Note that it cannot modify all attributes, only the ones specified above.

For example, the following will search for all files that have the Read-Only attribute set (/R), and then also sets their Hidden attribute.

FA /R /HID+

Alternatively, the following command searches for all files whose names begin with ORIG, and makes them Read-Only, so that they cannot be altered or deleted.

FA ORIG*.* /R+

If it is necessary to modify either the subdirectory or volume label attributes of a file, then the NU program must be used to edit the directory entries directly. This is discussed in more detail later in this chapter.

6.2.4 FF – FILE FIND

The FF command produces a report showing the location of all files with the specified name, even if they are in a different subdirectory. The full format of the command is:

FF [drive:] [filename] [switches]

- **[drive:]** specifies the drive to search.

- **[filename]** is the name of the file to be searched for. Wildcards can be used to find several similarly named files.

- **[switches]** controls the operation of the command:
  - /A   Search for the file on all drives, including floppies
  - /P   Pause after each screenful of information
  - /W   Display matching files in the wide format

The FF command is more useful than it may first appear to be. In many cases data is not destroyed, but misplaced. Providing the name of the file is known, or even a rough guess can be made, then the location of the file can be found quickly and easily.

6.2.5   FR – FORMAT RECOVER

FR is a very powerful command, allowing a high-level format to be reversed, and the data recovered. There are two ways in which FR can be used:

- Firstly, FR can be used to save the system information to a safe area of disk.
- Secondly, FR can be used after a high level format to recover the previous data.

Before considering how FR works, it is as well to examine exactly what the process of formatting a disk involves:

There are actually two types of format; a low-level format and a high-level format. The low-level format is entirely destructive, overwriting any previous information so that it is almost impossible to recover it. The low-level format is normally only performed on a new system, and usually involves the use of the FDISK command. The high level format, which is performed with the standard DOS FORMAT command, is much simpler. Rather than overwrite the entire disk, it just rewrites the data in the boot sector, FAT and directory structure, so that the system sees the disk as containing no data at all. The actual data area is left unaffected. FR attempts to recreate these areas when it is executed, either from the stored information, or just on a best-guess basis.

The format for the command is:

FR [drive:] [/SAVE] [/NOBAK]

- **[drive:]** specifies the drive on which the command is to be performed.
- **[/SAVE]** indicates that rather than attempt to recover the data, a copy is to be made of the system information. In fact two copies are made, one called FRE-COVER.DAT and one called FRECOVER.BAK.
- **[/NOBAK]** specifies that the production of the backup file is to be suppressed.

Thus to make a copy of the C: drive system area the command FR C: /SAVE is used. However, to initiate an attempt at reversing a format of the C: drive, the FR C: command is used. If the saved information is up to date then a full recovery will be made. If it is slightly out of date, or there was no saved information, then a partial recovery will be made. The success of such a partial recovery is dependent upon the usage of the disk, but generally speaking, all files situated in the root directory will be lost.

The FR command is very powerful, but can be disastrous if used at the wrong time. In many cases it is possible to achieve better results by manually unformatting the disk. However, if a copy has been made of the disk then there is no harm in first trying FR.

NOTE: FR does not work on a floppy disk, as the FORMAT process actually overwrites the data as well as the system area. FR is for hard-disk use only.

6.2.6 NDD – THE NORTON DISK DOCTOR

NDD is one of the two most powerful programs supplied in the Norton Utilities. Its purpose is to automatically detect and repair physical and logical errors on a floppy or hard disk. It checks the partition record, the boot sector, the FAT and the directory structure for any problems. Additionally it can be instructed to test the entire data area for bad sectors, and produce a report at the end detailing all of the results.

The format of the command is:

NDD [drive:.....] [switches]

- **[drive:.....]** specifies one or more drives on which the command is to be performed. NDD will start with the first, and then work through the list.

- **[switches]** control the operation of the command as follows:

  - /QUICK   Perform a quick test only, ie just test the system area
  - /COMPLETE   Perform a full test of both system and data areas
  - /R:filename   Send a report of the results to a file
  - /RA:filename   Append a report of the results to a file

If NDD is entered alone, then the program becomes menu controlled and allows the user to determine what it checks, and whether or not the errors are corrected. Figure 6.5 shows the opening menu for NDD.

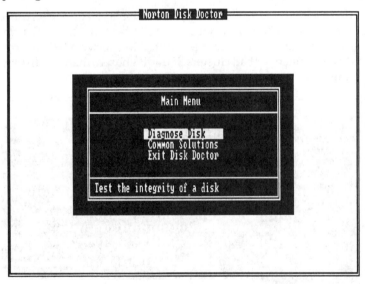

Figure 6.5   The Norton Disk Doctor opening menu

The choices at this point are Diagnose Disk, Common Solutions and Exit. Choosing Diagnose Disk brings another menu on to the screen, allowing the user to determine whether the entire disk or just the system area is to be tested. Once a choice is made, the test is carried out. Selecting Entire Disk causes the display shown in Figure 6.6 to be produced, indicating the area currently under test, as well as a variety of other disk information.

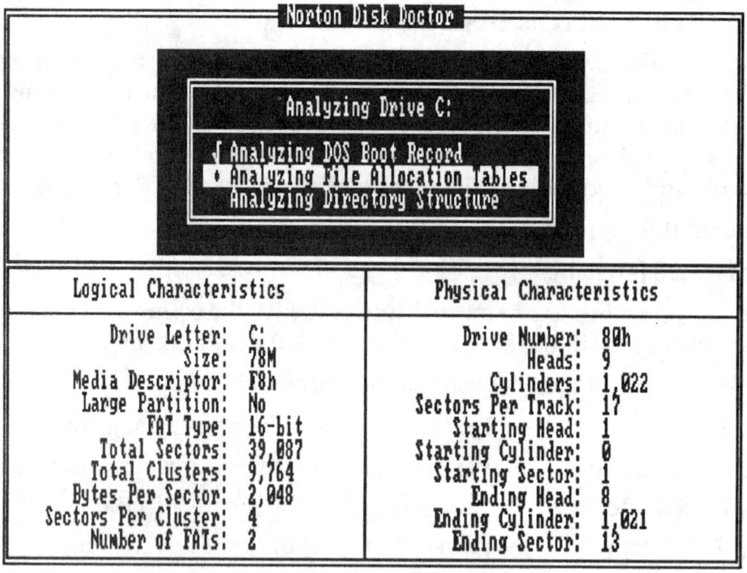

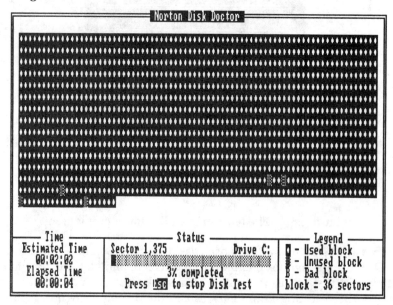

Figure 6.6   The NDD disk analysis display

Any errors that are detected at this point will be displayed on the screen, and the user is prompted to tell NDD whether or not they are to be corrected. After the initial disk analysis has been completed, the user is prompted to specify whether or not the entire disk surface is to be scanned for bad clusters. If this is chosen, then the display will appear as shown in Figure 6.7

Figure 6.7   The NDD surface analysis display

The system sequentially scans all clusters to determine whether or not they are usable. It is not very thorough in this, and in many cases will say that a cluster is usable when it is in fact suspect, or even unusable.

The most useful fact about NDD from a data recovery point of view is that it quickly scans the areas of most interest, notably the partition record, boot sector, FAT and entire directory structure. If required the results of these tests can be sent to disk in the form of a report.

Once any problems have been located by NDD, the user is then able to fix them much more easily using a disk editor. As the NDD repair techniques are quite rudimentary, they should not be trusted if an experienced user is able to recover the data manually.

6.2.7 QU – QUICK UNERASE

The QU command is what Norton Utilities is famous for. It allows one or more erased files to be quickly and easily recovered.

The form of the command is:

QU [filespec] [/A]

- **[filespec]** specifies the names of the files to unerase. It can include wildcard characters to perform multiple matches

- **[/A]** causes the command to be executed in automatic mode, and requires no user interaction.

When a file is deleted, DOS overwrites the first character of the filename, as discussed in Chapter 3. Therefore, to recover the file, QU needs to be told the letter that is to be used in this position. This can be specified in two ways:

- The filename can be specified when the command is issued, for example QU MYFILE.TXT

- The command can be run in interactive mode, in which case it prompts the user to choose the character for each file it unerases. Interactive mode is automatically selected unless the /A switch is specified.

For example,

- **QU MYFILE.TXT** unerases the file named ?YFILE.TXT, and assigns the letter M as the first character of the new filename. If there were several ?YFILE.TXT files in the current directory, then only the first is unerased.

- **QU \123*.WK1** runs QU in interactive mode, and unerases all files in the \123 directory with the extension .WK1. As each file is unerased, the user is prompted for the letter to be used as the first character of the filename.

- **QU** runs QU in interactive mode and unerases all files in the current directory, prompting for the first character of each filename as before.

Note that for QU to succeed, there must have been no changes made to the data on disk since the file was erased. If QU does not think it can unerase a file then a message will be displayed to this effect.

If more sophisticated unerasing facilities are required, then the UNERASE option in NU should be chosen.

6.2.8 SI – SYSTEM INFORMATION

The SI command provides a report containing general information about the system configuration, such as type and amount of memory, processor type, co-processor type, I/O ports, graphics adapters etc. It also calculates three performance indices: CI, the computing index; DI, the disk index; and PI, the overall performance index.

The form of the command is:

SI [drive:] [switches]

– **[drive:]** specifies which disk drive is to be used in the DI test.

– **[switches]** control the operation of the command:

- /A   ANSI machines; causes SI to skip all machine specific tests

- /LOG   Format the output for printer or file

- /N   Skip the live memory probe, a test which can cause problems on non-IBM machines if the system attempts to access non-existent memory

Figure 6.8 shows an example of a report produced by SI.

```
        Computer Name: IBM AT
      Operating System: DOS 3.30
      Built-in BIOS dated: Monday, 22 May 1989
        Main Processor: Intel 80386          Serial Ports: 2
          Co-Processor: None                Parallel Ports: 2
  Video Display Adapter: Monochrome (MDA)
      Current Video Mode: Text, 80 x 25 Monochrome
  Available Disk Drives: 3, A: - C:

DOS reports 640 K-bytes of memory:
    187 K-bytes used by DOS and resident programs
    453 K-bytes available for application programs
A search for active memory finds:
    640 K-bytes main memory    (at hex 00000-0A000)
    32 K-bytes display memory  (at hex 0B000-0B800)
    384 K-bytes extended memory (at hex 10000-16000)
ROM-BIOS Extensions are found at hex paragraphs: DC00

Computing Index (CI), relative to IBM/XT: 23.5
    Disk Index (DI), relative to IBM/XT: 2.6

Performance Index (PI), relative to IBM/XT: 16.5

Press any key to continue...
```

Figure 6.8   The System Information report

Note that the performance indices are relative to the original IBM PC/XT. Therefore, in this case the computing index indicates that the system is 23.5 times faster than the XT, whereas the DI index shows that disk operations are only performed at just over twice the XT speed.

6.2.9   UD – UNREMOVE DIRECTORY

The UD command is the opposite of the DOS RD command, ie it unremoves a directory in the same way that QU unerases a file. The format of the command is:

UD [directory pathname]

–   **[directory pathname]** is the full name and path of the previously removed directory.

UD is an important feature of Norton as the following example illustrates:

A hard disk on a system has been divided into sub-directories, one of which is called PLANDATA. The PLANDATA directory contains 10 Lotus 1-2-3 files, named PLAN00.WK1 through to PLAN09.WK1. The user deletes all of these files, thinking that they are no longer required, and then uses the DOS RD command to remove the PLANDATA directory.

It is now decided that the worksheet files need to be reinstated. However, it is not possible to unerase them using either Quick Unerase or NU as the directory has been removed. The only way to get the files back is to first issue the UD command:

UD PLANDATA

The directory is unremoved, and a report displayed on screen showing the files that it previously contained. The first letter of the filename of every file is always a ? as the file must have been erased in order that the directory could originally be removed.

The QU command can then be used (assuming no changes were made to the disk):

QU \PLANDATA\PLAN*.WK1

All erased files matching ?LAN*.WK1 are then unerased, and the letter P used for the first character of each name. The PLANDATA directory will now contain the files PLAN00.WK1, PLAN01.WK1 etc, up to PLAN09.WK1.

6.2.10   NU – NORTON UTILITY

This program is the core of the Norton Utilities package, and even shares the same name. It is a very sophisticated disk editor, offering the facility to unerase data, examine any part of the disk, modify areas of the disk, interpret the partition record, boot sector, FAT, root directory and subdirectories and much more.

The format of the command is:

NU [filespec] [switches]

–   **[filespec]** determines the file that is to be opened for editing when NU starts. If this is omitted then no file is opened, and one must be chosen with the menu commands.

–   **[switches]** control the operation of NU:

- /D0   Use the default screen driver, for 100% compatible machines

- /D1   Use the screen driver for BIOS-compatible systems

- /BW   Use the screen driver for a monochrome monitor with a CGA card

- /NOSNOW   Remove the fuzziness from the display of older
              CGA cards
- /EBCDIC   Use EBCDIC encoding for the data
- /WS   Use a WordStar format for file viewing
- /M   Maintenance mode - bypass DOS and perform all
             disk accesses at a hardware level. This is essential
             for reliable data recovery in many situations.
- /P   Only display printable characters

NU is menu driven, allowing all commands to be issued and choices to be made with a single key press. The opening menu is shown in Figure 6.9.

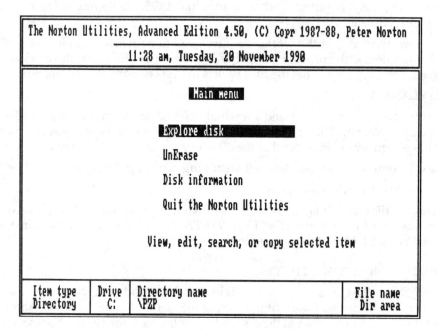

Figure 6.9   The NU opening menu

6.2.10.1   Explore Disk

Choosing the Explore Disk option produces a second menu with the following choices:

- Choose Item
- Information on Item
- Edit/Display Item
- Search Item for Data
- Write Item to Disk
- Return to Main Menu

Each of these choices are examined in detail in the following sections.

Choose Item

This menu option allows an item to be chosen so that it may later be edited, moved, copied or similar. The user selects one of the following:

- Change drive
- Change Directory
- File
- Cluster
- Sector
- Absolute Sector

The first two options, *Change Drive* and *Change Directory*, allow the current drive and directory to be altered. Choosing the directory is accomplished by moving the cursor through a graphical "tree" of the directory structure.

Choosing *File* lists all of the files in the current directory. If the current directory is the root, then entries for the Boot Sector, FAT and Root Directory are also listed.

Choosing *Cluster* allows the user to enter starting and ending cluster numbers, from 2 upwards. This is a quick and easy way to locate subdirectories and files according to their FAT entries.

Choosing *Sector* allows the user to enter starting and ending logical sector numbers, from 0 upwards. At the bottom of the screen is displayed a summary of the sector numbers for the areas that are used by the boot sector, FAT, root directory and files.

Choosing *Absolute Sector* provides a slightly different way of addressing the data. Rather than enter logical information, the user enters the physical address of the sectors that are to be examined. This data is entered as the Side, Cylinder, and Sector numbers for the starting position, and then the number of sectors that are to be examined. This option allows the user to address the entire disk, from PSN 0 upwards. Thus the partition record can be examined in this way by selecting Side 0, Cylinder 0 and Sector 1.

Information on Item

Once an item has been chosen, detailed information can be obtained by selecting this option. The information that is displayed is dependent upon what NU thinks the currently selected item is:

- If the item is a file or subdirectory, then the name, attributes, date and time, size in bytes and clusters, and starting cluster number are displayed. Additionally a pictorial map shows where the various clusters are situated.
- If the item is the boot sector, then a short description of the area is supplied, together with its starting sector number, usually 0.
- If the item is the FAT, then a short description of the FAT is displayed together with the starting and ending sector numbers. The FAT usually starts in sector 1.
- If the item is the Root Directory, then a short description is followed by the location of the root directory, in terms of starting and ending sector numbers.

Problems may occur with this option if the disk has become corrupted, when NU may think that the chosen item is actually something altogether different.

Edit/Display Item

This option provides the user with a comprehensive, easy to use disk editor. The program is semi-intelligent, displaying the data according to what it thinks the information represents. In fact there are five different ways of displaying the data:

- Hexadecimal Format. This is used when NU does not recognise the data as anything specific, ie none of the other formats. The data is represented in terms of its hexadecimal byte values. Additionally, the ASCII characters are shown to the right of the screen. Any changes can be made by entering either the hexadecimal or ASCII values. Figure 6.10 shows an example of the Hexadecimal display, in this case representing the boot sector of a hard disk.

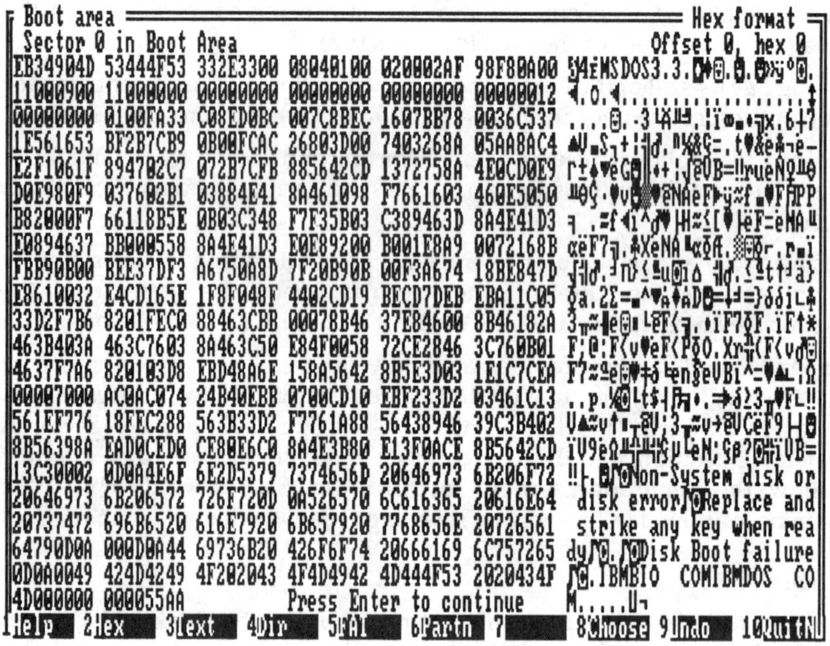

Figure 6.10   The Boot Sector in Hex format

- ASCII Format. This is used when NU sees the data as a text file, consisting mainly of the printable ASCII characters. The data is shown in the same way as it would appear in a word processor, with lines being terminated when NU encounters a line break character. Editing is performed by entering ASCII characters. Figure 6.11 shows an example of an ASCII display, and represents a simple text file.

- FAT Format. When the FAT is chosen as the current item, NU will display the data in a special format, allowing each FAT entry to be easily examined and altered. Changes are made by entering a new value for an entry. Hexadecimal notation is *not* used in this case, and all values are entered in decimal. Figure 6.12 shows an example of a FAT display.

```
┌ read.me ══════════════════════════════════ Text format ┐
  Cluster 1,139, Sectors 4,577-4,580           File offset 0, hex 0

   ▶Version 4.5 of the Norton Utilities - Advanced Edition◀
   ▶◀
   ▶We've added a few new commands to the Batch Enhancer,◀
   ▶program, have included new switches in Speed Disk, and◀
   ▶have made minor adjustments to the Norton Disk Doctor.◀
   ▶◀
   ▶◀
   ▶BATCH ENHANCER (BE)◀
   ▶==================◀
   ▶There are two additional subcommands available with the◀
   ▶Batch Enhancer program beyond those listed in the manual:◀
   ▶CLS and DELAY.◀
   ▶◀
   ▶        CLS◀
   ▶◀
   ▶     Purpose: To clear the screen and reposition the cursor◀
   ▶              at the home position.◀
   ▶     Format: BE CLS◀
   ▶◀
   ...more
                      Press Enter to continue
 1Help  2Hex  3Text  4Dir  5FAT  6Partn  7    8Choose 9Undo  10QuitNU
```

Figure 6.11   The ASCII text editor

```
┌ FAT area ══════════════════════════════════ FAT format ┐
  Sector 1 in 1st copy of FAT                  Cluster 2, hex 2

   3        4 <EOF>    6     7     8 <EOF>   10    11    12 <EOF> <EOF>
  <EOF> <EOF>   69 <EOF> <EOF> <EOF> <EOF> <EOF> <EOF> <EOF> <EOF> <EOF>
  <EOF> <EOF> <EOF> <EOF> <EOF> <EOF> <EOF> <EOF> <EOF> <EOF> <EOF> <EOF>
  <EOF> <EOF> <EOF> <EOF> <EOF> <EOF> <EOF> <EOF> <EOF> <EOF> <EOF> <EOF>
  <EOF> <EOF> <EOF> <EOF> <EOF> <EOF> <EOF>   97 <EOF> <EOF> <EOF> <EOF>
    79 <EOF> <EOF> <EOF> <EOF>  232 <EOF> <EOF> <EOF> <EOF> <EOF> <EOF>
  <EOF> <EOF> <EOF> <EOF> <EOF> <EOF> <EOF> <EOF> <EOF> <EOF> <EOF>  317
    99   100   101   102 <EOF>  104   105 <EOF> <EOF> <EOF>  109 <EOF>
  <EOF>  112   113   114   115 <EOF> <EOF>  118 <EOF> <EOF>  121 <EOF>
  <EOF>  124 <EOF> <EOF>  127   128 <EOF> <EOF>  131   132   133   134
   135   136   137   138   139   140   141   142   143   144   145   146
   147 <EOF> <EOF>  150   151   152   153   154   155 <EOF>  157   158
   159   160 <EOF>  162   163   164   165 <EOF>  167   168   169   170
   171   172   174 <EOF>  175   236   177 <EOF>  179   180   181   182
   183   184   185   186 <EOF> <EOF>  189   190   191   192   193   194
   195   196 <EOF> <EOF>  199   200   201   202   203   204   205   206
   207   208   209   210   211   212   213   214   215   216   217   218
   219   220   221   222   223   224   225   226   227   228   229   230
                      Press Enter to continue
 1Help  2Hex  3Text  4Dir  5FAT  6Partn  7    8Choose 9Undo  10QuitNU
```

Figure 6.12   The NU FAT editor

Directory Format .When the root directory or a subdirectory is chosen as the current item, NU displays the data in the form of a directory listing, showing all of the information in an easy to read format. Editing is achieved by entering new values in decimal for numeric sections, and ASCII characters for filename, extension etc. Figure 6.13 shows an example of a directory display.

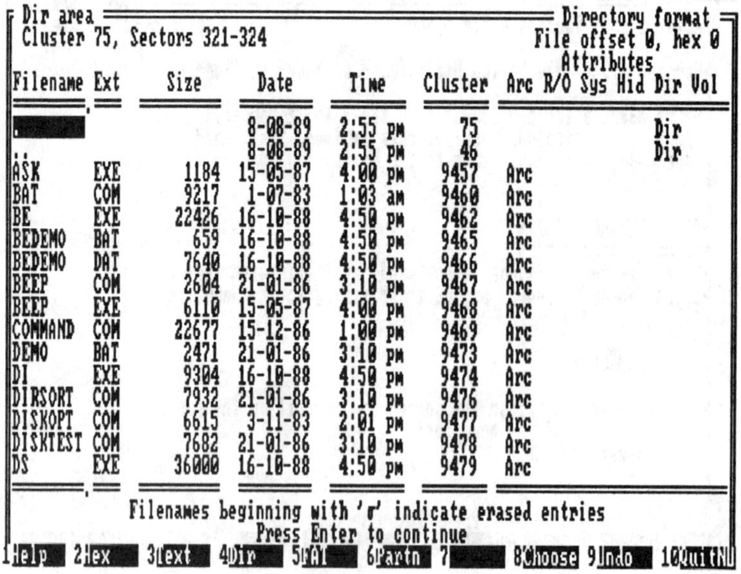

```
┌ Dir area ══════════════════════════════════════╤═ Directory format ═┐
│ Cluster 75, Sectors 321-324                     │  File offset 0, hex 0
│                                                 │     Attributes
│Filename Ext    Size     Date     Time    Cluster Arc R/O Sys Hid Dir Vol
│
│█                        8-08-89  2:55 pm    75                     Dir
│                         8-08-89  2:55 pm    46                     Dir
│ASK      EXE    1184    15-05-87  4:00 pm  9457   Arc
│BAT      COM    9217     1-07-83  1:03 am  9460   Arc
│BE       EXE   22426    16-10-88  4:50 pm  9462   Arc
│BEDEMO   BAT     659    16-10-88  4:50 pm  9465   Arc
│BEDEMO   DAT    7640    16-10-88  4:50 pm  9466   Arc
│BEEP     COM    2604    21-01-86  3:10 pm  9467   Arc
│BEEP     EXE    6110    15-05-87  4:00 pm  9468   Arc
│COMMAND  COM   22677    15-12-86  1:00 pm  9469   Arc
│DEMO     BAT    2471    21-01-86  3:10 pm  9473   Arc
│DI       EXE    9304    16-10-88  4:50 pm  9474   Arc
│DIRSORT  COM    7932    21-01-86  3:10 pm  9476   Arc
│DISKOPT  COM    6615     3-11-83  2:01 pm  9477   Arc
│DISKTEST COM    7682    21-01-86  3:10 pm  9478   Arc
│DS       EXE   36000    16-10-88  4:50 pm  9479   Arc
│
└═════════════════════════════════════════════════════════════════════
          Filenames beginning with 'r' indicate erased entries
                     Press Enter to continue
 1Help  2Hex   3Text  4Dir   5FAI   6Partn 7       8Choose 9Undo  10QuitNU
```

Figure 6.13   The NU directory editor

−   Partition Record Format. The Partition Record is always situated at PSN 0 on the disk, and as such must be chosen using the *Absolute Sector* option. NU displays the partition record information as shown in Figure 6.14, allowing any changes to be made simply by overwriting the existing values.

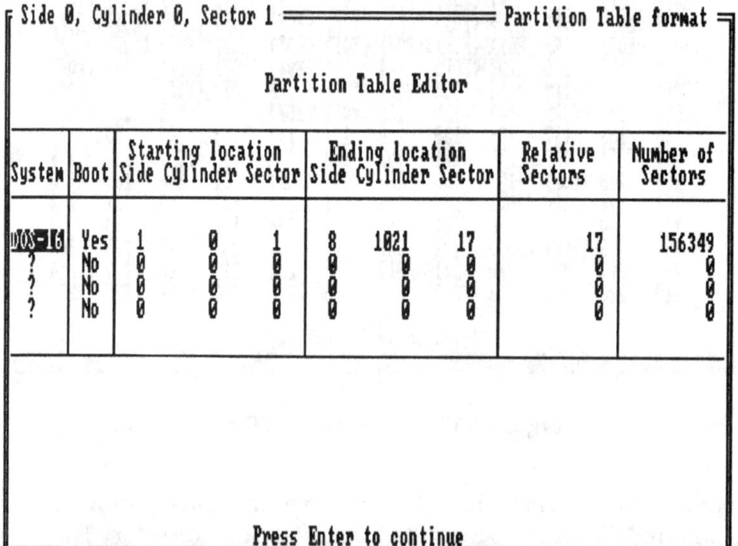

```
┌ Side 0, Cylinder 0, Sector 1 ═══════════════════ Partition Table format ═┐
│
│                         Partition Table Editor
│
│           Starting location     Ending location      Relative   Number of
│System Boot Side Cylinder Sector Side Cylinder Sector Sectors    Sectors
│
│DOS-16  Yes   1      0        1    8   1021    17       17        156349
│  ?     No    0      0        0    0      0     0        0             0
│  ?     No    0      0        0    0      0     0        0             0
│  ?     No    0      0        0    0      0     0        0             0
│
│
│
│
│
│                     Press Enter to continue
 1Help  2Hex   3Text  4Dir   5FAI   6Partn 7       8Choose 9Undo  10QuitNU
```

Figure 6.14   The NU partition record editor

The user can switch between different display formats by using the function keys. A bar at the bottom of the screen shows which key produces each display format. Thus to display the partition record in hexadecimal format, the [F2] function key is pressed, producing the display shown in Figure 6.15.

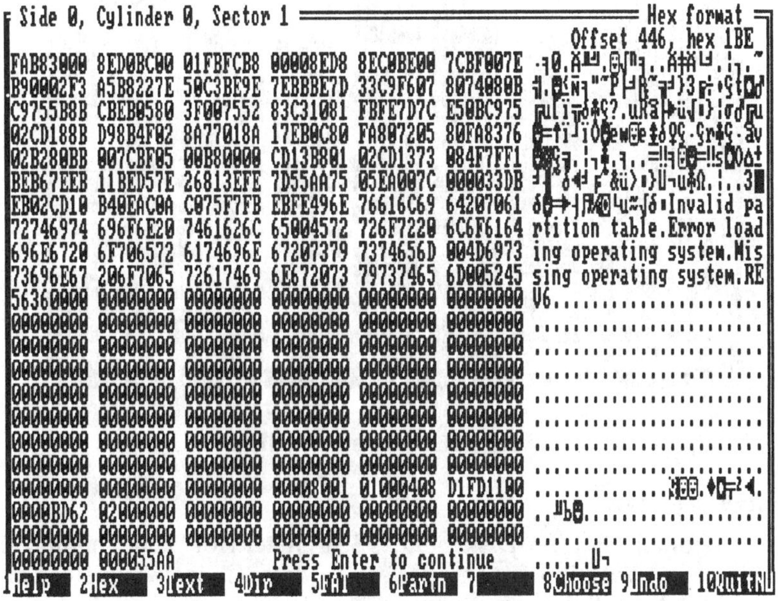

Figure 6.15   The partition record shown in hexadecimal format

Alternatively, the standard display produced when a text file is edited is shown in Figure 6.11. Pressing [F2] at this point will cause the data to be displayed in Hexadecimal format, as shown in Figure 6.16.

Note that all of the displays give considerably more information than just the data on disk. In every case, the top line of the screen identifies the item is that is represented. In the case of an absolute sector, such as the partition record, this is shown as Side, Cylinder and Sector numbers. Alternatively it may be identified as a FAT, directory, boot sector, or data file. The location of the item is also shown in the majority of cases, both in terms of its cluster address, and the sector numbers that it occupies.

Further information is given to locate the actual cursor position, so that the user can easily see whereabouts in the file any changes will be made. In the case of the Hexadecimal, ASCII and directory displays, the offset. ie the distance from the start of the sector, file etc, is shown in the top right hand corner. For the FAT display, the FAT entry number is shown.

The Edit/Display option is one of the most powerful features of the Norton Utilities, providing the user with an extremely informative, easy to use, versatile disk editor. The system automatically recognises and caters for both FAT types (16-bit and 12-bit), allowing the user to edit the entries with great ease. Any changes made are not immediately written to disk, as the user is prompted to confirm that the changes are correct before any permanent alterations are made.

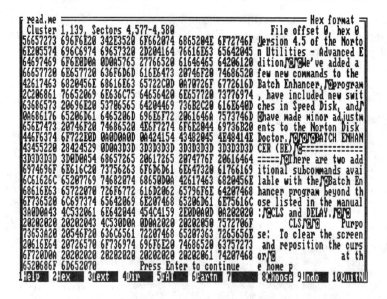

Figure 6.16   The hex editor

Search Item for Data

Another option from the Explore Disk menu is Search Item for Data. This allows the user to search the current selection for any pattern of data. Choosing this option leads to another menu with the following options:

– Where to search

– Text to search for

– Start search

– Display found text

– Continue search

– Leave search

The choice of *Where to Search* allows the user to select the entire disk, the data area only, the space used by erased files, or the currently selected item. Thus the search can be limited to any particular area that the data is thought to be contained in.

The *Text* for which to search can be entered either in the form of ASCII characters or hexadecimal byte values. This enables a search to be performed for non-printable characters and other data as well as the standard ASCII text characters.

Start Search causes the search procedure to be performed and the first occurrence of the search string to be located.

Display Found Text produces a display showing the sector containing the search string. This can be edited if required.

Continue Search causes the program to attempt to find the next occurrence of the search string. If it cannot find the string, then it produces a message to this effect.

Leave Search returns to the main menu.

Write Item to Disk

This option allows a copy of the current item to be written to any location on the current disk, or even another disk. Choosing this option produces another menu, from which the user must choose the mode of operation:

- File mode
- Cluster mode
- Sector mode
- Absolute Sector mode

The first of these, *File Mode*, is the safest of all. It uses the DOS file creation facilities to copy the current item to a file on disk. This ensures that the new data does not overwrite any existing files or system areas. Note that any item, whether it is a file, a number of clusters, sectors, or absolute sectors, can be written to a file in this way.

The last three options are more powerful, but contain no safeguards. They allow the current item to be written to a number of contiguous clusters, sectors or absolute sectors. As there are no safeguards, the data will overwrite anything that was on the disk previously. However, these options do allow new partition records, boot sectors, FATs and directory structures to be written to a disk. This is a very common necessity in data recovery, as will be seen in Chapter 7.

After choosing a mode the system prompts for the target location. The disk drive is selected first, and can be any of the devices attached to the system. The remaining information that is specified is dependent upon the mode:

- For file mode, the filename, including a full directory path, is entered.
- For cluster mode, the starting cluster is entered.
- For sector mode, the number of the first logical sector to be used is entered.
- For absolute sector mode, the user must specify starting values for the Head, Cylinder and Sector numbers.

The data is then written to the disk.

Return to Main Menu

This menu option simply returns control to the main menu.

6.2.10.2 Unerase

The unerase option is a more sophisticated version of the QU program, and allows the user to exercise much greater control over the data to be unerased than is possible with QU. Because of this, it requires the user to have a firm knowledge of how the data is stored to make the most of the features available.

The Unerase feature is menu driven, and is based around the menu options illustrated in Figure 6.17.

The first option, *Change Drive or Directory* functions in the same way as its counterparts in the other sections of NU; the drive is chosen by specifying its identifier, and the directory chosen from a pictorial tree denoting the available choices, as shown in Figure 6.18.

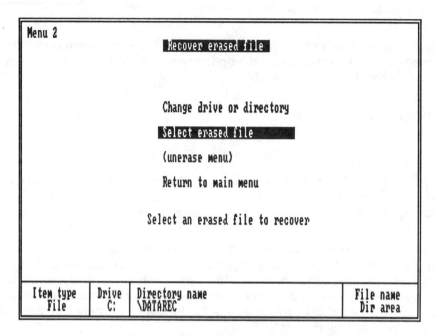

Figure 6.17   The Unerase menu

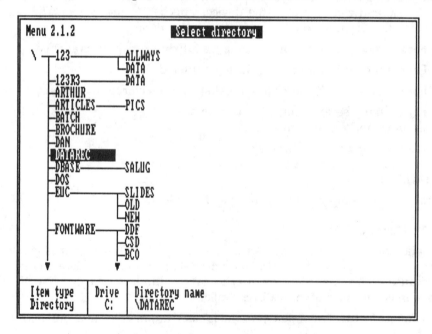

Figure 6.18   Selecting a directory

Once the drive and directory have been selected, the second option, *Select Erased File* can be chosen. A list of those files erased from the current directory is then displayed, as shown in Figure 6.19. The user selects one of the files from this list.

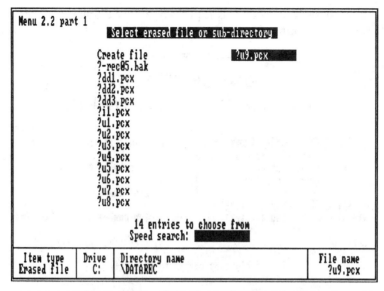

Figure 6.19   Selecting a file to unerase

Note, the first option in the list, *Create File*, is not the same as the others. It allows a new directory entry to be created, so that data can be unerased even if its original directory entry has been reused. If this entry is chosen, then the user is prompted for the name that will be assigned to the file.

Once a file has been selected, a report is produced giving information on the erased file. The report also indicates whether or not the successful unerasure of the file is possible. At this point, the user is prompted to enter the first character of the filename, as shown in Figure 6.20.

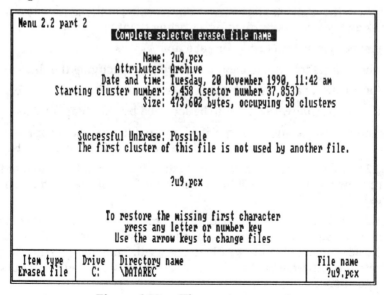

Figure 6.20   The unerase report

After the above steps have been accomplished, a new display appears as shown in Figure 6.21. These menu options control the way in which the file's data is recovered.

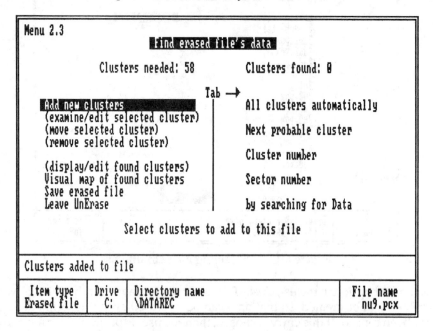

Figure 6.21   The second level menu

The first option, *Add New Clusters*, allows the user to specify which clusters are to be used, and how they will be pieced together to form the file. The right hand side of the screen shows the possible methods.

–   The first of these selects all clusters automatically, in the same way as QU. This is a quick and easy way of providing a starting point for the operation.

–   The second selects the clusters one at a time

–   The third allows the user to choose a cluster, by specifying the cluster number

–   The fourth allows a cluster to be chosen according to its sector number

–   The final choice allows a cluster to be specified by searching for data.

Note that until clusters have been specified, most of the remaining options on the left hand side of the screen are unavailable, and are shown enclosed in brackets.

Figure 6.22 shows the effect of selecting clusters automatically. Note that the cluster numbers are shown at the bottom of the screen in the form of a list, and that one of them is highlighted.

The second option, *Examine.edit selected cluster*, can now be used to look at or modify the highlighted cluster. This is very useful as it allows the user to determine what a particular cluster contains before the file is unerased. Thus it is possible to determine whether or not this cluster actually belongs to the file, as well as whereabouts in the file it should be positioned.

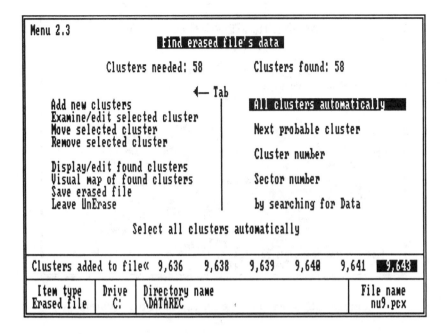

Figure 6.22   Selecting clusters

The third option, *Move selected cluster*, allows the order of the clusters to be altered. The highlighted cluster can be moved through the list until its correct position is found.

The fourth option, *Remove selected cluster*, allows a cluster to be removed from the list, particularly useful if inspection of the cluster reveals that it is not actually a part of the file to be unerased.

The fifth option, *Display/edit found clusters* allow the data in the clusters to be viewed on screen one cluster at a time. Any alterations that are required can be made at this point. This differs from the second option as it allows all of the selected clusters to be examined, in the order in which they appear in the list at the bottom of the screen.

The sixth option, *Visual map of found clusters*, produces a pictorial representation of the clusters' locations on disk. An example of such a map is shown in Figure 6.23.

This map allows the user to quickly see whereabouts the different clusters are situated, and to decide whether it is feasible that these locations are correct. If the clusters that were thought to make up the file are scattered widely over the disk, then it is likely that an error has been made in the selection. However, if the clusters are grouped together, as in this example, then it is very likely that they are correct, and the file unerasure can proceed successfully.

Finally, before leaving the system, the unerased file must be saved to disk with the seventh option, *Save erased file*. Until this command is chosen, the file is held only in memory, and is not present on disk except in its deleted form.

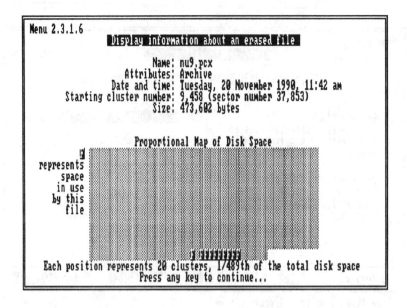

Figure 6.23   Map of the locations of the clusters

6.2.10.3   Disk Information

The final option from the main menu, *Disk Information*, provides two types of report on the disk drives. The first of these is a pictorial map of the usage of the disk surface. This map shows space in use, unused space, and any bad sectors that have been marked. Figure 6.24 shows an example of such a map.

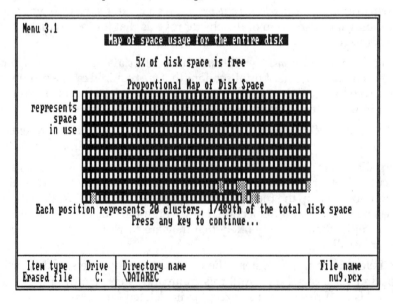

Figure 6.24   Pictorial map of disk usage

The second option produces a technical report on the disk, giving information such as capacity and logical dimensions, as shown in Figure 6.25.

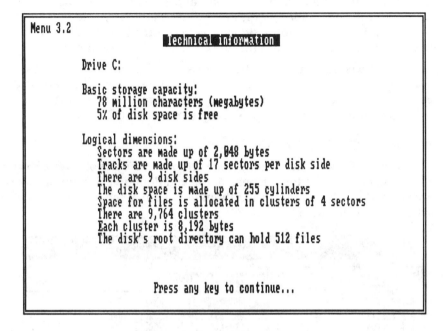

Figure 6.25   The NU technical report

6.2.10.4   Maintenance Mode

Whilst NU is indeed very powerful and versatile, problems can occur in some situations, especially where it is used on a non-standard system. A typical example of this is when NU is used to edit the disk on a system using Large Logical Sectors (see Chapter 3). NU does not always recognise the presence of LLSs on a hard disk, and can create problems of its own if it is used to edit such a device.

In situations such as this, NU has the ability to go into *Maintenance Mode*, a special operational mode that causes all disk accesses to be made at BIOS level, thus circumventing the problem of the LLS. However, this means that all selections must be made within NU using the Cluster, Sector or Absolute Sector options, as Files and Directories are no longer recognised. Additionally, although NU will attempt to identify the various data areas that are encountered, it is unwise to rely on this identification to any great degree. Thus all editing and examination should be performed in Hexadecimal format, otherwise serious problems may be encountered.

A further restriction imposed in maintenance mode is that certain other commands are made unavailable, most noticeably the unerasing facility from the main menu. Therefore, maintenance mode should only be used when using NU for low-level editing of non-standard disks and DOS versions.

6.3 PC TOOLS

Norton Utilities and PCTools are the market leaders in the area of disk management and utilities. Each has advantages over the other, and generally speaking, any facilities provided by one will be provided by the other when it is next upgraded. Thus, the task of choosing between them is not easy, as it is necessary to determine which of the products currently offers the features that are deemed to be most important.

As the two products are very similar, the discussion of PCTools will be limited to those features that differ most from the Norton Utilities. This means that there are no detailed discussions of every menu command, as the procedures for using features that are common to both products are much the same in Norton and PCTools.

6.3.1 WORKING ENVIRONMENT

One area in which PCTools does differ from Norton is in the use of a WIMPS environment. WIMPS stands for Windows, Icons, Mouse and Pulldown Screens, implying that all commands and functions are selected through the use of the mouse rather than the keyboard. Figure 6.26 shows the initial PCTools screen.

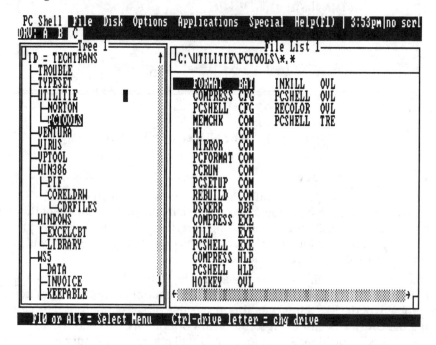

Figure 6.26   The PCTools Display

As can be seen, the screen is divided into two main areas. The left hand side shows a diagrammatic representation of the directory structure, and the right hand side lists the files in the current directory. Across the top of the screen are the menu titles. An menu is selected by moving the cursor to one of the titles and clicking the mouse button. The menu choices then drop down, allowing the user to select the desired command. Figure 6.27 shows the File menu commands.

Figure 6.27   The File menu options

To select one of the commands, the cursor is moved to the appropriate entry and the mouse button clicked again. Many of the commands work with files, and these are selected by clicking on the file name in the right hand window, prior to selecting the command. Thus to rename the file COMPRESS.CFG to SQUEEZE.CFG, the following is required:

- Click on the file COMPRESS.CFG in the right hand window. A 1 is displayed to the side of the filename to indicate that this is the first selected file.

- Click on the File menu bar, to bring down the menu of file commands.

- Click on the Rename option.

- Follow the instruction displayed on screen to rename the file

Many commands can be carried out on multiple files in one go, simply by selecting several files rather than just one. This is achieved simply by clicking on the required filenames, one after another. The first file will be shown with a 1 by the side of it, the second with a 2 and so on.

Many of the more powerful features of PCTools are situated under other menu options, namely Disk, Applications and Special:

6.3.2   DISK MENU

The Disk menu contains all commands that directly affect the disk, as opposed to those that operate on files or memory. The majority of these commands are involved in disk management, rather than disk modification. However, the disk editor is situated in this menu under the heading of *Disk View/Edit*. Figure 6.28 shows the display produced when this command is selected.

Figure 6.28   The PCTools disk editor

The disk editing ability of PCTools is not as comprehensive as that of Norton, and does not offer the sophisticated automatic identification and display formats for different areas. Additionally, the disk editor accesses the disk through DOS, and is thus restricted to working within the DOS partition. Therefore there is no way that the partition record can be altered using PCTools.

On the positive side, the disk editor is very easy to use, and provides a no-fuss method of altering disk data. Many users find the display produced by PCTools to be more readable than that from Norton, although this is purely a matter of personal preference. The other inherent bonus is that the mouse can be used to move the cursor, removing the necessity for the user to be forever pressing keys.

6.3.3 APPLICATIONS MENU

The Applications menu contains commands to run programs that are external to PCTools. Figure 6.29 shows the standard options provided by the Applications menu.

The five options are all external programs, meaning that they are held on disk as executable files and simply called up by PCTools when they are required. They are all disk orientated programs, and operate as follows:

6.3.3.1 Compress Disk

This is a file defragmenter, similar to Norton's SpeedDisk program. Fragmentation occurs when the clusters in use by a particular file are not contiguous. This can cause disk-intensive applications, such as databases, to be slowed down slightly. However, the performance loss is very slight, and may not be noticed by the majority of users.

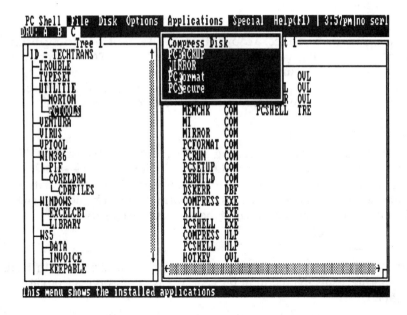

Figure 6.29   The Applications menu

Compress Disk will defragment the entire disk, and position files and directories where it thinks the system can access them with a minimum of delay. This involves reading every cluster on the disk, and writing it to a new location. This is quite a lengthy process, and even on the fastest disks will take in excess of 15 minutes.

The problem with defragmentation programs is that they continually update the FAT as well as the actual data on the disk, as they record the new position of a cluster whenever it is moved. If there were a power failure while the FAT was being written, or after the cluster was moved but before the FAT was updated, then it is very likely that information on the disk will be corrupted. In the worst case, it will be the FAT itself that is corrupted.

It is therefore recommended that disk defragmentation programs are used as little as possible, and should not be used at all unless a serious performance degradation has become obvious. If performance is suffering, then it is perhaps time to consider upgrading the hard disk of the system to a faster device, rather than using the stop-gap solution of the defragmenter.

A commonly held belief is that defragmenting a disk increases the amount of free space. This is totally untrue when considering IBM and compatible systems, as no extra space is created by defragmenting the disk.

There is one benefit to defragmenting a disk; as all of the files are moved into contiguous areas, it is much easier to recover them if they are accidentally deleted. Thus the process of unerasing large numbers of files is made significantly easier.

6.3.3.2   PC Backup

PC Backup is an easy to use backup utility, for making copies of data on either hard or floppy disks. Being menu driven means that the user need have no knowledge about the backup process, and will be given step by step instruction on what to do.

6.3.3.3 Mirror

Mirror is a program that produces a copy of the system area of the current disk, and stores this copy in a safe area. It is very similar to Norton's Format Recover command, except that the data is used in the undeleting process as well as the unformatting command. Selecting Mirror from the Applications menu causes the data file to be created; it does not unformat the disk as a separate command is used for this procedure.

6.3.3.4 PC Format

PC Format is an intelligent disk formatting utility. It detects the capacity of the disk drive that is to be used to format a disk, and automatically informs the user of this on screen. This is of particular interest to those users with several different capacity floppy disk drives connected to a single machine, as the information can be used to check that the correct density disk is being formatted in the correct density drive.

6.3.3.5 PC Secure

PC Secure is a rudimentary security program. It can be overcome with relative ease. However, it achieves its main aim in preventing casual observers from accessing confidential data.

6.3.3.6 Adding Applications

One area in which PCTools is ahead of Norton Utilities is the way in which new applications can be added to this menu. The purpose of this is to allow novice users to select their favourite spreadsheet, database or word processor just by pointing to it with the mouse.

Any application program can be added to the menu through the *Modify Application List* command in the *Options* menu. When this command is chosen, a form is produced on screen for the user to complete. This includes the name and location of the program, any parameters that must be specified on the command line, any other information that is needed, and the file extensions for the data files. As this form need only be completed once, the data can be entered by an experienced user. Any novice can then execute the program by clicking on its name, or on one of the data files that are recognised by the application. This can significantly reduce the number of problems that are encountered due to finger trouble.

Another way of executing the program is available if the data file extensions are specified in the form. If the user clicks on any file with a known extension, then the appropriate application is automatically executed.

This simple to use *front end* system may not immediately be thought of as an aid to data recovery. However, it falls into the category of preventative measures, by making it easier for the user to access applications in the correct way, thus reducing errors and possible problems.

6.3.4 SPECIAL MENU

The Special menu contains a number of commands that would not be required by the novice, but which are of interest to experienced users, particularly those involved with data recovery. Figure 6.30 shows the Special menu options.

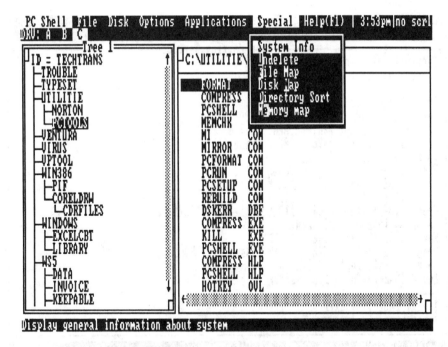

Figure 6.30   The Special menu options

- The first of these, *System Info*, is much the same as Norton's SI command, and provides exactly the same information, albeit in a slightly different layout.

- The second option, *Undelete*, is also very similar to Norton's facilities. However, rather than have three separate commands as in Norton, PCTools has grouped the three processes of Automatic file recovery, Manual file recovery, and Subdirectory recovery into one. Thus it is easier to use, and generally quicker for simple unerasures. However, PCTools does not provide the same degree of flexibility as Norton, especially in terms of being able to find clusters by searching for data etc. In this respect, Norton is a definite winner.

- *File Map* and *Disk Map* both produce pictorial representation of space usage in the same way as Norton.

- *Directory Sort* is also very similar to Norton, allowing directory entries to be sorted by any combination of name, extension, size, date and time.

- The final option, *Memory Map*, is very useful, and has no equivalent in Norton. It produces a report showing how the memory of the computer is being used, and what the programs are that are using it. This is invaluable in the process of tracking down and identifying TSR programs, and in particular viruses. Figure 6.31 shows an example of a memory map.

Overall, PCTools is seen by many users to offer a much more user-friendly interface than Norton, and for them this benefit outweighs the disadvantage of having less sophisticated data recovery tools. However, in the majority of cases, PCTools is as functional as Norton is terms of data recovery, it just requires more effort from the user to achieve the desired results.

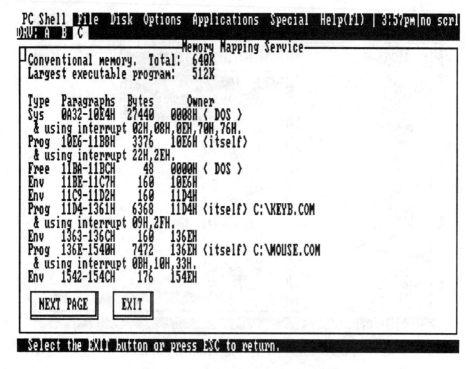

```
PC Shell File Disk Options Applications Special Help(F1) | 3:57pm|no scrl
DRV: A B C
                      ┌───────Memory Mapping Service───────┐
                      Conventional memory. Total:  640K
                      Largest executable program:   512K

                      Type  Paragraphs  Bytes      Owner
                      Sys   0A32-10E4H  27440     0008H ( DOS )
                       & using interrupt 02H,08H,0EH,70H,76H.
                      Prog  10E6-11BBH   3376     10E6H (itself)
                       & using interrupt 22H,2EH.
                      Free  11BA-11BCH     48     0000H ( DOS )
                      Env   11BE-11C7H    160     10E6H
                      Env   11C9-11D2H    160     11D4H
                      Prog  11D4-1361H   6368     11D4H (itself) C:\KEYB.COM
                       & using interrupt 09H,2FH.
                      Env   1363-136CH    160     136EH
                      Prog  136E-1540H   7472     136EH (itself) C:\MOUSE.COM
                       & using interrupt 0BH,10H,33H.
                      Env   1542-154CH    176     154EH

                      ┌──────────┐   ┌──────┐
                      │NEXT PAGE │   │ EXIT │
                      └──────────┘   └──────┘
                      └──────────────────────────────────────┘
Select the EXIT button or press ESC to return.
```

Figure 6.31   The memory map report

6.4   DISK EXPLORER

The Disk Explorer is a disk editing utility produced by Quaid Software Ltd, in Canada. The most recent version of the program was produced in 1987, and therefore may seem to be somewhat dated compared to its competitors. Also to its disadvantage is the fact that it concentrates solely on disk editing; it supplies no options for sorting directories, de-fragmenting disks etc, in the same way that Norton, PCTools and many others do.

However, the disk explorer is an excellent utility for editing disk data, and in particular floppy disk data. Its abilities far surpass the facilities available in Norton and PCTools, as it allows extremely accurate changes to be made to stored data. More importantly though, it has one other major advantage over most of the other utilities available - it tells the user exactly what is happening, exactly what is on the disk and exactly what it is about to do. Other packages tend to insulate the user from such details, employing their own 'user-friendly' jargon for terms and techniques that are thought to be beyond the knowledge of the inexperienced.

This does mean that the user is assumed to be familiar with the technical aspects of disk storage, and understands such terms as CRC, LSN, PSN, head, cylinder, sector etc. The manual supplied with Disk Explorer is very helpful in this area, as it contains a full glossary of technical terms and definitions.

Disk Explorer is menu driven, although the layout of the menu options is very different from the majority of the packages on the market. On executing the program, the initial display appears as shown in Figure 6.32.

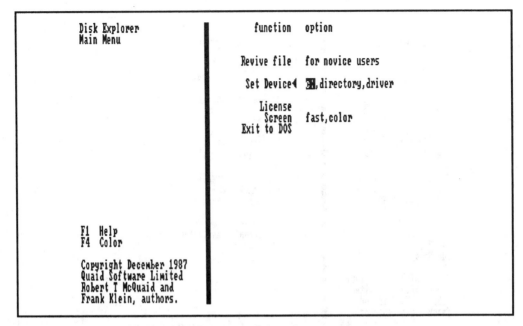

```
Disk Explorer                   function   option
Main Menu

                                Revive file   for novice users

                                Set Device◀  ▓,directory,driver

                                License
                                  Screen   fast,color
                              Exit to DOS




    F1  Help
    F4  Color

    Copyright December 1987
    Quaid Software Limited
    Robert T McQuaid and
    Frank Klein, authors.
```

Figure 6.32   The Disk Explorer opening menu

6.4.1   OPENING MENU OPTIONS

The menu options are *Revive File, Set Device, License, Screen* and *Exit to DOS*.

Revive File is the option name for file unerasure. The procedure is very simple, and is much akin to the Unerase option in NU. The system automatically guides the user through the steps required to recover the data, but still provides a great degree of flexibility allowing experienced troubleshooters to perform more complicated recoveries.

Set Device is the option used to specify which drive is to be examined and how it is to be treated. As can be seen, the system defaults to referencing the current drive, which in this case is C:. This is changed through a single key press for the other drives. Disk Explorer can recognise any number of drives connected to the computer, although each of them must be either a 360K, 720K, 1.2M or 1.44M floppy, or a hard disk. The drive can be treated as a non-DOS disk, in which case no interpretation is performed, or it can be viewed by the system as a DOS disk, in which case it can be examined at DOS level, BIOS level, or can simply be analysed to produce summary information.

License Screen produces a page of text on screen outlining the copyright agreement. It gives a full contact address for any unauthorised users to send payment to, in order that they can become registered and receive the full manual etc.

Exit to DOS returns control to DOS, removing the program from memory and allowing further applications to be executed.

6.4.2   MAIN MENU

Once the Set Device option has been chosen and a drive specified, the main menu options are displayed on the screen, as shown in Figure 6.33.

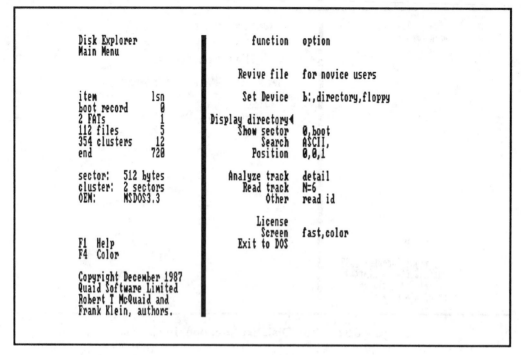

```
Disk Explorer                    function   option
Main Menu

                                Revive file   for novice users

item            lsn             Set Device   b:,directory,floppy
boot record      0
2 FATs           1          Display directory◄
112 files        5            Show sector   0,boot
354 clusters    12                 Search   ASCII,
end            720               Position   0,0,1

sector:   512 bytes            Analyze track   detail
cluster:  2 sectors             Read track   N=6
OEM:      MSDOS3.3                   Other   read id

                                   License
                                    Screen   fast,color
F1  Help                        Exit to DOS
F4  Color

Copyright December 1987
Quaid Software Limited
Robert T McQuaid and
Frank Klein, authors.
```

Figure 6.33   The Disk Explorer main menu

As can be seen, the display now contains much more information. On the left of the screen is some summary information regarding the layout and geometry of the disk. This allows the user to confirm that Disk Explorer has indeed interpreted the disk layout correctly. The right hand side of the screen contains the main menu options, which allow all of the examination and editing options to be carried out.

Menu options are chosen with the cursor keys, and the settings under each one can be selected with the + and – keys to the right of the numeric keypad. Once the relevant menu option has been chosen, and the desired settings have been specified, pressing Enter causes the command to be executed. As this method of selecting commands is very different to other packages, users might find it difficult to come to terms with at first. However, it does allow a great deal of information and a large number of menu choices to be displayed on screen at once, without cluttering the screen excessively. Once experience has been gained with the system, it is often found that commands can be issued much more quickly with this method than with the techniques employed by Norton and PCTools.

6.4.3   DISPLAY FORMATS

One of the advantages of Disk Explorer is that it can display data in a wide variety of formats, allowing modifications to be made at any time.

6.4.3.1   Directory Format

Figure 6.34 shows the screen display for a directory listing.

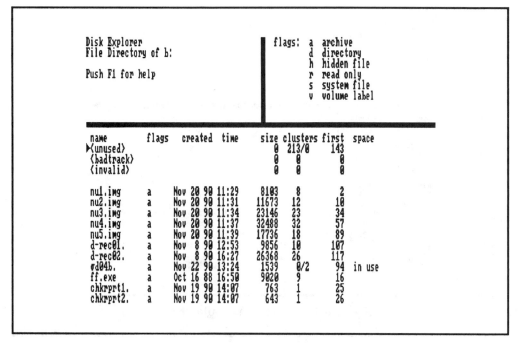

Figure 6.34   The directory display/editor

The information is given in a very similar format to that provided by Norton. However, further information is given at the top of the screen relating to clusters that are unused or corrupt, allowing the user to instantly determine the overall usage and condition of the disk.

6.4.3.2   FAT Format

The FAT editor/display is unique to Disk Explorer. It is the only true FAT editor that allows clusters to be picked up and moved, viewed and edited all with a minimum of effort. Figure 6.35 shows the FAT display for a disk.

As can be seen, the FAT entries are displayed in a very easy to read format, with each chain of clusters displayed next to the associated filename. This allows the exact cluster usage to be seen at a glance.

The cursor keys work slightly differently when editing the FAT, as they also allow the user to pick up, move and delete cluster entries at any point in any FAT chain. This allows FAT modifications to be made extremely easily.

6.4.3.3   Data Format

Data for any file, track or sector can be displayed just as easily. For example Figure 6.36 shows the display for a text file.

Disk Explorer can in fact display data in four different formats.

– Text format displays all of the bytes in a sector, each represented as its ASCII character, as shown in Figure 6.36.

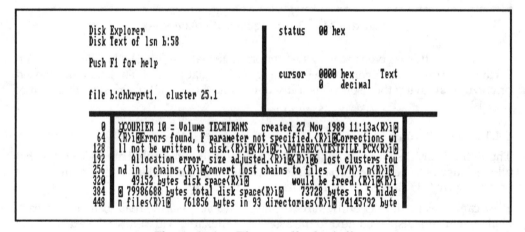

Figure 6.35   The FAT display/editor

Figure 6.36   The text display/editor

–   Book format displays all the bytes as ASCII characters, but advances to a new line at each carriage return character. Thus the display appears similar to that produced by a word processor.

–   Roman format shows the values in hexadecimal notation, and writes them in the traditional format of left to right.

–   Arabic format shows the bytes in hexadecimal notation, but writes them from right to left. Additionally lower case letters are used to make the difference between Arabic and Roman more obvious. The use of Arabic format makes the interpretation of little-endian data considerably easier.

Figure 6.37 shows the Roman display format.

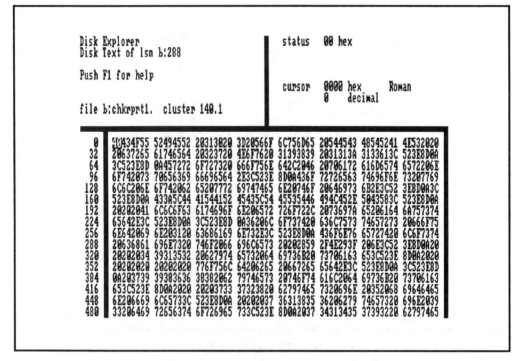

Figure 6.37   The Roman data display format

Sophisticated editing options are provided which allow subtle modifications to be made to the data. These include the typical change, insert and overwrite options, but also more powerful bit-editing commands. These are useful if the disk has become slightly corrupted by a magnetic field, or if the original disk drive was faulty.

6.4.4   TRACK ANALYSIS

Disk Explorer has a number of built-in diagnostic routines, for automatically identifying faults that it finds on the disk. Unlike many other packages, Disk Explorer tells the user exactly what the fault is. This means that with the appropriate knowledge, it is simple to remedy the problem.

For example, when faced with a sector containing a CRC error, most other utilities report a Data Error when attempting to access the data. This information is of little or no use, as it gives insufficient information to allow the problem to be identified. However, if Disk Explorer detects a CRC error, it says so. Figure 6.38 illustrates the report produced when the Track Analysis option is used on a disk containing a CRC error.

The list of errors at the bottom left of the screen highlights any faults that are found. Note that there are some situations, notably involving copy-protected disks, in which such errors are normal.

The information at the top of the screen gives the exact location of the faulty sector. In this case it reports that it is the first sector on the track. This area is used by the CHKRPRT1 file.

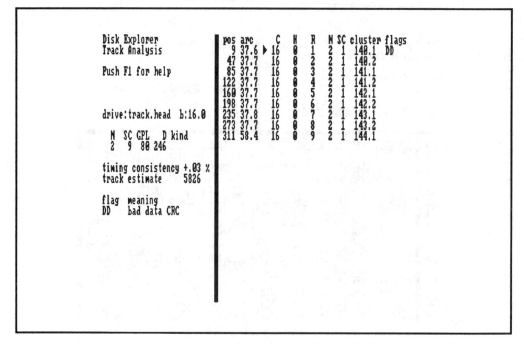

Figure 6.38   The track analysis report

If an attempt to access this file is made from DOS, then the following error will be reported:

```
Data error reading drive B
Abort, Retry, Ignore, Fail?
```

Disk Explorer can be used to remedy the problem. With the display as shown in Figure 6.38 above, pressing the Enter key places Disk Explorer into sector edit mode. If the F5 function key is pressed, the sector is written back to the disk with a correct CRC value. Thus the data can now be accessed from DOS with no problems.

There may be situations in which it is desirable to create errors on disks, for example when testing suspect hardware and software. Disk Explorer can be used to create such errors, just as easily as it can be used to fix them. In fact, it can be used to write sectors with incorrect CRCs, deleted address marks, weak bits etc. Thus a diagnostic disk can be created to test the correct operation of either hardware or software.

6.4.5 RESTRICTIONS OF DISK EXPLORER

Disk Explorer can be unreliable when used with some modern hard disks, in particular those that use large logical sectors. In such cases it may appear that the disk geometry has been correctly recognised, but further investigation reveals that Disk Explorer is not using this information correctly. These problems occur most noticeably when performing low-level operations such as absolute disk read/write operations, and in particular when the Track Analysis options are used. Therefore, it is recommended that the use of Disk Explorer is restricted to floppy disks only, where it remains the most powerful utility available.

6.5 SHAREWARE UTILITIES

Shareware is a recently developed method for individual software developers and small software houses to market their software. The concept of shareware is that the programs are provided free of charge, for an initial trial period. The only fees that are charged are for the actual disks and the labour element in producing the copy.

If at the end of the trial period the software is still in use, then a registration fee must be sent to the authors. The payment of the registration fee licences the software for further use, in exactly the same way as if it was bought from a dealer.

By distributing software in this way, the authors are able to reduce overheads, and thus produce a greater variety of different programs than if traditional marketing techniques had been used. This means that the user benefits by having a very wide choice of applications, utilities, operating systems etc, many of which are of excellent quality, equal in fact to commercially available programs.

Disk Utilities are no exception, and there are many specialised programs available. These range from disk editors and disk management programs to sophisticated hardware testing systems. Many of these programs duplicate features that are available in Norton, PC Tools, Disk Explorer etc. However, one program of particular interest is TestDrive.

TestDrive is a special program written to allow the testing and fault diagnosis of 5.25" 360K floppy disk drives. Many problems and faults occur with floppy disks due to actual problems with the hardware. These may not be breakages or mechanical failures, but are usually caused through mis-adjustment and general wear and tear. TestDrive checks the most essential factors, producing a detailed technical report and more useful Pass/Fail results for each test.

Many of the TestDrive tests require the use of a special disk produced by Dysan, known as the Dysan Diagnostic Disk (DDD). The DDD is provided free of charge to a user when they register their purchase of the shareware. Using the DDD, TestDrive is able to check the following:

- Spindle speed
- General write/read operations
- Head alignment
- Hysteresis
- Head azimuth
- Hub centring
- Continuous alignment

Even though some of these terms may be beyond the comprehension of many users, it is essential to be able to diagnose problems in these areas when fault finding disk problems. TestDrive allows this to be done by users who have little or no technical knowledge. A qualified engineer can then be contacted to determine whether or not it is economic to repair the device or whether it should be replaced.

TestDrive is controlled through the use of the function keys, and produces an opening display as shown in Figure 6.39.

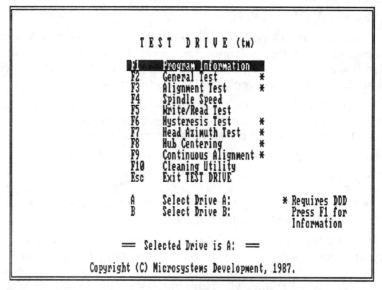

Figure 6.39   The TestDrive opening menu

Each of the options performs one or more tests, and usually produces a graphical display showing the results. The following sections describe each of these tests.

6.5.1   GENERAL TEST

The general test causes six of the other tests to be performed sequentially, producing pass or fail results for each one. In addition to the pass/fail result, the actual measured values and the criteria will be displayed, showing the degree to which the drive does not meet the required standards.

Figure 6.40 shows a sample display produced by the general test for a bad drive. The separate sections below give more information on each individual test.

The general test is a good option to choose as the first stage in problem diagnosis as it highlights any faults that are present, allowing further inspection using the individual commands below.

6.5.2   HEAD ALIGNMENT AND SENSITIVITY

The alignment test measures the position of the read/write head over the centre of each track on the disk. This is often referred to as *radial alignment*.

A standard 360K disk has 48 tracks per inch (TPI), each of which is 1/48th of an inch wide (0.020833 inches wide). The alignment test attempts to read data from the DDD which has been written in a special way, so that it gets continuously further from the centre of the track. When the test fails, the position is measured and hence the sensitivity is measured. The test is performed for adjustments towards and away from the disk hub, and thus two limits are produced. The criteria for the disk to pass the test is that the head must be able to read data that is 8 milli-inches from the track centre, both toward and away from the hub. The degree to which the sensitivity for each track varies towards and away from the disk centre is a measure of the alignment

```
                       TEST DRIVE
                      General Test


                                   Criteria    Test     Result
                                   --------  ----------  --------
     Alignment /    Track  0 Head 0   +/- 8    + 6 -12    Fail
     Sensitivity    Track  0 Head 1   +/- 8    +11 -10    Pass
                    Track 19 Head 0   +/- 8    + 7 -11    Fail
                    Track 19 Head 1   +/- 8    +11 - 9    Pass
                    Track 39 Head 0   +/- 8    + 6 -11    Fail
                    Track 39 Head 1   +/- 8    + 8 - 9    Pass


     Hysteresis     Track 19 Head 0     1.5      2.0      Fail


     Spindle Speed  . . . . . . . .  295 - 305   309      Fail


     Hub Centering  . . . .  Head 0   0 Errors  2 Errors  Fail


     Head Azimuth   . . . .  Head 0   +/- 39'   +42 -42   Pass
                             Head 1   +/- 39'   +42 -21   Fail
```

Figure 6.40   The General Test report

The display produced by the alignment test for an acceptable drive is shown in Figure 6.41. Those areas shown with a ~~~~ have been read correctly, those shown with an *erXX* entry have not been read, the XX indicating the error number.

```
                      TEST DRIVE Alignment Test


           Track  ---------------------------
           39   30   19   16    5    0       0    5    16   19   30   39

  - 13 er02 er02 er02 er02 er02 er02     er02 er02 er02 er04 er10 er04
  - 12 er02 er02 er02 er02 er02 er02     er02 er02 er02 er02 er02 er02
  - 11 er02 er02 er02 er02 er02 er02     er02 er02 er02 er02 er02 er02
  - 10 ~~~~ ~~~~ ~~~~ ~~~~ ~~~~ ~~~~     ~~~~ ~~~~ ~~~~ ~~~~ er02 er02
  -  9 ~~~~ ~~~~ ~~~~ ~~~~ ~~~~ ~~~~     ~~~~ ~~~~ ~~~~ ~~~~ ~~~~ er02
  -  8 ~~~~ ~~~~ ~~~~ ~~~~ ~~~~ ~~~~     ~~~~ ~~~~ ~~~~ ~~~~ ~~~~ ~~~~
  -  7 ~~~~ ~~~~ ~~~~ ~~~~ ~~~~ ~~~~     ~~~~ ~~~~ ~~~~ ~~~~ ~~~~ ~~~~
  -  6 ~~~~ ~~~~ ~~~~ ~~~~ ~~~~ ~~~~     ~~~~ ~~~~ ~~~~ ~~~~ ~~~~ ~~~~
                  Head   0                         Head   1
  +  6 ~~~~ ~~~~ ~~~~ ~~~~ ~~~~ ~~~~     ~~~~ ~~~~ ~~~~ ~~~~ ~~~~ ~~~~
  +  7 ~~~~ ~~~~ ~~~~ ~~~~ ~~~~ ~~~~     ~~~~ ~~~~ ~~~~ ~~~~ ~~~~ ~~~~
  +  8 ~~~~ ~~~~ ~~~~ ~~~~ ~~~~ ~~~~     ~~~~ ~~~~ ~~~~ ~~~~ ~~~~ ~~~~
  +  9 ~~~~ ~~~~ ~~~~ ~~~~ ~~~~ ~~~~     ~~~~ ~~~~ ~~~~ ~~~~ ~~~~ ~~~~
  + 10 er02 er02 er02 ~~~~ ~~~~ ~~~~     ~~~~ ~~~~ ~~~~ ~~~~ ~~~~ er02
  + 11 er02 er02 er02 er02 er02 er02     er02 er02 er02 er02 er02 er02
  + 12 er02 er02 er02 er02 er02 er02     er02 er02 er02 er02 er02 er02
  + 13 er02 er04 er04 er04 er04 er04     er04 er04 er02 er02 er04 er02
```

Figure 6.41   The Head Alignment report

6.5.3   SPINDLE SPEED

The spindle speed is the speed at which the disk rotates. For a 360KB disk, this must be between 295 and 305 revolutions per minute (RPM). Some manufacturers specify tighter constraints, and therefore it is always best to adjust the spindle speed to be as near to 300 RPM as possible. The TestDrive documentation includes full instructions on how the drive speed is adjusted.

The results of the spindle speed test for an acceptable drive will appear as shown in Figure 6.42.

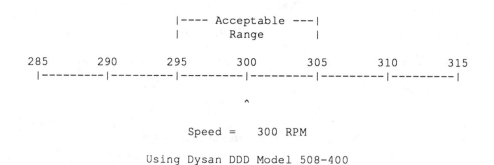

```
      TEST DRIVE Spindle Speed Measurement


               |---- Acceptable ---|
               |        Range      |

285        290        295        300        305        310        315
 |---------|---------|---------|---------|---------|---------|
                               ^


               Speed =    300 RPM

         Using Dysan DDD Model 508-400
```

Figure 6.42   The Spindle Speed report

6.5.4   GENERAL WRITE/READ OPERATIONS

This test measures the ability of the drive to write and read information on each sector of the disk. Thus it can be used to test a drive, by using a good diskette, or it can be used to test a suspect diskette by running the test on a drive that is known to be good.

The test requires the use of a pre-formatted scratch diskette, and writes 512 random bytes of data to each sector on the disk. It then reads back each sector and compares what was read with what was written. Should the test fail, and the diskette is known to be good, then it is likely that the disk drive requires significant servicing or replacement.

Figure 6.43 shows the results of the write/read test for an unacceptable drive. Note the presence of errors on many tracks, indicating that discrepancies were encountered between the written and read data.

6.5.5   HYSTERESIS

Hysteresis is a measure of the drive's ability to position the head in exactly the same position over a specified track from either direction. The test moves the head to an inner track, and then seeks to the middle of the disk. The alignment is measured at this point. The head is then moved to the outer track, and the middle track sought a second time. Again the alignment is measured, and the hysteresis value calculated from the difference. The test is performed again for a different track.

Errors in this test indicate possible problem with the head positioning mechanism, requiring professional repair. Figure 6.44 shows the hysteresis display for an acceptable drive, indicating the alignment measurement after each test.

```
                    TEST DRIVE Write / Read Test

          Sector-+   Track --
                 |   0 - - -  9  - - - 19 - - -  29 - - -  39
                 1 - ~~C~~~~~~~~~~~~~~~~~~~~~~~~~~~~~~~~~~~~~~-
                 2 - ~~~~~~~~~~~~~~~~~~~~~~~~~~~~~~~~~~~~~~~~~|
~ = Sector OK    3 - W~~~~~~~~~~~~~~W~~~~~~~~~~~~~~~~~~~~~~~~~|
                 4 - WR~~~~~~~~~~~~~~~~~~~~~~~~~~~~~~~~~~~~~~~|
                 5 - WR~~~~~~~~~~~~~~~~~~~~~~~~~~~~~~~~~~~~~~~| Head
W = Write error  6 - WW~~~~~~~~~~~~~W~~~~~~~~~~~~~~~~~~~~~~~~~|  0
                 7 - WR~~~~~~~~~~~~~~R~~~~~~~~~~~~~~~~~~~~~~~~|
R = Read error   8 - R~~~~~~~~~~~~~~~~~~~~~~~~~~~~~~~~~~~~~~~~~|
                 9 - ~~~~~~~~~~~~~~~~~~~~~~R~~~~~~~~~~~~~~~~~~|
C = Compare error 1 - ~~~~~C~~~~~~~~~~~~~~~~~WR~~~~~~~~~~~~~~~-
                 2 - ~~~WRW~~~~~~~~~~~~~~~~~WWR~~~~~~~~~~~~~~|
                 3 - ~~~WWWW~~~~~~~~~~~~~~~~~~~~~~~~~~~~~~~~~|
Total errors = 54 4 - ~~~WWWW~~~~~~~~~~WWW~~~~~~~~~~~~~~~~~~~|
                 5 - ~~~WWRW~~~~~~~~~~WWW~~~~~~~~~~~~~~~~~~~| Head
                 6 - ~~~~RWW~~~~~~~~~~~~~~~~~~~~~~~~~~~~~~~~~|  1
                 7 - ~~~~WRR~~~~~~~~~~~~~~~~~~~~~~~~~~~~~~~~~|
                 8 - ~~~~~RR~~~~~~~~~~~~~~~~~~~~~~~~~~~~~~~~~|
                 9 - ~~~~~RRWC~~~~~~~~~~~~~~~~~~~~~~~~~~~~~~~-
```

Figure 6.43   The Write/Read Test report

```
                  TEST DRIVE Hysteresis Test

                  m i l l i - i n c h e s ----------
H Tr Dir Error   -13-12-11-10 -9 -8 -7 -6 +6 +7 +8 +9+10+11+12+13
- -- --- -----   |--|--|--|--|--|--|--|--|--|--|--|--|--|--|--|
0 16 --                 ~~~~~~~~~~~~~~~~~~~~~~~~~~~~~~
     0.0            ~~~~~~~~~~~~~~~~~~~~~~~~~~~~~~~~

1 16 --                  ~~~~~~~~~~~~~~~~~~~~~~~~~~~~~
     0.5            ~~~~~~~~~~~~~~~~~~~~~~~~~~~~~~~

0 19 --              ~~~~~~~~~~~~~~~~~~~~~~~~~~~~~~~~~~
     0.5          ~~~~~~~~~~~~~~~~~~~~~~~~~~~~~~~~

1 19 --              ~~~~~~~~~~~~~~~~~~~~~~~~~~~~~~~~
     0.0          ~~~~~~~~~~~~~~~~~~~~~~~~~~~~~~~
```

Figure 6.44   The Hysteresis report

6.5.6   HEAD AZIMUTH

Head azimuth is a measure of the angle of the head relative to the track centreline. If the head is rotated or twisted away from this line then problems may occur in transferring disks between drives.

The DDD has a special azimuth track used for this test, which allows the azimuth of a particular drive head to be checked. Figure 6.45 shows the display produced by the azimuth test for an unacceptable drive, the X entries indicating those areas of the track that could not be read.

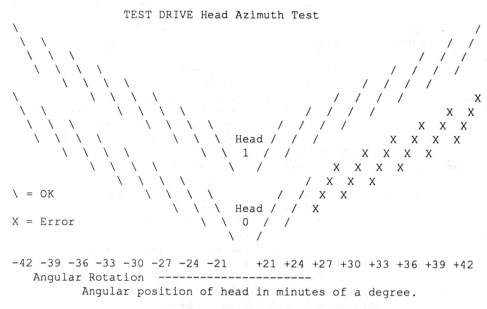

Figure 6.45   The Head Azimuth report

6.5.7   HUB CENTRING

This test measures how well the disk is clamped, and how near to a perfect circular pattern it is rotated in. The eccentricity of the drives rotational pattern is measured in terms of milli-inches, and displayed in a graphical form, as shown in Figure 6.46.

This example shows the centring ability for a good disk drive. Note that there is still a single error present, even though the drive is deemed to be in good shape. In fact the drive is said to be acceptable as long as there are no errors on the 7 milli-inch line.

6.5.8   CONTINUOUS ALIGNMENT

The continuous alignment test repeatedly performs the single alignment test, allowing the user to choose which track it is performed on.

This means that the alignment of the drive can be adjusted while the test is running, allowing the results of each small adjustment to be seen instantly. Figure 6.47 shows the graphical results of the continuous alignment test.

6.5.9   CLEANING UTILITY

The cleaning utility is designed to be used in conjunction with a standard head cleaning diskette. Rather than just leave the drive head in one position, as is the case with the traditional method of entering a DIR command to spin the disk, the head cleaning utility causes the head to be moved from the inside to the outside track repeatedly, thus ensuring that it is cleaned evenly.

The utility also allows the user to determine how long the disk is to be spun for. In general it is recommended that the drive cleaning diskette is used for no longer than 30 seconds at a time, as the abrasive nature of the surface can cause problems if used for longer periods.

```
TEST DRIVE Hub Centering Head 0


              ~     ~
         ~              ~
        ~                        ~
    ~          ~     ~
       ~             ~          X
                        ~
9 --  ~   ~       ~    ~                              ~
             ~              ~        ~    ~
                       ~                        ~    ~
8 --  ~   ~                      ~
                            ~    ~         ~        ~
                                            ~    ~      ~    ~
7 --  ~                            ~
                         ~         ~              ~
                                    ~    ~       ~
~ = OK  X = Error                   ~                 ~
                                         ~    ~

    One Disk Revolution  --------------------
```

Figure 6.46   The Hub Centring report

```
TEST DRIVE Continuous Alignment Test

    m i l l i - i n c h e s ----------
    -13-12-11-10 -9 -8 -7 -6 +6 +7 +8 +9+10+11+12+13
    |--|--|--|--|--|--|--|--|--|--|--|--|--|--|--|

Current        ~~~~~~~~~~~~~~~~~~~~~~~~~~~~~~~~~~
Previous       ~~~~~~~~~~~~~~~~~~~~~~~~~~~~~~~~~~~
               ~~~~~~~~~~~~~~~~~~~~~~~~~~~~~~~~~~
               ~~~~~~~~~~~~~~~~~~~~~~~~~~~~~~~~~~
               ~~~~~~~~~~~~~~~~~~~~~~~~~~~~~~~~~~
               ~~~~~~~~~~~~~~~~~~~~~~~~~~~~~~~
               ~~~~~~~~~~~~~~~~~~~~~~~~~~~~~~~~~~
               ~~~~~~~~~~~~~~~~~~~~~~~~~~~~~~~~~~
               ~~~~~~~~~~~~~~~~~~~~~~~~~~~~~~~~~~
               ~~~~~~~~~~~~~~~~~~~~~~~~~~~~~~~~~~
               ~~~~~~~~~~~~~~~~~~~~~~~~~~~~~~~~
               ~~~~~~~~~~~~~~~~~~~~~~~~~~~~~~~~~
```

Use the up & down arrows   Head 0   Track 19   Use the left & right
to switch heads   arrows to switch tracks

Figure 6.47   The Continuous Alignment report

6.6 COPYIIPC

COPYIIPC is a disk duplication program produced by Central Point Software Inc. COPYIIPC has been available for many years, and has steadily increased in versatility whilst still remaining easy to use. There are many rivals to COPYIIPC which offer similar facilities and abilities, CopyWrite being one of the more famous. However, COPYIIPC has shown itself to be of greater use in data recovery, as it can copy even seriously corrupted disks without any trouble.

COPYIIPC produces an exact image copy of the source disk, including any anomalies that it may detect. However, it will alert the user to these problems, and ask if they are to be corrected or left as they are. For this reason the program is of particular use in data recovery, as it allows an exact copy to be made of any possibly corrupted disks. Attempts at data recovery can then be performed using the copy, leaving the original unchanged. If things should go wrong and the data on the copy is damaged, then it is a simple matter to make another copy from the original.

The program is used from the DOS command line:

COPYIIPC [source drive] [target drive]

The user is prompted for disk changes etc, as well as any further information that may be required. Such prompts usually require Yes or No answers to specific questions.

6.6.1 DATA RECOVERY USING COPYIIPC

COPYIIPC can be used in its own right for recovering information. A common cause of data loss or corruption is the CRC. This checksum value is used by DOS to determine whether or not data on the disk has been corrupted in any way. If the CRC read from the disk does not match the CRC calculated from the data, then DOS reports a *Data error reading drive X:*, and prevents access to that data.

If COPYIIPC is used to copy a floppy disk that has a CRC error, then it will report an error when it comes to read the faulty sector. The user is then prompted to specify whether or not this error is to be corrected. Giving a positive reply will cause the CRC error to be remedied in the copy, making the sector readable again. Specifying that the error is not to be corrected will cause the CRC error to be present in the copy, thus allowing the user to diagnose and remedy the fault manually.

COPYIIPC can be used to remedy other types of errors, such as loss of address mark etc. However, it is essential that these faults are correctly diagnosed before attempting to rectify them. Failure to do this will almost certainly result in an even greater amount of data being destroyed on the copy.

6.7 PROGRAMMING LANGUAGES

Whilst most data recovery tasks can be tackled using products such as those described above, there are some situations which will defy all attempts using such tools. In these cases, it will be necessary to resort to using dedicated programs, written specifically to solve the problem in hand. The only way to produce such programs is to use a programming language.

There are many different programming languages available for personal computers, although three of the most common are:

- BASIC
- Pascal
- C

BASIC is the simplest language of the three, and is sometimes supplied when a new computer system is purchased. BASIC stands for Beginners All-purpose Symbolic Instruction Code, and was designed in the late 1960s to allow novice programmers to use computer systems. It is very easy to learn, and uses English words as commands.

Pascal is more sophisticated than BASIC, but takes a correspondingly longer time to learn fully. Pascal is a procedural language, whereby any task is broken down into separate blocks, each of which can be easily programmed.

C is a language that is used for the creation of powerful applications software. It is not an easy language to learn, and is of more use to systems programmers than to those in data recovery.

Standard versions of Pascal and BASIC offer very similar facilities in terms of accessing disk information etc. However a version of Pascal from Borland (called Turbo Pascal) enhances the standard by providing a range of very powerful BIOS level commands for accessing disk information. This means that Turbo Pascal is ideal for creating simple programs for specific data recovery tasks. Additionally there is a wide range of backup products for Turbo Pascal, providing a variety of specialised facilities. For these reasons it is recommended that anyone interested in learning a programming language should strongly consider Turbo Pascal, as it offers many advantages over BASIC for data recovery applications.

6.8 SUMMARY

This chapter has only briefly touched on a few of the many thousands of utilities and programs available for data recovery. As many of these programs work at such a low level, in particular when performing absolute disk accesses, it is recommended that only proven packages be given consideration. In fact, it may be wise to avoid superficial upgrades for packages such as Norton and PCTools as they do little to increase the functionality of the system, and in many cases actually make it harder for the experienced user to perform the required operations.

All of the products examined in this chapter are excellent at performing specific tasks; Norton and PCTools work very well for general examination and modification of hard and floppy disks, Disk Explorer provides a number of unique facilities for editing floppy disk data, TestDrive offers a complete diagnostic test of any floppy disk, COPYIIPC produces image copies of just about any floppy disk, and the programming languages mentioned can be used to fill in any gaps left by the other products.

However, it should always be remembered that these products are just tools, and that it will often be necessary to use several tools in any one data recovery situation. Thus it is essential to gain a good working knowledge of how a variety of such programs can be used for data recovery purposes, as this will allow the greatest number of problems to be successfully tackled.

7   Case Studies Of Disaster Recovery

7.1   GUIDELINES

Previous chapters have provided background information and descriptions of the tools and programs that are required for data recovery. However, the process of recovering the data is not always as simple as selecting a program and using it to perform a predetermined sequence of steps. There are some situations in which this approach can be used, but most data recovery tasks are more complicated, requiring the user to apply interpretive skills to solve the problems. In many cases there may be several possible solutions, and it will be necessary to exercise discretion and eliminate the least likely.

Therefore, it is impossible to provide a rigid procedure which solves all data recovery problems, although a set of general guidelines will help in steering the user towards likely solutions. The following forms a basis for most data recovery attempts.

7.1.1   CHECK FOR A BACKUP

The first step is to see if there is an up-to-date backup copy of the data. If there is, then it is pointless to try and restore the corrupt data unless there is a very important reason for doing so. Also, the backup should not be restored before checking that the original media is sound, as the problem may recur if there is a physical defect.

Before restoring the backup, a copy should be made. Thus if problems occur and the first backup is damaged during the process of restoring it, then the second is still available. One problem that may occur, especially with tape backups, is destruction of the media by the drive. If this happens and the first backup is destroyed or damaged, then the second backup should not be restored on the same device; a different drive must be used, otherwise the same thing may happen.

Assuming there is no backup available, it will be necessary to face the problem of actually recovering the information that was lost or corrupted on the original media.

7.1.2   OBTAIN BACKGROUND INFORMATION

Rushing headlong into a data recovery problem is the worst thing of all to do, as simple solutions may not be obvious to start with.

It is very important to find out *exactly* what happened. This means talking to the person who was using the machine when the failure was noticed, and if possible anyone who

123

was using the machine previously. It is often very confusing to listen to people's opinions about what happened; it is much safer to rely only on hard facts.

It will be necessary to know what the machine was doing at the time, what software was in use both at the time the loss was noticed and beforehand, as well as what the lost or corrupted data was supposed to represent. For example, was the data a spreadsheet file, text file, database file or program file? How large was the data file? What did it contain? Which application was used to create the file? When was the data last accessed? Who last altered the data? Has any major tidying up of the disk been performed recently?

These facts should provide a rough outline so that the data recoverer will know what to look for, and how to go about the job of recovering the information.

7.1.3 LIST ALL POSSIBILITIES

All possible causes of data loss should be listed, together with the actions that are needed to recover the data in each case. For some situations there may be many different reasons, and an even greater number of solutions. In such cases the possibilities should be listed in terms of likelihood, or alternatively by listing the easiest solutions first.

7.1.4 TAKE A COPY

A copy of the media should always be made. Whilst this is relatively easy for floppy disks, it can be considerably more difficult for hard disks. In the case of floppy disks, the original disk should be write protected, before the copy is made, with a write-protect tab. Although it is possible to write protect hard disks by disconnecting the wire that carries the write enable signal, in most cases this will not be considered a necessity. Nevertheless users should take extreme care to ensure nothing is written to the original disk, at least before an accurate diagnosis as to the source of the problem has been made.

Methods of creating a copy of a hard disk include the following:

– The connection of another hard disk to the computer, allowing the original disk to be copied to the new one.

– The use of a network to transfer the contents of the disk to another computer system.

– Copy the contents to a Bernoulli drive, DataPac or other demountable storage unit.

– If no other options exist, copy the data to floppy, or even magnetic tape. This option is far from ideal as it is no longer an image copy.

Software to create such an image copy may have to be written specifically. Alternatively, it may be possible to use a proprietary program such as NU, PCTools, Disk Explorer, Debug etc to achieve a similar effect.

7.1.5 TRY EACH SOLUTION IN TURN

Each possible solution should be tried in turn, starting with the most likely or simplest. There are certain solutions that are commonly encountered, and it may be worth trying some of these first:

– SETUP. Checking the specifications for SETUP may reveal a problem, especially if the disk type or geometry appears to be incorrectly specified. In many cases it will prove fruitless to attempt any further operations if the SETUP data is wrong.

- If the FAT has been corrupted, then it is possible that the second copy is still OK. A disk editor can be used to copy the good version of the FAT onto the corrupted one, or it may be necessary to combine different parts of each copy to achieve the desired results.

- Has a utility been used to make a copy of the system area? Two common examples are the FR command in Norton, and the Mirror command in PCTools. The data files for these utilities are named FRECOVER.DAT and MIRROR.FIL respectively, and could provide useful information.

- Dirty Buffers. As a file is created and written to disk, it is stored in an area of memory called a buffer. When each one becomes full, or the file is closed, the buffer is flushed to disk and the information recorded permanently. When a small file is created in this way, it only occupies a small section of the buffer, leaving the previous contents to occupy the remainder. Closing the file causes the entire buffer to be written to disk, including the unwanted data. This unwanted data may be FAT information, directory information, or miscellaneous data. Therefore, quickly scanning the clusters for small files may reveal useful data which can be used to recover information.

- If the partition record is corrupt, the disk will not be read at all by DOS. This can be easily overcome by patching a good partition record over the corrupted one, again using a disk editor. If there were several partitions on the disk then it will be necessary to reinstate the partition information manually. The only way to obtain the required addresses and sizes is to locate the start of each partition on disk, by looking for the boot sector. This can be recognised by the signature of 55AAh in the last two bytes, and will always be located at a position where the head number is 0 and the sector number is 1.

- If the boot sector has been corrupted then it will be necessary to modify the data using a sector editor. The main code can be copied from any disk, but the data relating to the disk dimensions must be patched manually.

- CHKDSK will give information about lost clusters. This is quite a tell-tale sign when files and directories have been corrupted. CHKDSK /F will create directory entries for such files, or the undelete systems in NU or PCTools can be used.

- When undeleting, try to undelete single cluster files before working on large ones. This makes the task much easier. To undelete a file, find the first cluster from the directory entry, then attempt to manually find the next one. This can be achieved by looking at the data in the first cluster and matching it to the next. Repeat this until the entire file is found.

- Files with a length of 0 bytes can be patched by editing the directory entry, then confirming that the FAT chain is correct.

- Unformatting is a major operation. Subdirectories should be undeleted first, and then undeletion techniques used to recreate the files. This is one of the most time consuming data recovery tasks, and can often be performed efficiently by Norton etc. However, the results of such an automated recovery should always be thoroughly tested before the data is assumed to be correct.

- Make copies of the data that is recovered during the recovery exercise, not just at the end. These copies must be produced on separate media, usually floppy disks.

—   In many cases it is necessary to know the format for the data files in order to make a full recovery. Some common file formats are given in the appendices, although in many cases it will be necessary to contact the vendor to obtain this information. Once this information has been acquired, it is possible to recreate files, even if they have been severely damaged.

7.1.6   ADMIT DEFEAT

It is essential to realise when it is unlikely that data will be successfully recovered. In such cases it is much safer to pass the problem to someone who has more experience in such matters. Although the fee they charge may be large, there is a much greater chance that the data will be recovered. If the recovery process is continued by someone who is unsure of what to do next, then it is likely that the data may be irreparably destroyed.

7.2   WHEN HAS SUCCESSFUL RECOVERY BEEN ACHIEVED?

The task of the troubleshooter is to attempt to recover as much data as possible from the source media. However, it may be impossible to determine whether or not the relevant data has been recovered, and hence whether or not the recovery operation is complete. It is therefore important to liaise with the original user of the system, as they are often the only person who can decide whether or not the recovery operation is complete.

They may also be able to supply useful information during the recovery process. For example, they can often identify data as belonging to a particular file, which may in turn allow the troubleshooter to determine exactly how the data should be formatted.

7.3   SIX COMMON DATA RECOVERY SCENARIOS

The following scenarios are typical examples of the problems that may be encountered. Each scenario starts with details of the problem, as related by the user. All information that is known has been listed. The approach to the problem is then planned, and the data recovery attempted. The Norton Utilities (Version 4.5) package has been used as the primary tool for working through the examples, as this has proved to be the most flexible and adaptable for such operations. Any other similar integrated package such as PCTools, Mace Utilities or Bakers Dozen could have been used in its place, and it is recommended that users select the system they are most familiar with.

All of the examples used in these scenarios are based on floppy disks. However, all of the techniques and methods employed are equally applicable to hard disks.

7.3.1   SCENARIO 1

7.3.1.1   The Problem

A user reports that they have accidentally deleted all of the files on a floppy disk they were given by entering DEL *.* from the DOS prompt. They know there were four or five files on the disk, and that two of them were Lotus 1-2-3 worksheet files. They think the other files may be from WordStar, but cannot be sure. The worksheet files are known to be called WIDGET89.WK1 and STAFF.WK1, the first of which contains a profit and loss account and the second contains a staff database. It is thought that no file was greater than 5KB in size.

7.3.1.2 The Solution

At first glance this appears to be fairly straightforward. The disk contained relatively few files all of which were quite small. Therefore it seems likely that the Norton quick unerase (QU) utility can be used to recover the information. Failing this it will be necessary to use the Unerase option in Norton to perform this manually. As the cause of the loss is known to be human error, it is unlikely that there are any further complications to the problem.

The first step in solving the problem is to make a copy of the original disk. This can be made with diskcopy, COPYIIPC etc, but it is essential to write-protect the original before it is even inserted into the disk drive, to prevent any further losses from occurring. Once the copy has been made, it can be used to recover the data.

The Norton QU utility will be tried first; the working copy of the disk is inserted into a drive (either A: or B depending on the drive and diskette densities), and the following command entered from DOS:

QU B:

This assumes that the Norton utilities have been correctly installed on a hard or floppy disk, and the Norton directory is current or has a path specified. QU will produce the display shown in Figure 7.1.

```
C:\>qu b:
QU-Quick UnErase, Advanced Edition 4.50, (C) Copr 1987-88, Peter Norton

Directory of B:\
    Erased file specification: *.*
    Number of erased files: 4
    Number that can be Quick-UnErased: 4

    Erased files lose the first character of their names.
    After selecting each file to Quick-UnErase, you will be
    asked to supply the missing character.

    ?emo.bak          256 bytes     1:04 pm  Fri 23 Nov 90
Quick-UnErase this file (Y/N) ?
```

Figure 7.1   Using QU to recover lost data

QU has reported that there are four deleted files on the disk, and that it is possible to recover all of them. Therefore the prompts on-screen should be followed to undelete the files one at a time. For each file it is necessary to state whether or not it is to be undeleted, and if so, what the first letter of the filename is to be. Two of the files are specified as ?EMO and ?EMO.BAK. From this it appears likely that they were previously named MEMO and MEMO.BAK, and so the first letter of the filename can be supplied. The third file is specified as ?TAFF.WK1, and is obviously the STAFF.WK1 worksheet.

This operation appears to be entirely successful for the first three files, but QU fails on the fourth, reporting that it cannot be undeleted as the data in the first cluster is in use by another file. This report is shown in Figure 7.2.

It is still not known whether Norton has undeleted the first three files correctly, or whether it has failed completely in this operation. This can be ascertained by looking at the data in the files, preferably in the same way that they would be used normally.

```
C:\>qu b:
QU-Quick UnErase, Advanced Edition 4.50, (C) Copr 1987-88, Peter Norton

Directory of B:\
   Erased file specification: *.*
   Number of erased files: 4
   Number that can be Quick-UnErased: 4

   Erased files lose the first character of their names.
   After selecting each file to Quick-UnErase, you will be
   asked to supply the missing character.

   ?emo.bak          256 bytes      1:04 pm  Fri 23 Nov 90
 'memo.bak' Quick-UnErased

   ?emo              256 bytes      1:04 pm  Fri 23 Nov 90
 'memo' Quick-UnErased

   ?taff.wk1       2,098 bytes      1:02 pm  Fri 23 Nov 90
 'staff.wk1' Quick-UnErased

   ?idget89.wk1    4,750 bytes     12:56 pm  Fri 23 Nov 90
It is not possible to Quick-UnErase this file
Its data space is being used by another file
Press any key to continue...
```

Figure 7.2   Failure of QU to recover last file

The first two files that were undeleted are called MEMO and MEMO.BAK. They are likely to be the WordStar files, and so can be viewed on screen with the DOS TYPE command:

TYPE B:MEMO

This lists the contents of the MEMO file on the screen, as shown in Figure 7.3. Viewing the MEMO.BAK file produces the same result.

```
From: Admin Dept

To:   D. Smithson
      B. Anderson
      K. Setton

Enclosed on disk are files in spreadsheet format. Please view
in 1-2-3 and advise of any changes.
```

Figure 7.3   The text of the recovered MEMO file

The STAFF.WK1 file is obviously a worksheet, and thus must be loaded into Lotus 123 to view the data. Therefore Lotus 123 is executed, and the file retrieved in the normal manner:

123 (E)
/F(ile) R(etrieve) B:STAFF.WK1 (E)

However, rather than load the file into memory, Lotus reports an error, as shown in Figure 7.4.

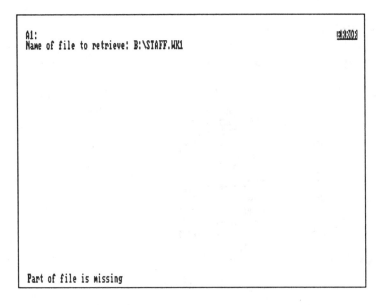

Figure 7.4 Lotus error message on attempting to load the file

According to Lotus a part of the file is missing. This error is actually produced in most cases when the system does not think the data file is in the correct format. Thus it can be assumed that the STAFF.WK1 file has not been recovered correctly.

It is now necessary to backtrack one step, as an incorrect operation has been performed on the data. The safest way to do this is to start on the recovery again, by making another copy of the original diskette, and then undeleting only the MEMO and MEMO.BAK files. Once this has been done, the recovery process can be resumed.

As the QU utility has failed, it is necessary to adopt the second line of action and use the Unerase facility from Norton. However, before starting on this it is advisable to obtain some background information about the disk format. This is achieved with the DI command:

DI B:

A report is produced detailing the important disk parameters, as shown in Figure 7.5.

From this report it can be seen that the sectors are 512 bytes, and each cluster is made up of two sectors. Thus the minimum allocation unit is 1KB, or 2 sectors.

The next step is to obtain more information about the files themselves. As they have only been deleted, the directory entries for them will still be available in the root directory sector. This can be viewed through NU:

NU B:

The *Explore Disk* option is chosen, followed by *Choose Item* and *File*. *Root directory area* is then chosen from the list of available files. On selecting *Edit/display item* the display will appear as shown in Figure 7.6, with the root directory data shown in directory format.

```
Press any key to continue...

C:\>di b:
DI-Disk Information, Advanced Edition 4.50, (C) Copr 1987-88, Peter Norton

    Information from DOS        Drive B:        Information from the boot record
--------------------------------------------------------------------------------
                                system id       'MSDOS3.3'
                         media descriptor (hex)      FD
              1                  drive number
            512              bytes per sector         512
              2             sectors per cluster         2
              2               number of FATs            2
            112           root directory entries      112
              2               sectors per FAT           2
            354             number of clusters
                             number of sectors        720
              1                offset to FAT            1
              5            offset to directory
             12               offset to data
                             sectors per track          9
                                  sides                 2
                              hidden sectors            0
```

Figure 7.5   Disk information for drive B:

From this it can be seen that the file sizes and locations are as follows:

Filename	Size (bytes)	Size (clusters)	First cluster
STAFF.WK1	2098	3	2
WIDGET89.WK1	4750	5	3
MEMO	256	1	10
MEMO.BAK	256	1	11

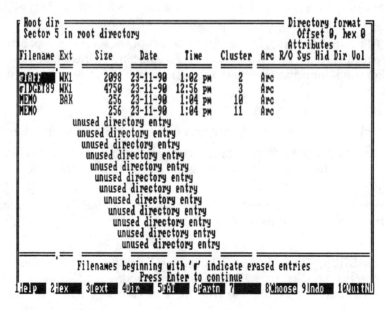

Figure 7.6   Directory listing for the data

As STAFF.WK1 and WIDGET89.WK1 have not yet been unerased, the only areas of the disk in use are clusters 10 and 11, which are occupied by the previously unerased MEMO and MEMO.BAK files. This can be confirmed by selecting and viewing the FAT, which produces the display shown in Figure 7.7.

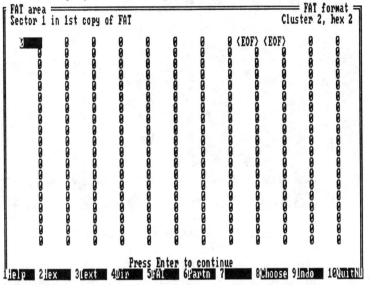

Figure 7.7   Listing of the disk FAT

Notice that the FAT entries displayed in Figure 7.7 have been converted to decimal by Norton, with the <EOF> markers representing the FFFFh entries at the end of each FAT chain.

The next step in the recovery process is to determine where the remainder of the two deleted files can be found. It is known that clusters 2 and 3 are used by the start of the two files, thus the next cluster that needs to be considered is cluster 4. This can be viewed on screen by selecting *Choose item, cLuster 4*, as shown in Figure 7.8.

The bottom section of Figure 7.8 shows some readable text mixed in with a variety of numbers and other data. In particular, it identifies the data as being a staff database for the Widget company. Thus it can be assumed that this cluster is a part of STAFF.WK1. Viewing the 2nd sector of cluster four shows the layout of the data in the file, and it can be seen that there is a fairly repetitive pattern, as many of the entries in any Lotus database will use similar formats.

Cluster 5 can also be viewed in the same way, and it can be seen from the layout of the data that it is actually a continuation of the file. Therefore, the 3 clusters that make up the STAFF.WK1 file have all been identified as clusters 2, 4 and 5. The NU Unerase facility can now be used to unerase the file. Each of the clusters to be added must be individually specified, as problems will be caused if the automatic specification is used.

Once the file has been unerased it should again be checked by attempting to retrieve the data into 123. However, unlike the previous attempt which produced an error, the file will now load correctly and will be seen to be complete with no data loss or corruption whatsoever.

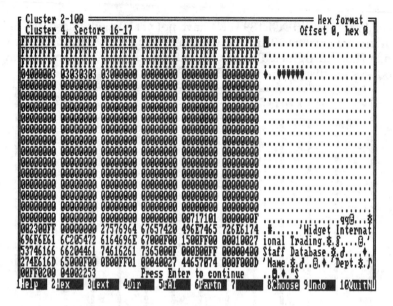

Figure 7.8   Data stored in cluster 4

The final step is to unerase the WIDGET89.WK1 file. As success has been achieved using the Unerase option from NU for the first file, it is recommended that the same approach be used for the second file.

The first cluster of the file is known from the directory entry to be cluster 3, and so it is necessary to locate the next cluster in the chain by examination. The next free cluster is number 6, and so this should be examined using the NU Explore disk options. It can be seen that the data is actually part of a profit and loss account worksheet, which is indeed what WIDGET89.WK1 contained prior to deletion. The format and layout of the data is not so obvious in this case, although a pattern is still recognisable. Figure 7.9 shows the data in cluster 6.

As this pattern continues in clusters 7, 8 and 9 it can be safely assumed that these clusters form the remainder of the file. Therefore the file can be recovered using the NU Unerase command, specifying each cluster manually for safety. Figure 7.10 shows a visual map indicating the positioning of the clusters for the file.

The file should be tested as before by loading the file into 123, when it will be found to be totally recovered, with no data corruptions at all.

7.3.1.3 Summary

This scenario has illustrated the problems associated with even apparently simple unerasing exercises. The assumption that automatic tools such as QU will work in all cases is a very dangerous one, and this example has illustrated that even when QU appears to work, there are situations in which it actually produces incorrect results.

However the sophisticated file format employed by Lotus makes manual unerasure of worksheet data quite difficult, and it may be found that the task of differentiating between several clusters containing such data is almost impossible for the inexperienced.

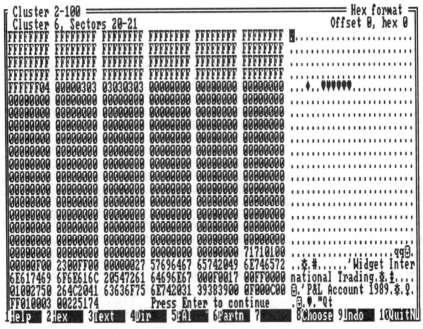

Figure 7.9   Data stored in cluster 6

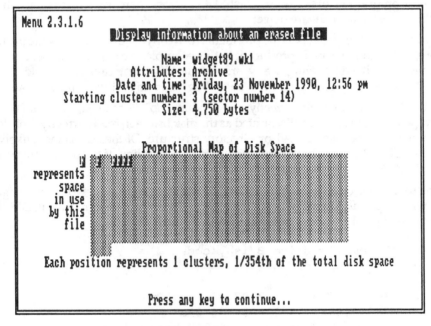

Figure 7.10   Cluster locations of WIDGET89.WK1 data

7.3.2 SCENARIO 2

7.3.2.1 The Problem

A user reports that their disk appears to have been corrupted. It previously contained five files; two worksheet files by the names of WIDGET89.WK1 and STAFF.WK1, a WordStar memo and its backup, and a recently created test file called NEWFILE. They have no idea how the disk was corrupted, but are desperate to retrieve all of the data. They cannot even obtain a directory listing of the contents; the command appears to work but all that is displayed on the screen is garbage.

7.3.2.2 The Solution

There is little information provided in this scenario that can be used to deduce a cause for the fault. The user has not even been able to define what they mean by corrupt, so there is a very large range of possibilities in the case. One pointer that may be helpful is the inability to obtain a meaningful directory listing, even though the DIR command appears to work. This implies that the disk is readable, but appears to have been corrupted. Thus the most likely causes and actions are:

Corruption of directory and/or FAT	Requires directory and FAT data to be reinstated.
Corruption of boot sector	Requires boot sector data to be recreated.
Disk crash in directory/FAT area	Data area must be extracted to a new disk as this one is physically damaged.

The first two of these possibilities could be caused by any number of factors including application program errors, system crash, DOS errors, hardware errors etc. The last possibility is due to a hardware defect.

The first stage in the recovery is the production of a copy. The original is write protected as before, and then the copy is produced. In this example, the copying process is part of the recovery, as it will highlight any area of the disk that cannot be read. Thus if COPYIIPC is used, any data errors will be highlighted and rectified on the copy.

COPYIIPC is found to work perfectly, and produces no error messages at all. Therefore the third possible cause can be discounted as the disk has been read correctly. This leaves corruption of the boot sector, FAT or directory structure. Of these, it is most likely that either the FAT or directory have been corrupted as corruption of the boot sector usually renders the disk entirely unreadable.

As the user reported that the DIR command does not work, it is worth investigating exactly what happens. Therefore, with the copy of the corrupt disk in drive B, DIR B: can be entered, and produces the display shown in Figure 7.11.

```
Volume in drive B is y code
Directory of  B:\

ds, M   996540   2-00-80   8:00p
4278194688  17-01-05   6:02a
          2 File(s)     351232 bytes free
```

Figure 7.11   Results of the DIR B: command

Obviously this is total garbage, and implies that the data in the directory structure is incorrect. CHKDSK can be used to obtain a first impression of the condition of the FAT. It will highlight any errors that are found, particularly if there are any lost chains. These lost chains may well relate to the data files if the directory entries are corrupt. Entering CHKDSK B: produces the report shown in Figure 7.12.

```
Volume y code created 12 Jan 1996 1:51p
Errors found, F parameter not specified.
Corrections will not be written to disk.
B:\alary
    First cluster number is invalid,
     entry truncated.
B:\y code
    First cluster number is invalid,
     entry truncated.
B:\     First cluster number is invalid,
     entry truncated.
B:\
    First cluster number is invalid,
     entry truncated.
B:\ds, M
    Allocation error, size adjusted.
B:\
    First cluster number is invalid,
     entry truncated.

6 lost clusters found in 4 chains.
Convert lost chains to files  (Y/N)? n
    6144 bytes disk space
         would be freed.

362496 bytes total disk space
     0 bytes in 3 hidden files
     0 bytes in 1 directories
  5120 bytes in 2 user files
351232 bytes available on disk

655360 bytes total memory
568064 bytes free
```

Figure 7.12   Results of the CHKDSK B: command

Seemingly, this report also consists of garbage, as the names of the files contain illegal characters etc. However, it can be seen that some of the names contain readable text. For example, the volume label is specified as *y code*, and one of the files is named *alary*. Furthermore, although there is a date displayed, it is clearly incorrect. This would tend to indicate that the most likely cause of the problem is that a data file has been written over the directory area, with certain parts of the file now being incorrectly interpreted by DOS as file names and specifications. CHKDSK has however found some lost chains, which may possibly relate to the lost data files. It is unwise to automatically assume that this is so, and careful examination is required before a decision is taken.

As DOS seems unable to interpret this data, it will be necessary to use NU to examine it. NU is executed as before, and the root directory area chosen and viewed on screen. The display appears as shown in Figure 7.13.

```
┌ Root dir ════════════════════════════════════════ Directory format ┐
│ Sector 5 in root directory                             Offset 0, hex 0 │
│                                                         Attributes      │
│ Filename Ext    Size     Date      Time     Cluster  Arc R/O Sys Hid Dir Vol │
│ ▬▬▬▬▬▬▬ ═══  ══════  ════════  ═══════   ═══════  ═══ ═══ ═══ ═══ ═══ ═══ │
│             , not a proper directory entry                             │
│ y code *  ◄    589839  12-01-96   1:51 pm     65     Arc R/O Sys Hid Dir Vol │
│             not a proper directory entry                               │
│             not a proper directory entry                               │
│             not a proper directory entry                               │
│             not a proper directory entry                               │
│             unused directory entry                                     │
│ ◦ ä▇ ◦ L ¼▇              0-08-07   1:40 am      4                    Vol │
│             not a proper directory entry                               │
│             not a proper directory entry                               │
│             unused directory entry                                     │
│             not a proper directory entry                               │
│             not a proper directory entry                               │
│             unused directory entry                                     │
│             not a proper directory entry                               │
│             not a proper directory entry                               │
│ ══════ , ══ ══════ ══════ ══════ ══════ ══════ ══════ ══════ ══════ │
│           Filenames beginning with 'σ' indicate erased entries         │
│                    Press Enter to continue                             │
│1Help  2Hex   3Text  4Dir   5FAT   6Partn  7      8Choose 9Undo  10QuitNU│
```

Figure 7.13   Viewing the root directory in NU

The data is obviously meaningless, and Norton displays the *Not a proper directory entry* message for the majority of the entries. Viewing the data in hexadecimal format produces the display shown in Figure 7.14. It can be seen that the data currently occupying the root directory area is actually part of a data file, probably a part of the Lotus 1-2-3 staff database worksheet.

In order to know the extent of the corruption, it will be necessary to view some of the adjacent areas. Figure 7.15 shows the 2nd sector of the root directory, which can be seen to be blank. Thus it can be assumed that this area is unaffected.

Examination of the other sectors in the root directory area reveal that all are blank, and thus unaffected by the disk corruption. It is also essential to view the FAT data to determine whether any problems have been encountered. Figure 7.16 shows a listing of the FAT.

Whilst it is difficult to determine whether or not this is correct, the data appears to be feasible. The values can be compared with the second copy of the FAT, and will be found to be identical. Thus it is likely that the FAT is unaffected. Therefore, from the investigations carried out so far, the only area that seems to be affected is the first sector of the root directory. If this proves to be true, then recovery is straightforward, but time consuming.

Figure 7.14   The root directory area viewed in hexadecimal format

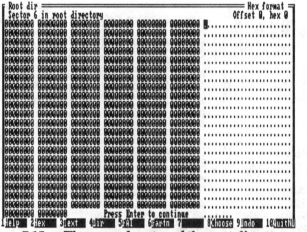

Figure 7.15   The second sector of the root directory area

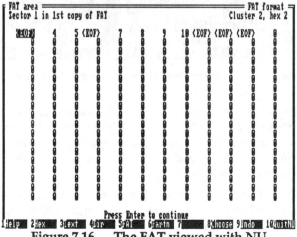

Figure 7.16   The FAT viewed with NU

To double check the validity of the FAT, it is advisable to examine each of the chains of clusters in turn, to determine whether or not they appear to form valid data files. It can be seen from the FAT that there are in fact five chains, two of which are multi-cluster and three of which consist of single clusters:

2

3-5

6-10

11

12

This would seem to correspond to the five files that were originally on the disk, although further examination is required to confirm this. Figure 7.17 shows a hexadecimal display of the data held in cluster 2.

```
┌Cluster 2-355 ═══════════════════════════════════════ Hex format ═┐
│ Cluster 2, Sectors 12-13                          Offset 511, hex 1FF│
│46726F6D 3A204164 6D696E20 44657074 0D0A0D0A 546F3A09 From: Admin Dept♪♂♀To:0│
│442E2053 6D697468 736F6E0D 0A09422E 20416E64 6572736F D. Smithson♪♂0B. Anderso│
│6E0D0A09 4B2E2053 6574746F 6E0D0A0D 0A456E63 6C6F7365 n♪♂0K. Setton♪♂♀Enclose│
│64206F6E 20646973 6B206172 65206669 6C657320 696E2073 d on disk are files in s│
│70726561 64736865 65742066 6F726D61 742E2050 6C656173 preadsheet format. Pleas│
│65207669 65770D0A 696E2031 2D322D33 20616E64 20616476 e view♪♂in 1-2-3 and adv│
│69736520 6F662061 6E792063 68616E67 65732E1A 1A1A1A1A ise of any changes.→↑↑↑↑│
│1A1A1A1A 1A1A1A1A 1A1A1A1A 1A1A1A1A 1A1A1A1A 1A1A1A1A →↑↑↑↑↑↑↑↑↑↑↑↑↑↑↑↑↑↑↑↑↑↑↑↑│
│1A1A1A1A 1A1A1A1A 1A1A1A1A 1A1A1A1A 1A1A1A1A 1A1A1A1A →↑↑↑↑↑↑↑↑↑↑↑↑↑↑↑↑↑↑↑↑↑↑↑↑│
│1A1A1A1A 1A1A1A1A 1A1A1A1A 1A1A1A1A 1A1A1A1A 1A1A1A1A →↑↑↑↑↑↑↑↑↑↑↑↑↑↑↑↑↑↑↑↑↑↑↑↑│
│1A1A1A1A 1A1A1A1A 1A1A1A1A 1A1A1A1A 44414E20 20202020 →↑↑↑↑↑↑↑↑↑↑↑↑↑↑↑↑DAN│
│20202010 00000000 00000000 00006856 F7145200 00000000 ▶.........hV≈⌐R....│
│44415441 52454320 20202010 00000000 00000000 0000427F DATAREC  ▶.........B⌐│
│49151A05 00000000 44424153 45202020 20202010 00000000 I§→♣....DBASE    ▶....│
│00000000 0000A165 15131D00 00000000 444F5320 20202020 ......ie§!↕......DOS│
│20202010 00000000 00000000 0000FB88 03130D00 00000000 ▶.........√δ♥!!♪.....│
│45554320 20202020 20202010 00000000 00000000 0000734A EUC             .....sJ│
│3C153C01 00000000 464F4E54 57415245 20202010 00000000 <§<☺....FONTWARE  ▶....│
│00000000 0000014E 1715C604 00000000 46504220 20202020 ......⌐N↕§╞♦....FPB│
│20202010 00000000 00000000 0000EB7E 0E155500 00000000 ▶.........δ~♫§U.....│
│47524150 48494353 20202010 00000000 00000000 0000A471 GRAPHICS  ▶.........ñq│
│89140F00 00000000       Press Enter to continue       ë¶☼....▌│
1Help   2Hex   3Text   4Dir   5FAT   6Partn  7         8Choose 9Undo  10QuitNU
```

Figure 7.17 Hexadecimal listing of the data in cluster 2

This appears to be a memo, and could be either the main WordStar file or its backup. Note that there is also further data after the text of the memo. This is actually an example of a dirty buffer. It can be seen that it contains a number of directory entries, which can be viewed more legibly by selecting directory format with the F4 function key. The display will appear as shown in Figure 7.18

Unfortunately this directory information does not appear to relate to the data that is to be recovered; it is most likely directory information from a hard disk, due to the high proportion of sub-directory entries.

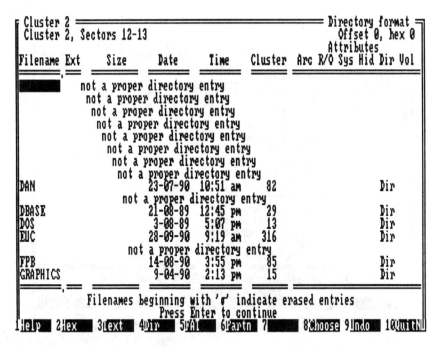

Figure 7.18   Cluster 2 data shown in directory format

Examining the other chains will allow them to be identified as follows:

Cluster	Usage
2	Memo or backup
3–5	Staff database
6–10	Profit and loss account
11	Memo or backup (same as 2)
12	Single line text file

Note that in the case of the Lotus worksheet file and the dBase staff database, it is necessary to know and recognise the file formats employed by these packages before the content of the data becomes obvious.

In the last case, cluster 12, the text itself appears to be only 9 characters. The remainder of the sector is filled with another dirty buffer, which again appears to be directory data. This can be viewed in directory format, and will appear as shown in Figure 7.19.

It can be seen from this listing that there is a strong likelihood that the data is in fact a directory for this disk. Therefore, the data can be copied to the first sector of the root directory in an attempt to recover the data. This can be achieved as follows:

– Firstly select sector 32 as the current item with the *Choose item, Sector, 32* series of commands.

– Choose the *Write item to disk* command, and follow the prompts on screen to specify the mode as Sector mode and the destination to be drive B, sector 5.

– When the warning screen is displayed, as shown in Figure 7.20, respond *Yes* to the prompt to write the data to the new location.

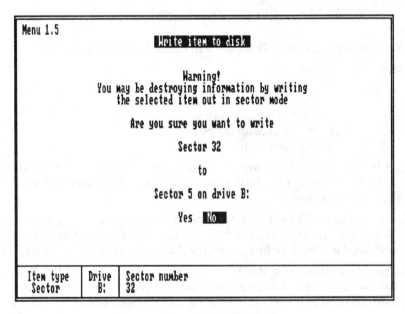

```
┌ Cluster 2-355 ════════════════════════════════ Directory format ═┐
│ Cluster 12, Sectors 32-33                              Offset 0, hex 0 │
│                                                           Attributes   │
│Filename Ext    Size     Date      Time    Cluster  Arc R/O Sys Hid Dir Vol│
│════════════════════════════════════════════════════════════════════════│
│TestFile eAK     256    23-11-90   1:04 pm      2    Arc                 │
│STAFF    WK1    2098    23-11-90   1:02 pm      3    Arc                 │
│WIDGET89 WK1    4750    23-11-90  12:56 pm      6    Arc                 │
│MEMO             256    23-11-90   1:04 pm     11    Arc                 │
│              unused directory entry                                    │
│              unused directory entry                                    │
│              unused directory entry                                    │
│              unused directory entry                                    │
│              unused directory entry                                    │
│              unused directory entry                                    │
│              unused directory entry                                    │
│              unused directory entry                                    │
│              unused directory entry                                    │
│              unused directory entry                                    │
│              unused directory entry                                    │
│              unused directory entry                                    │
│══════════════════════════════════════════════════════════════════════│
│          Filenames beginning with 'ỿ' indicate erased entries         │
│                     Press Enter to continue                            │
│ 1Help  2Hex  3Text  4Dir  5Fat  6Partn  7▓▓  8Choose  9Undo  10Quit&NU│
```

Figure 7.19   Cluster 12 data shown in directory format

```
┌─────────────────────────────────────────────────────────────────┐
│ Menu 1.5                                                          │
│                       ▐ Write item to disk ▌                     │
│                                                                  │
│                            Warning!                              │
│          You may be destroying information by writing            │
│               the selected item out in sector mode               │
│                                                                  │
│                   Are you sure you want to write                 │
│                                                                  │
│                           Sector 32                              │
│                                                                  │
│                               to                                 │
│                                                                  │
│                      Sector 5 on drive B:                        │
│                                                                  │
│                          Yes  ▐ No ▌                            │
│                                                                  │
│                                                                  │
│ ┌───────────┬───────┬──────────────────────────────────────────┐│
│ │ Item type │ Drive │ Sector number                             ││
│ │ Sector    │ B:    │ 32                                        ││
│ └───────────┴───────┴──────────────────────────────────────────┘│
└─────────────────────────────────────────────────────────────────┘
```

Figure 7.20   Warning screen

Once the data has been copied, it can be viewed by selecting *Choose item, File, root directory area*. The display appears as shown in Figure 7.21.

The name for the first directory entry is obviously incorrect, and should be changed to its correct value of MEMO.BAK. Once this has been altered, NU can be exited and a DIR command entered from DOS. This produces a report as shown in Figure 7.22.

```
┌Root dir ════════════════════════════════ Directory format ═┐
│ Sector 5 in root directory                      Offset 0, hex 0 │
│                                                    Attributes    │
│ Filename Ext    Size     Date     Time   Cluster  Arc R/O Sys Hid Dir Vol │
│ ┌──────┐                                                         │
│ │est fil│ eAK     256  23-11-90   1:04 pm    2    Arc           │
│ STAFF   WK1     2098  23-11-90   1:02 pm    3    Arc           │
│ WIDGET89 WK1    4750  23-11-90  12:56 pm    6    Arc           │
│ MEMO            256  23-11-90   1:04 pm   11    Arc           │
│           unused directory entry                                │
│           unused directory entry                                │
│           unused directory entry                                │
│           unused directory entry                                │
│           unused directory entry                                │
│           unused directory entry                                │
│           unused directory entry                                │
│           unused directory entry                                │
│           unused directory entry                                │
│           unused directory entry                                │
│           unused directory entry                                │
│           unused directory entry                                │
│                                                                 │
│       Filenames beginning with 'σ' indicate erased entries      │
│                   Press Enter to continue                        │
│ 1Help  2Hex  3Text  4Dir  5Al  6Partn  7   8Choose 9Undo 10QuitNU │
```

Figure 7.21   New root directory data

```
Volume in drive B has no label
Directory of  B:\

MEMO      BAK      256   23-11-90    1:04p
STAFF     WK1     2098   23-11-90    1:02p
WIDGET89  WK1     4750   23-11-90   12:56p
MEMO               256   23-11-90    1:04p
        4 File(s)      351232 bytes free
```

Figure 7.22   Directory listing for recovered data

Note that all appears to be correct, other than the fact that there are only four files listed. The fifth file, NEWFILE, is not on the directory listing at all. The reason for this is that the dirty buffer was only written to disk when NEWFILE was created, which was before its directory entry was inserted. Therefore, the directory entry must be created in some other way.

It is possible to do this manually, using NU to edit the root directory. However, CHKDSK does the job automatically, as the data on disk is still considered to be a lost chain. Executing the CHKDSK B: command produces a report as shown in Figure 7.23.

If this is repeated with the /F option, then a file will be created called FILE0000.CHK which contains the data for the lost chain. This is shown in Figure 7.24.

```
      Errors found, F parameter not specified.
      Corrections will not be written to disk.


      1 lost clusters found in 1 chains.
      Convert lost chains to files  (Y/N)? n
            1024 bytes disk space
                 would be freed.

         362496 bytes total disk space
          10240 bytes in 4 user files
         351232 bytes available on disk

         655360 bytes total memory
         524080 bytes free
```

Figure 7.23   Result of the CHKDSK command

```
      Volume in drive B has no label
      Directory of  B:\

      MEMO       BAK      256   23-11-90     1:04p
      STAFF      WK1     2098   23-11-90     1:02p
      WIDGET89 WK1      4750   23-11-90    12:56p
      MEMO                256   23-11-90     1:04p
      FILE0000 CHK      1024   26-11-90     3:51p
                5 File(s)      351232 bytes free
```

Figure 7.24   Directory listing including recovered file

All that remains to be done is to edit the directory entry to correct the name, and also the length of the file. This can be achieved in NU, as shown in Figure 7.25.

The recovery is now complete, as all of the data has been recovered and is provided in a usable format.

The discovery of the dirty buffer was very fortunate in this example as it allowed the directory data to be easily created. If this had not been available, then it would have been necessary to re-create the data as follows:

–   Firstly, the corrupted directory data would have to be zeroed out, by copying the second (blank) directory sector onto the first.

–   CHKDSK is then used to attach directory entries to the chains of lost clusters.

–   Each of the files produced by CHKDSK is identified by viewing the data on screen or through NU, and then renamed appropriately.

–   The data in the files must then be tested by loading them into the appropriate application program.

–   As the NEWFILE data is only 9 bytes long and does not contain an EOF marker, it is necessary to modify the file length manually, as before.

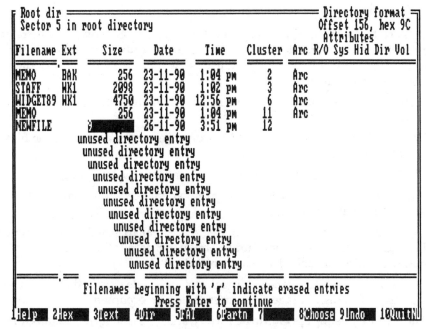

Figure 7.25   Editing the root directory entry

7.3.2.3   Summary

This scenario has illustrated the value of finding dirty buffers on disk, as it allowed almost immediate recovery of the directory data. The value of these areas increases dramatically when working with hard disks and full floppies, as there will be many files and possibly sub-directories. In such situations the manual method becomes very laborious and more prone to error.

If the FAT had also been corrupted, then the discovery of a dirty buffer containing relevant data would have been even more important, as the manual creation of large amounts FAT data is a very time consuming and complicated task.

The scenario has also illustrated the relative ease with which seemingly corrupted data may be recovered. Many users faced with a similar situation would run CHKDSK, but would probably resign themselves to the fact that the data was lost when faced with the initial CHKDSK report, as shown in Figure 7.12.

7.3.3   SCENARIO 3

7.3.3.1   The Problem

A user reports problems with the floppy disk. It contains just four files, two of 256 bytes, one of just over 2K, and one of just under 5K. Thus the total amount of disk space occupied is around 10K. However, when a DIR command is issued, the files are listed correctly, but DOS reports that there are 0 bytes free. Also, two of the files (the larger ones) which are worksheets can no longer be read into 1-2-3, although the smaller word processor files can be accessed without problem.

7.3.3.2 The Solution

At first glance this appears to be a fairly odd problem. DOS knows that there are four files on the disk, and apparently lists their names and specifications correctly. However, it still thinks that there are 0 bytes available on disk. Furthermore, some of the files can be accessed and some can't.

It is useful to look for connections between files when some can and some can't be read. In this case, there are two obvious differences:

- The files that can be read are both word-processor files, whereas the files which are unreadable are worksheets.

- The files which can be read are both very small, but the unreadable files are larger.

There are several pointers here which help the experienced troubleshooter to diagnose this problem almost immediately:

- DOS reports the number of bytes of free space available on disk by referencing the FAT rather than the directory entries. Thus if there are 0 bytes free, then this implies that the FAT is full, and all clusters are indicated as being in use.

- Furthermore, the files that can be accessed are single cluster files, as they require less than 1K of disk storage. The unreadable files occupy more than one cluster.

- The directory listing appears to be correct, and gives the correct details for the files

These facts all contribute to identifying the FAT as the cause of the problems. Thus it is the FAT that will be given first priority in examination and diagnosis.

The first step in remedying the fault is to produce a copy. DISKCOPY, COPYIIPC or any other proprietary image copier can be used, and it will be found that all produce perfect copies of the data and report no errors.

A DIR listing of the disk is useful, to confirm that the details are indeed correct. This is shown in Figure 7.26. CHKDSK may also be used to provide information on the state of the directory and FAT. The report produced by CHKDSK is shown in Figure 7.27.

```
Volume in drive B has no label
Directory of  B:\

MEMO      BAK      256   23-11-90    1:04p
MEMO               256   23-11-90    1:04p
STAFF     WK1     2098   23-11-90    1:02p
WIDGET89 WK1      4750   23-11-90   12:56p
         4 File(s)            0 bytes free
```

Figure 7.26   Directory listing showing the corrupt files

Note that CHKDSK reports a large number of clusters in lost chains, adding weight to the conclusion that the FAT is the cause of the problems.

It is wise to double check exactly what happens when Lotus 1-2-3 attempts to load one of the worksheet data files. Figure 7.28 shows the error message that is produced in this situation.

```
Errors found, F parameter not specified.
Corrections will not be written to disk.

B:\STAFF.WK1
    Allocation error, size adjusted.
B:\WIDGET89.WK1
    Allocation error, size adjusted.

350 lost clusters found in 350 chains.
Convert lost chains to files   (Y/N)? n
    358400 bytes disk space
            would be freed.


    362496 bytes total disk space
      4096 bytes in 4 user files
         0 bytes available on disk
```

Figure 7.27   CHKDSK report for corrupt disk

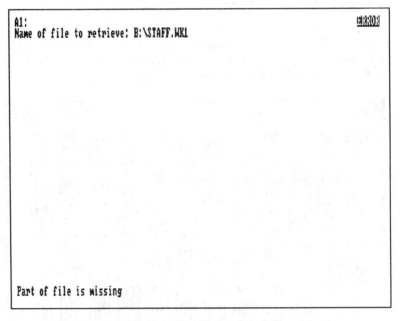

Figure 7.28   Lotus 1-2-3 file retrieval error message

A disk editor may be used to view the data at a lower level. Figure 7.29 shows the display produced when NU is used to view the directory data. From this it can be seen that DOS is reporting the correct details for the files, and that there have never been any other files on the disk.

```
┌ Root dir ══════════════════════════════════════════ Directory format ┐
│ Sector 5 in root directory                             Offset 0, hex 0 │
│                                                           Attributes    │
│ Filename Ext    Size    Date    Time    Cluster  Arc R/O Sys Hid Dir Vol│
│ .                                                                        │
│ MEMO    BAK      256   23-11-90  1:04 pm     2    Arc                   │
│ MEMO             256   23-11-90  1:04 pm     3    Arc                   │
│ STAFF   WK1     2098   23-11-90  1:02 pm     4    Arc                   │
│ WIDGET89 WK1    4750   23-11-90 12:56 pm     7    Arc                   │
│                 unused directory entry                                  │
│                 unused directory entry                                  │
│                 unused directory entry                                  │
│                 unused directory entry                                  │
│                 unused directory entry                                  │
│                 unused directory entry                                  │
│                 unused directory entry                                  │
│                 unused directory entry                                  │
│                 unused directory entry                                  │
│                 unused directory entry                                  │
│                 unused directory entry                                  │
│                 unused directory entry                                  │
│ ═══════.═══════════════════════════════════════════════════════════════│
│            Filenames beginning with 'r' indicate erased entries         │
│                      Press Enter to continue                            │
│ 1Help  2Hex   3Text  4Dir   5FAT   6Partn  7        8Choose 9Undo  10QuitNU│
```

Figure 7.29   Root directory data displayed with NU

Therefore, the FAT is examined, to determine what exactly has happened to it. NU is again used to view the data, and display it in FAT format. Figure 7.30 shows the first sector of the FAT data displayed on screen.

```
┌ FAT area ════════════════════════════════════════════ FAT format ┐
│ Sector 1 in 1st copy of FAT                          Cluster 2, hex 2 │
│                                                                        │
│   <EOF> <EOF> <EOF> <EOF> <EOF> <EOF> <EOF> <EOF> <EOF> <EOF> <EOF> <EOF>│
│   <EOF> <EOF> <EOF> <EOF> <EOF> <EOF> <EOF> <EOF> <EOF> <EOF> <EOF> <EOF>│
│   <EOF> <EOF> <EOF> <EOF> <EOF> <EOF> <EOF> <EOF> <EOF> <EOF> <EOF> <EOF>│
│   <EOF> <EOF> <EOF> <EOF> <EOF> <EOF> <EOF> <EOF> <EOF> <EOF> <EOF> <EOF>│
│   <EOF> <EOF> <EOF> <EOF> <EOF> <EOF> <EOF> <EOF> <EOF> <EOF> <EOF> <EOF>│
│   <EOF> <EOF> <EOF> <EOF> <EOF> <EOF> <EOF> <EOF> <EOF> <EOF> <EOF> <EOF>│
│   <EOF> <EOF> <EOF> <EOF> <EOF> <EOF> <EOF> <EOF> <EOF> <EOF> <EOF> <EOF>│
│   <EOF> <EOF> <EOF> <EOF> <EOF> <EOF> <EOF> <EOF> <EOF> <EOF> <EOF> <EOF>│
│   <EOF> <EOF> <EOF> <EOF> <EOF> <EOF> <EOF> <EOF> <EOF> <EOF> <EOF> <EOF>│
│   <EOF> <EOF> <EOF> <EOF> <EOF> <EOF> <EOF> <EOF> <EOF> <EOF> <EOF> <EOF>│
│   <EOF> <EOF> <EOF> <EOF> <EOF> <EOF> <EOF> <EOF> <EOF> <EOF> <EOF> <EOF>│
│   <EOF> <EOF> <EOF> <EOF> <EOF> <EOF> <EOF> <EOF> <EOF> <EOF> <EOF> <EOF>│
│   <EOF> <EOF> <EOF> <EOF> <EOF> <EOF> <EOF> <EOF> <EOF> <EOF> <EOF> <EOF>│
│   <EOF> <EOF> <EOF> <EOF> <EOF> <EOF> <EOF> <EOF> <EOF> <EOF> <EOF> <EOF>│
│   <EOF> <EOF> <EOF> <EOF> <EOF> <EOF> <EOF> <EOF> <EOF> <EOF> <EOF> <EOF>│
│   <EOF> <EOF> <EOF> <EOF> <EOF> <EOF> <EOF> <EOF> <EOF> <EOF> <EOF> <EOF>│
│   <EOF> <EOF> <EOF> <EOF> <EOF> <EOF> <EOF> <EOF> <EOF> <EOF> <EOF> <EOF>│
│   <EOF> <EOF> <EOF> <EOF> <EOF> <EOF> <EOF> <EOF> <EOF> <EOF> <EOF> <EOF>│
│   <EOF> <EOF> <EOF> <EOF> <EOF> <EOF> <EOF> <EOF> <EOF> <EOF> <EOF> <EOF>│
│   <EOF> <EOF> <EOF> <EOF> <EOF> <EOF> <EOF> <EOF> <EOF> <EOF> <EOF> <EOF>│
│                      Press Enter to continue                           │
│ 1Help  2Hex   3Text  4Dir   5FAT   6Partn  7        8Choose 9Undo  10QuitNU│
```

Figure 7.30   FAT entries displayed with NU

As can be seen, the entire sector is comprised of <EOF> entries, whereas the majority should in fact be comprised of 0 to indicate that it is unused. It can therefore be deduced that the FAT has been corrupted in some way. The extent of this corruption must be determined. The second sector can be viewed with NU to determine whether or not it too has been affected. Figure 7.31 shows the second sector of the FAT in hexadecimal format. All of the entries are FF, representing <EOF>. Thus the second sector has also been corrupted.

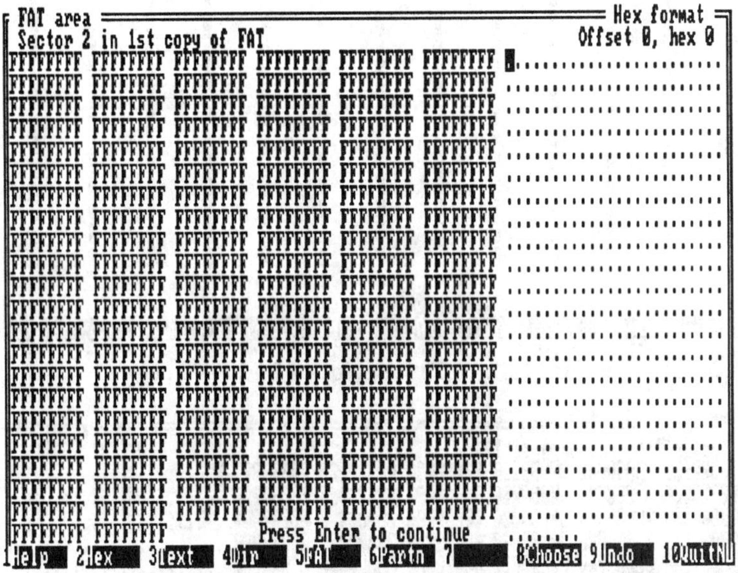

Figure 7.31   Second sector of the FAT displayed in hexadecimal

The FAT is one of the most important areas of the disk, as it controls space allocation for files, programs etc. Therefore, it is generally catastrophic if the FAT is corrupted in this way, as some or all of the data will be unreadable and the files will be incomplete. For this reason, DOS makes two copies of the FAT, the first of which it uses for the ongoing filing tasks, and the second of which is kept as a backup copy.

Therefore, the next step in remedying the problem is to check for the existence and condition of the second copy of the FAT. This is situated in the sectors immediately after the first copy. Viewing the first sector of the second copy produces the display shown in Figure 7.32.

It seems highly probable that the data in this copy of the FAT is correct, as there are in fact four chains corresponding to the original four files. The directory entries can be cross-referenced, and it will be found that the chains are in the correct positions, and are of the correct lengths for the files listed.

As both sectors of the first copy of the FAT were corrupted, it is necessary to check both sectors of the second copy. Figure 7.33 shows the second sector of the second copy in hexadecimal format. (The reference to Sector 3 at the top of this display relates to the third overall sector in the FAT, ie the first copy occupies sectors 1 and 2, and the second copy sectors 3 and 4). It can be seen that all of the entries are 00, indicating that the clusters are empty and available for use.

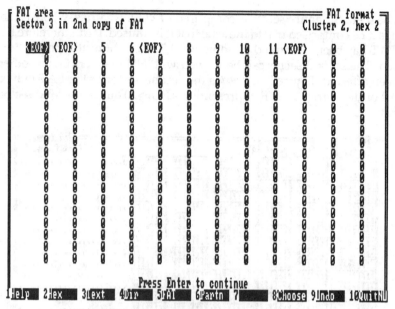

Figure 7.32   First sector of 2nd FAT copy

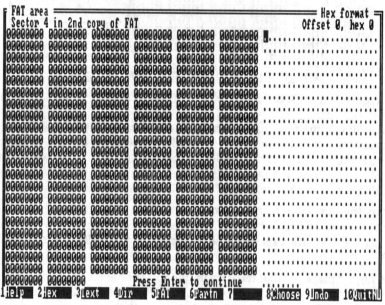

Figure 7.33   Second sector of 2nd FAT copy

The problem can therefore be remedied by copying the data in the second copy of the FAT onto the first. This is achieved as follows:

– Firstly the second copy of the FAT is chosen to be the current item. The commands *Choose item, Sector* are issued, and sectors 3 and 4 specified as the start and end points. Figure 7.34 shows the dialogue box produced at this point.

```
Menu 1.1.5
                    Select sector
          You may select sectors numbered from 0 through 719

                    Starting sector: 3

                    Ending sector: 4




                Outline of Sector Usage on This Disk

              0          Boot area       (used by DOS)
            1 - 4        FAT area        (used by DOS)
            5 - 11       Root Dir. area  (used by DOS)
           12 - 719      Data area       (where files are stored)

  Item type   Drive  Sector range
   Sector      B:    3-4
```

Figure 7.34   Selecting the FAT for copying

– These sectors are then written over the first copy of the FAT. The commands required are Write item to disk, Sector mode, B: starting sector 1.

– The warning prompt should be confirmed by entering *Yes* in response. The prompt is shown in Figure 7.35.

```
Menu 1.5
                    Write item to disk


                         Warning!
             You may be destroying information by writing
                the selected item out in sector mode

                 Are you sure you want to write

                         Sector 3-4

                            to

                 Sectors 1-2 on drive B:

                      Yes   No


  Item type   Drive  Sector range
   Sector      B:    3-4
```

Figure 7.35   Copying FAT sectors 3&4 to sectors 1&2

The disk has now been fully corrected, and can be checked with DIR, CHKDSK, and by loading the two worksheet files into 1-2-3.

7.3.3.3   Summary

Although the operation of the FAT is fundamental to DOS, in many cases it is not difficult to manipulate and modify if problems are encountered. This is made even easier as there are two copies of the data stored on disk.

If in this example the second copy had also been corrupted, then recovery would not have been as straightforward. It would have required the troubleshooter to try and rebuild the FAT data manually, in much the same way as for the first scenario considered in this chapter. In this case, the FAT entries for the two single cluster files would have been created first, followed by the FAT entries for the two worksheets. Note that care must be taken to ensure that appropriate clusters of data are allocated to the two worksheet files as Lotus will refuse to retrieve the file if it contains any errors.

Note that manual modification of FAT entries on floppy disks is extremely laborious, as 12-bit FATs are used. Thus the task of editing a floppy disk FAT is best accomplished using a FAT editor such as that supplied in NU. However, there are circumstances where this is unadvisable, especially where hard disks are involved. The geometry of the hard disk is more sophisticated than a floppy, and NU can occasionally mis-read the data, especially where large logical sectors are implemented. This in turn means that when NU displays the FAT and allows it to be modified, it may actually write the modified data incorrectly. Therefore, if there is any doubt regarding NUs interpretation of the FAT data, the absolute sector mode should be used to edit the data, thus ensuring that all of the areas are correctly positioned.

7.3.4   SCENARIO 4

7.3.4.1   The Problem

A very serious problem is reported; a user has a floppy disk that contained two WordStar files and two 1-2-3 worksheets, but they accidentally started to format it. However, as soon as they realised what they had done, they pressed Ctrl+C to force the formatting process to stop.

Unfortunately, the disk cannot now be read at all, and produces General Failure error messages if any programs that require access to the disk are executed. An attempt at using CHKDSK revealed over 300 lost clusters. They know that the text files are less than 1K each, although the worksheets are larger and are thought to be about 3K and 5K.

7.3.4.2   The Solution

The formatting process is destructive for floppy disks, and overwrites the entire disk surface. Thus if the process has proceeded too far before it was stopped, then it will be impossible to make a full recovery.

It is certain that the formatting process had at least started, as the disk is now unusable, so the first step in the recovery must be to find out exactly how far it had been allowed to continue.

The next stage will be to re-instate the system areas, or to copy the data to another already formatted floppy. This choice is dependent upon the extent of the formatting.

Once the system areas are OK, the recovery of the data can proceed, in exactly the same way as if the FAT and Directory entries had been corrupted.

A working copy of the disk must be made first, as in all data recovery situations. It is best to use COPYIIPC, although if tried, DISKCOPY will be found to work perfectly well in this situation. No errors are reported by either program, hence it can be assumed that the formatting process terminated gracefully, and did not part-format a track.

If the DIR or CHKDSK commands are tried, a number of General failure error messages are displayed. However, replying *Retry* to each of these forces the system to try and read the disk, and produces the results shown in Figures 7.36 and 7.37.

```
General Failure error reading drive B
Abort, Retry, Fail? r
 Volume in drive B has no label
 Directory of  B:\

File not found
```

Figure 7.36   DIR listing for partially formatted disk

```
General Failure error reading drive B
Abort, Retry, Fail? r

Probable non-DOS disk.
Continue  (Y/N)? y

Errors found, F parameter not specified.
Corrections will not be written to disk.

B:\vvvvvvvv.vvv
    First cluster number is invalid,
      entry truncated.

General Failure error reading drive B
Abort, Retry, Fail? r

B:\vvvvvvvv.vvv
    First cluster number is invalid,
      entry truncated.

B:\vvvvvvvv.vvv
    First cluster number is invalid,
      entry truncated.

354 lost clusters found in 354 chains.
Convert lost chains to files  (Y/N)? n
    362496 bytes disk space
            would be freed.

    362496 bytes total disk space
         0 bytes in 64 directories
         0 bytes available on disk
```

Figure 7.37   CHKDSK report for partially formatted disk

As DOS is obviously interpreting the data incorrectly, it is wise to try an alternative method. NU can be used to view the data, and is invoked by entering NU B:. However, even NU fails to recognise the disk, and requires that it be re-started in *Maintenance mode*, so that it uses BIOS level disk accesses rather than DOS level operations. The NU error message is shown in Figure 7.38.

```
C:\PZP)nu b:
The Norton Utilities, Advanced Edition 4.50, (C) Copr 1987-88, Peter Norton
```

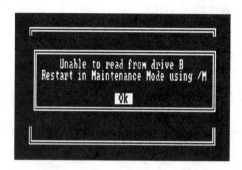

Figure 7.38   NU error message when reading partially formatted disk

Starting NU in maintenance mode causes several of the features to be disabled. The most obvious is the unerase facility, although all of the *Explore Disk* options that deal with files or directories are also unavailable. These disabled options are displayed in parenthesis, as shown in Figure 7.39.

```
The Norton Utilities, Advanced Edition 4.50, (C) Copr 1987-88, Peter Norton
                  1:48 pm, Tuesday, 27 November 1990

                            Main Menu

                           Explore disk

                           (unerase)

                           Disk information

                           Quit the Norton Utilities

                    View, edit, search, or copy selected item

 Item type   Drive   Sector number
 Sector      B:      0
```

Figure 7.39   Maintenance mode main menu

The reason that some of the features are no longer available is because when in maintenance mode, NU does not support the concepts of files or directories. All it recognises are the BIOS level allocation units of clusters, logical sectors and absolute sectors. Therefore any operation that relates to a file or directory, such as unerasing, is no longer valid.

One of the first things to check in NU is whether the disk geometry has been correctly recognised. If this is not the case, then it is fruitless to attempt any further operations until the problem is rectified. The disk information option in NU will provide the relevant information, as shown in Figure 7.40.

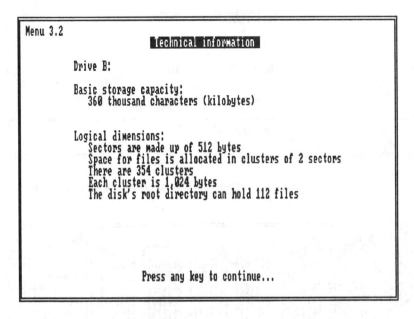

Figure 7.40   Technical information for drive B:

As can be seen, NU does indeed recognise the disk correctly, seeing it as a 360K floppy with 354 clusters of 1K each. Therefore the process of recovery can begin.

The boot sector can be examined by selecting physical sector 0 as the current item. Figure 7.41 shows the options available under the *Choose item* menu, and the selection that is required is *Sector*, with the start sector specified as 0 and the ending sector specified to allow a reasonable range to be scanned, for example 100.

Choosing the *Edit/display item* option will cause sector 0 to be displayed, as shown in Figure 7.42. As can be seen, the entire boot sector is filled with values of F6, which is the format pattern used for floppy disks.

This indicates that sector 0 has been completely formatted, hence making the disk unreadable by DOS. If the subsequent sectors are viewed, it will be seen that this pattern continues to fill all sectors up to and including sector 8. However, sector 9 is full of 0 values, as shown in Figure 7.43.

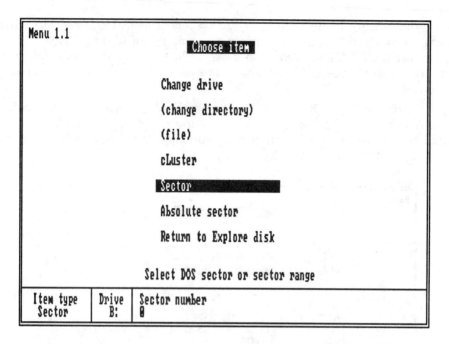

Figure 7.41   The maintenance mode options for item choice

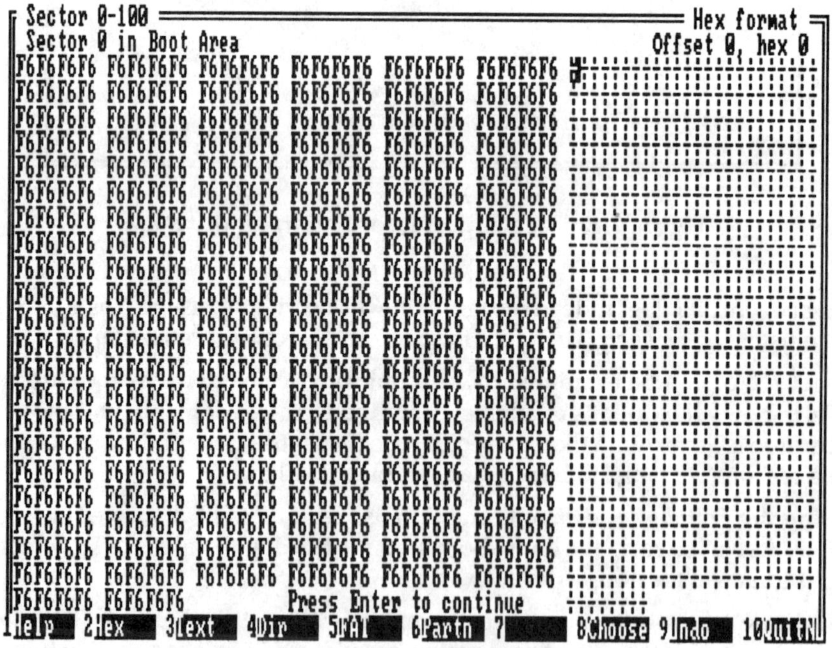

Figure 7.42   Boot sector of partially formatted disk

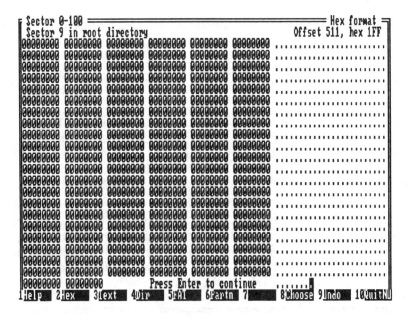

Figure 7.43   Sector 9 of partially formatted disk

Sector 9 is a part of the root directory area, and would be filled with 0s if the entries were unused. Thus the presence of the 0 values in this area indicates that this sector was not reformatted. The 0s continue to fill sectors 10 and 11, but sector 12 actually contains data, as shown in Figure 7.44.

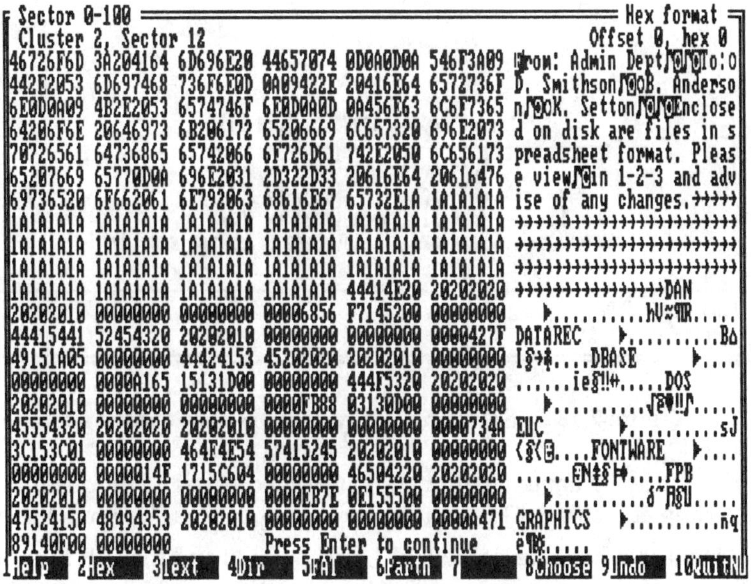

Figure 7.44   First cluster of the data area

Sector 12 is actually the first sector of the data area, and corresponds to the first sector of cluster number 2. Thus the data displayed in this sector must be a part of a data file. In fact it can be seen that the data is actually a text file, and contains a memo. It can therefore be assumed that this is the first WordStar file on disk. More importantly, it indicates that this sector has not been formatted, and hence the remainder of the data area has not been formatted either.

From this inspection, the extent of the reformatting is known to be only sector 0 through 8. This is actually the entire first track on the disk (track 0 - the system area). Therefore the formatting process was stopped very quickly indeed, as only this area was affected. As only a small amount of data needs to be reinstated, it is quicker and easier to copy the system area from a formatted blank diskette to the working disk, rather than copy the data area of the work disk to the formatted diskette.

To do this, it is first necessary to have a blank formatted diskette available. This diskette is placed into drive A:, and the work disk in drive B:. The *Choose item, Change drive, A:, Sector* commands are then issued, and the start and end sectors specified as 0 and 11 respectively. Note that this is greater than the area that was formatted, and is actually the entire system area. Figure 7.45 shows the dialogue box for this operation.

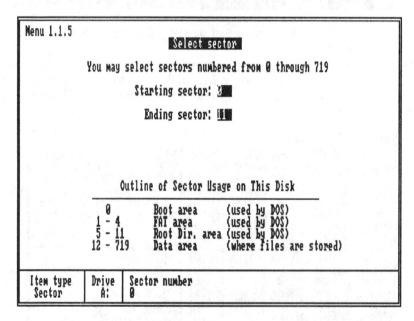

Figure 7.45   Selecting the system area for copying

The *Write item to disk, Sector mode* commands are issued next, and the destination chosen as drive B:, starting at sector 0. The warning screen appears as shown in Figure 7.46.

Once the system area has been copied, NU can be exited and the DIR B: and CHKDSK B: commands issues to determine whether the operation has been successful. Both of these commands produce results indicating that the disk is entirely blank, as the directory and FAT contain no entries at all.

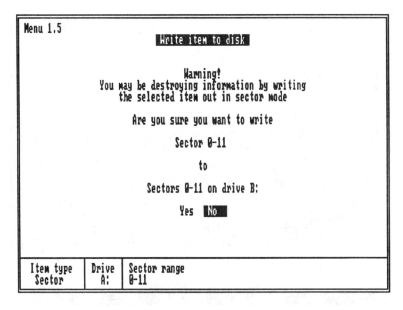

Figure 7.46   Warning screen produced when copying

NU can then be restarted, but this time it is not necessary to use maintenance mode as the disk is readable by DOS. The benefit of this is that the Unerase feature may now be used to manually recover the data from the disk.

The following steps will be required for each file that is to be unerased:

- Choose the *Select erased file* command, and then select the *Create file* option.
- Specify a name for the file. As the contents of the file will not be known until the disk in examined, it is advisable to use a name such as FILE01, FILE02 etc. The files can later be renamed appropriately.
- Choose the *Add new clusters* command from the unerase menu, and select *Next probable cluster* as a starting point.
- Examine the data in the chosen cluster, and determine whether it is relevant.
- If it is, add it to the list of clusters for the file.
- Repeat the above three steps until all the clusters for the file have been found.
- Save the file to disk.

Thus for the first file, the name is specified as FILE01, and on choosing the *Next probable cluster*, *Display/Edit data* commands, cluster 2 will be displayed on screen, as it is the first currently unused cluster on the disk. This is shown in Figure 7.47.

It can be seen that this cluster contains some text, and therefore is most likely to be a part of one of the word processed files. It is assigned to the file by selecting the *Add clusters to file* command. As both text files are less than 1K in size, each occupies a single cluster. Therefore, there are no further clusters to locate for this file, and it can be saved to disk with the *Save erased file* command.

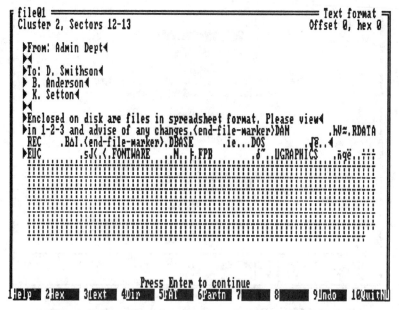

Figure 7.47   Data in cluster 2 shown as ASCII text

At this point a warning screen is displayed, as shown in Figure 7.48. This alerts the user to the fact that the size of the recovered file is different to the size recorded in the directory. As a file produced with the *Create file* option will have had no previous directory entry, its size is indicated as 0 clusters. Hence this message screen appears for all files created in this way.

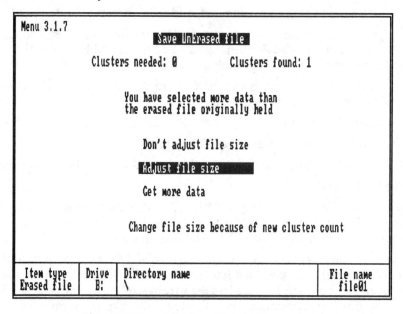

Figure 7.48   File length warning screen

Replying *Yes* to the prompt causes the directory entry to be written to disk, and the FAT entries for the cluster created as appropriate. A short report is displayed on screen to inform the user of the successful unerasure of the file, as shown in Figure 7.49.

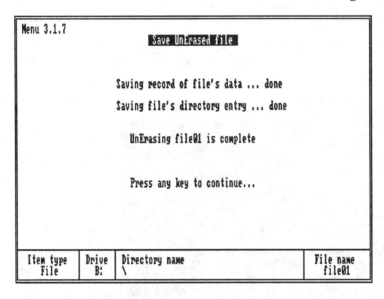

Figure 7.49   Message produced once the file has been saved

The process of recovering the data is repeated for the three remaining files. However, it is not a simple matter to recognise which file cluster 3 belongs to. When the cluster is displayed on screen, it appears as shown in Figure 7.50.

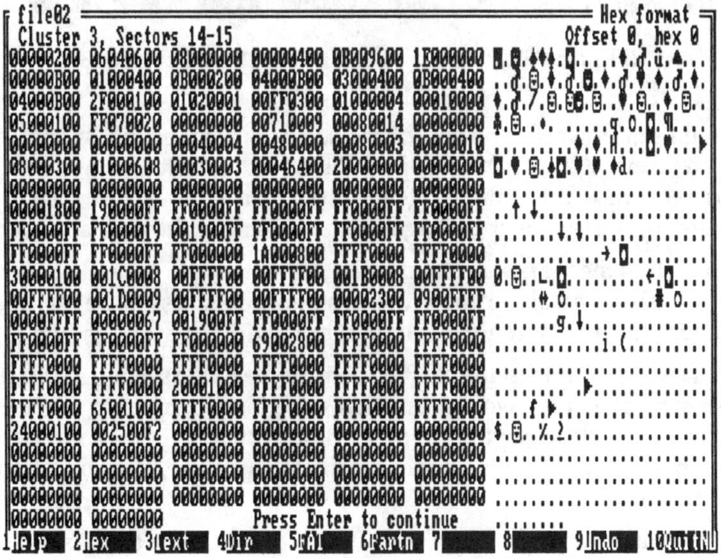

Figure 7.50   Data in first sector of cluster 3

This is definitely not a WordStar text file, and so is likely to be one of the worksheet files. This is confirmed by the presence of the values 00 00 02 00 as the first four bytes of data. These values will always be found at the start of a Lotus worksheet, and will be followed by two bytes indicating the version number, in this case 06 04 which corresponds to version 2.2.

The identification of the cluster as worksheet data can be further confirmed by examining the second sector in the cluster, which appears as shown in Figure 7.51.

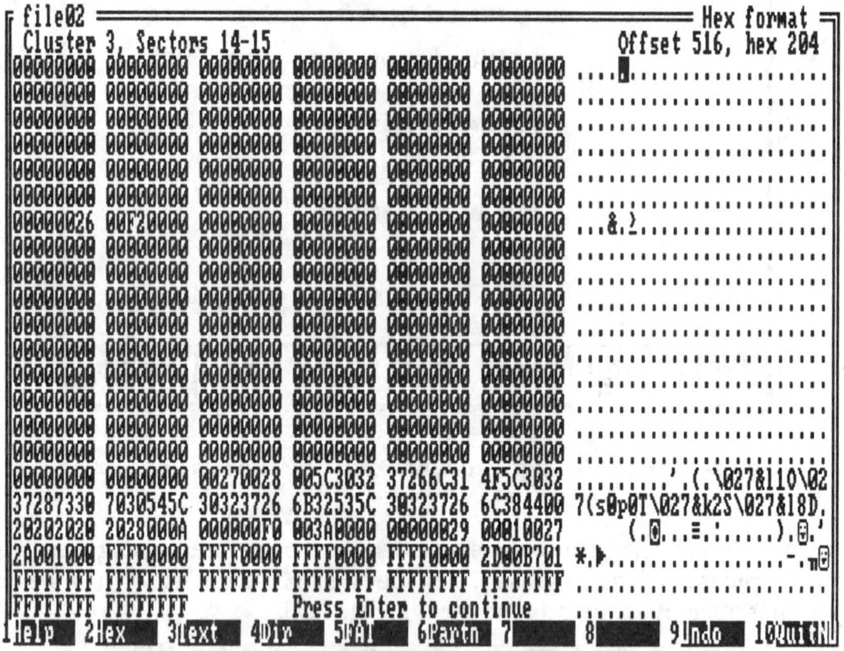

Figure 7.51   Data in second sector of cluster 3

It can be seen that towards the end of the sector is a collection of values that form a string of text reading \027&l10\027(s0p0T\027&k2S\027&l8D. Any user familiar with 1-2-3 should recognise this immediately as being a printer setup string. These are commonly used by spreadsheet packages, and so identify the data as a worksheet.

As it is known that the worksheet files are both greater than 1K and hence occupy more than one cluster, it is necessary to locate the remaining clusters for the file. The next cluster that is unused is cluster 4, and if viewed on screen will appear as shown in Figure 7.52.

The values toward the end of the cluster identify the data as being a staff database, and this is known to be one of the worksheets that were lost. Examining the second sector in this cluster reveals a repetitive pattern for the data, indicating that it is indeed a database comprised of many records with a similar format. Therefore, cluster 4 should be added to the list of clusters.

Cluster 5 contains only a small amount of data, but it can be seen that this follows the same pattern as cluster 4 and so is likely to be a part of the same file. The majority of cluster 5 is filled with values of 0, indicating that the space is perhaps unused. In fact,

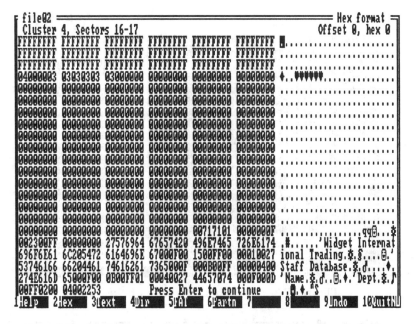

Figure 7.52.   Cluster 4 data, identifying the file as a worksheet

this is the last cluster in the chain that forms the data file as indicated by the Lotus 1-2-3 end of file sequence of 01 00 00 00 at the end of the data. Therefore, after adding this cluster to the existing list, the file can be saved to disk as before.

The third file is created in exactly the same way as the first two. The next available cluster is number 6, and on viewing this it will be seen to contain the text of a memo. Hence it can be assumed that this is the other wordstar text file, which can be immediately saved to disk as it is known to be only 1 cluster long.

The fourth file is similarly created, and starts with cluster 7. The first few bytes of data identify the cluster as forming the start of a worksheet file, as shown in Figure 7.53.

The next cluster, number 8, can be seen to contain the worksheet heading. These labels identify the file as a profit and loss account worksheet, as shown in Figure 7.54.

The recovery process can be performed as before, although there are a total of five clusters for this file.

Once the unerasure of the fourth file has been achieved, the data recovery procedure is almost complete. All that needs to be done is to rename the recovered files with descriptive names so that the user can access their data with the appropriate applications programs.

The first and third files were found to be memos, and so should be renamed as MEMO1 and MEMO2 or similar. The second file was the staff database worksheet, and so should be called STAFF.WK1. The last file was the 1989 profit and loss account, and so should be named as PROFIT89.WK1 or similar. It is essential to complete this final step as many users would not know how to retrieve the files into Lotus if they were left with names of FILE02 and FILE04. Figure 7.55 shows a directory listing of the recovered data.

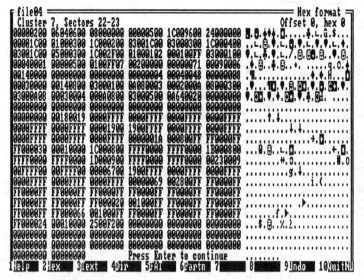

Figure 7.53   Data in first sector of cluster 7

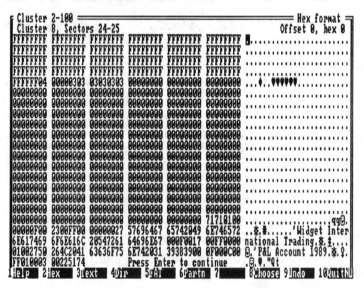

Figure 7.54   Data in first sector of cluster 8

```
Volume in drive B has no label
Directory of  B:\

MEMO1              1024   27-11-90   2:08p
STAFF    WK1       3072   27-11-90   2:12p
MEMO2              1024   27-11-90   2:18p
WIDGET89 WK1       5120   27-11-90   2:19p
         4 File(s)      352256 bytes free
```

Figure 7.55   Directory listing for the recovered data

7.3.4.3 Summary

The recovery of a partially formatted floppy, or wholly formatted hard disk, may seem to be an impossible task. However, this scenario has shown it to be merely a case of taking things one step at a time, starting with an examination of the extent of the damage, proceeding through the reinstatement of the system areas and finishing up with the recovery of the actual data files.

Such a process can however be very time consuming, as with a hard disk there may be many hundreds or thousands of files to undelete in this way. The task is made easier when subdirectories are employed, as the directory entries for files in these subdirectories are left intact, making unerasure much simpler because the first cluster number and file size are known for each one.

In fact, as the format process on a hard disk is not destructive in the same way as it is on a floppy disk, the utility packages all provide a means of reinstating the system areas and files without having, in most cases, to resort to manual methods. However, if utilities such as Norton's Wipedisk are used to reformat a disk, the effect is similar to that of using format on floppies.

Note that it is impossible to achieve results in cases of partial formatting if a tool such as NU, PCTools or Disk Explorer is not available. This is because all DOS-based utilities, such as Debug, will fail to read the disk data once the system areas have been erased, and therefore there is no way of reinstating the system areas or copying the usable data areas.

7.3.5 SCENARIO 5

7.3.5.1 The Problem

A user complains of a problem on their diskette when they attempt to display a text file on the screen. The file is called D-REC02, and contains around 26K of word processed text. On issuing the TYPE D-REC02 command, the message *General Failure reading drive B:* is displayed. All of the other files on the disk can be accessed without any problems.

7.3.5.2 The Solution

As the problem appears to be confined to a single file, it would seem most likely that a disk crash has occurred. This would cause the data in one or more sectors on the disk to become unreadable, producing the above error. Therefore, the main aim of the recovery exercise is to copy all of the data from the existing diskette to a new, good disk.

An alternative solution is that for some reason the disk cannot be read by the user's computer, and so an attempt may be made to read the disk using a different drive.

First of all, it is advisable to view the directory listing to determine what files are on the disk. Figure 7.56 shows this information.

Next, an attempt to access the file using different hardware should be made. Issuing the TYPE B:D-REC02 however produces the following message:

```
General Failure error reading drive B
Abort, Retry, Fail?
```

As this fails, the second possible solution proves incorrect. Thus it is necessary to attempt to make a copy of the data onto a good, error-free disk.

As it is known that DOS fails to read the disk correctly, it is not worth attempting to use the DISKCOPY utility for this purpose. Even if it did work, it is unlikely that the copied data would be correct. Therefore, either NU or COPYIIPC should be used instead.

```
Volume in drive B has no label
Directory of  B:\

NU1       IMG       8103    20-11-90    11:29a
NU2       IMG      11673    20-11-90    11:31a
NU3       IMG      23146    20-11-90    11:34a
NU4       IMG      32488    20-11-90    11:37a
NU5       IMG      17736    20-11-90    11:39a
D-REC01             9856     8-11-90    12:53p
D-REC02            26368     8-11-90     4:27p
FF        EXE       9020    16-10-88     4:50p
CHKRPRT1            763     19-11-90     2:07p
CHKRPRT2            643     19-11-90     2:07p
CHKRPRT3            447     19-11-90     2:07p
      11 File(s)     218112 bytes free
```

Figure 7.56   Directory listing for the entire disk

On executing NU with the command NU B: and selecting the file D-REC02 as the current item, a problem arises when the system attempts to access sector 257, and NU displays the message shown in Figure 7.57.

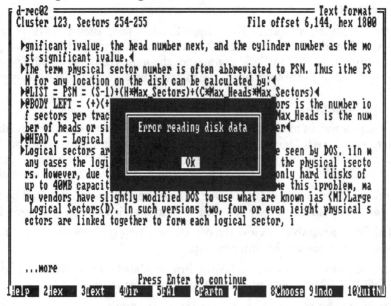

Figure 7.57   NU error message

This indicates that NU is unable to read the data correctly, and so should be discarded in favour of COPYIIPC. Issuing the COPYIIPC A: B: command starts the operation.

On attempting to copy sector 257, the system reports a data error, and prompts the user to specify whether or not it should be corrected. As this is known to be the faulty sector, specifying *Yes* will cause the data to be corrected when it is written to the new diskette.

Once the copying process has been completed, an attempt to access the file can again be made, this time using the copy. On issuing the TYPE B:D-REC02 command the contents of the file are correctly displayed on screen.

7.3.5.3 Summary

Bad sectors and disk crashes cause many problems for floppy disk users, especially if the floppies are mis-handled. However, the simple remedial action illustrated in this example has shown just how easy it can be to recover the data. COPYIIPC is very powerful in this respect, and can be forced to read data from badly damaged disks. Care must of course be taken once the data has been recovered to ascertain that it is correct and complete, as there are some situations in which perfect data recovery is impossible.

The example has also illustrated the importance of trying several different utilities to access the data. There are many situations in which one program will read data from a disk that another cannot interpret. Hence it is essential to try all possibilities for any situation before deciding that data recovery is impossible.

7.3.6   SCENARIO 6

7.3.6.1   The Problem

A user reports a strange problem with one of the utilities that they regularly use. The program is the FindFile utility supplied with Norton. Rather than execute correctly, it reports a *Directory Too Complex* error. The problem only appears to occur when one particular disk is in use, as the utility works correctly for all other disks. They have also encountered problems using other utilities such as CHKDSK and TREE with the disk. A number of subdirectories have been used on the disk, and it is thought that some data has been lost from these although the names and sizes of the files are not known.

7.3.6.2   The Solution

The cause of these problems is not immediately obvious, and may at first glance appear to be due to program malfunction. However, the fact that the utilities work correctly for other disks implies that this is probably not the cause. The second possibility is that the disk has become corrupted in some way, preventing the utilities from accessing the data. This is more likely, as it is thought that some data has also been lost.

The way in which the corruption has occurred will require detailed investigation, as it appears not to fall into any of the categories seen so far. Therefore, the remedial action will have to be preceded by an in-depth examination of the data on the disk, to determine exactly what has happened, and hence how it can be rectified.

As in all situations, a copy is made of the disk. DISKCOPY can be used, as it is known that DOS can read the disk data, even if it interprets it incorrectly. The examination of the data can then commence, starting with a look at the listings for the root and sub-directories. Figure 7.58 shows the listing for the root directory.

Figure 7.59 shows the listing for the MYDATA subdirectory.

```
Volume in drive B has no label
Directory of  B:\

MYDATA          <DIR>      23-11-90    5:44p
JOHN90          <DIR>      23-11-90    5:44p
WIDGET88        <DIR>      23-11-90    5:44p
WIDGET89        <DIR>      23-11-90    5:44p
FF        EXE      9020    16-10-88    4:50p
          5 File(s)    335872 bytes free
```

Figure 7.58   Listing for the root directory

```
Volume in drive B has no label
Directory of  B:\MYDATA

.               <DIR>      23-11-90    5:44p
..              <DIR>      23-11-90    5:44p
PERSONAL        <DIR>      23-11-90    5:45p
WORK            <DIR>      23-11-90    5:45p
          4 File(s)    335872 bytes free
```

Figure 7.59   Listing for the MYDATA subdirectory

Figure 7.60 shows the listing for the JOHN90 subdirectory.

```
Volume in drive B has no label
Directory of  B:\JOHN90

MYDATA          <DIR>      23-11-90    5:44p
JOHN90          <DIR>      23-11-90    5:44p
WIDGET88        <DIR>      23-11-90    5:44p
WIDGET89        <DIR>      23-11-90    5:44p
FF        EXE      9020    16-10-88    4:50p
          5 File(s)    335872 bytes free
```

Figure 7.60   Listing for the JOHN90 subdirectory

Figure 7.61 shows the listing for the WIDGET88 subdirectory.

```
Volume in drive B has no label
Directory of  B:\WIDGET88

.               <DIR>      23-11-90    5:44p
..              <DIR>      23-11-90    5:44p
          2 File(s)    335872 bytes free
```

Figure 7.61   Listing for the WIDGET88 subdirectory

Figure 7.62 shows the listing for the WIDGET89 subdirectory.

```
Volume in drive B has no label
Directory of  B:\WIDGET89

    .             <DIR>      23-11-90    5:44p
    ..            <DIR>      23-11-90    5:44p
FORECAST          <DIR>      23-11-90    5:45p
ACTUAL            <DIR>      23-11-90    5:45p
OTHER             <DIR>      23-11-90    5:46p
          5 File(s)     335872 bytes free
```

Figure 7.62   Listing of the WIDGET89 subdirectory

Further examination of the directory structure reveals that there are several cross-references, where a subdirectory actually references itself, or its parent. These are known as *recursive subdirectories*, and are caused by the subdirectory data becoming corrupted. From the examinations, it can be seen that the directory structure is similar to that shown in Figure 7.63.

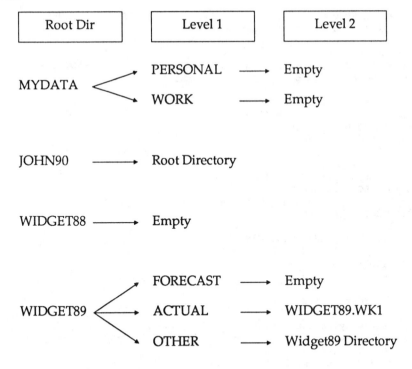

Figure 7.63   Diagrammatic representation of the directory structure

Experimentation with the FindFile and CHKDSK programs illustrates the problems encountered by the user. Figure 7.64 shows the result of issuing the FF WIDGET89.WK1 command, and Figure 7.65 shows an extract from the CHKDSK report for the disk.

```
FF-File Find, Advanced Edition 4.50, (C)
Copr 1987-88, Peter Norton


Directories too complex
```

Figure 7.64   Results of the Norton FF utility

```
Errors found, F parameter not specified.
Corrections will not be written to disk.

B:\JOHN90
    Invalid sub-directory entry.

    Convert directory to file  (Y/N)? n
B:\WIDGET89\OTHER
    Invalid sub-directory entry.

B:\WIDGET89\OTHER\OTHER
    Invalid sub-directory entry.
    .

    .
B:\WIDGET89\OTHER\OTHER\OTHER\OTHER\OTHER\OTHER\OTHER\OTHER
    Invalid sub-directory entry.

Cannot CHDIR to
B:\WIDGET89\OTHER\OTHER\OTHER\OTHER\OTHER\OTHER\OTHER\OTHER\FORECAST
   tree past this point not processed.

5 lost clusters found in 3 chains.
Convert lost chains to files  (Y/N)? n
     5120 bytes disk space
           would be freed.

B:\WIDGET89
    Is cross linked on cluster 5
B:\WIDGET89\FORECAST
    Is cross linked on cluster 8
B:\WIDGET89\ACTUAL
    Is cross linked on cluster 9
B:\WIDGET89\ACTUAL\WIDGET89.WK1
    Is cross linked on cluster 10
B:\WIDGET89\OTHER
    Is cross linked on cluster 5
B:\WIDGET89\OTHER\FORECAST
    Is cross linked on cluster 8

    362496 bytes total disk space
      7168 bytes in 36 directories
     14336 bytes in 10 user files
    335872 bytes available on disk

    655360 bytes total memory
    568064 bytes free
```

Figure 7.65   Extract from the CHKDSK report

The problems that have been encountered are due to corruption of the data in the subdirectory entries. As this data can still be accessed DOS reports no errors, although any programs or utilities accessing the information will find it to be incorrect. As in previous examples, NU can be used to obtain a low-level view of the data held on the disk. Figure 7.66 shows the NU display of the root directory data.

```
┌ Root dir ═══════════════════════════════════════ Directory format ═┐
│ Sector 5 in root directory                          Offset 0, hex 0 │
│                                                       Attributes     │
│ Filename Ext    Size     Date     Time    Cluster  Arc R/O Sys Hid Dir Vol│
│                                                                      │
│ ▓WDATA▓                23-11-90  5:44 pm     2                    Dir │
│ JOHN90                 23-11-90  5:44 pm                          Dir │
│ WIDGET88               23-11-90  5:44 pm     4                    Dir │
│ WIDGET89               23-11-90  5:44 pm     5                    Dir │
│ FF        EXE   9020   16-10-88  4:50 pm    19     Arc                │
│            unused directory entry                                    │
│            unused directory entry                                    │
│            unused directory entry                                    │
│            unused directory entry                                    │
│            unused directory entry                                    │
│            unused directory entry                                    │
│            unused directory entry                                    │
│            unused directory entry                                    │
│            unused directory entry                                    │
│            unused directory entry                                    │
│            unused directory entry                                    │
│ ═══════════════════════════════════════════════════════════════════ │
│         Filenames beginning with 'σ' indicate erased entries         │
│                   Press Enter to continue                            │
│ 1Help  2Hex   3Text  4Dir   5Al   6Partn  7      8Choose 9Undo  10QuitNU│
```

Figure 7.66   Listing of root directory data

The five entries correspond to those reported by the DIR command before, implying that there are no deleted or hidden subdirectories. However, it can be seen that the entry for JOHN90 has no starting cluster specified, indicating that the value is recorded as 00. Cluster 00 corresponds to the root directory, and thus this value can be assumed to be incorrect.

The cluster number for the JOHN90 subdirectory needs to be changed to reference the appropriate subdirectory cluster. This can be located by inspection, but it should be noted that the directory entries before and after JOHN90 tend to imply that the data can be found in cluster 3. An examination of cluster 3 reveals that it does in fact contain a directory entry, albeit an empty one. Figure 7.67 shows the data held in cluster 3, displayed in directory format.

The probability that this is the correct cluster is confirmed by the fact that cluster number 0 is referenced as the address of the .. entry, ie the parent directory for this entry is root. As there were no other deleted entries in the root directory to which this cluster may apply, it is certain that it is in fact the subdirectory data for JOHN90.

Thus the root directory is selected as the current item, and the cluster number for JOHN90 is changed to 3. The data is written to disk to make the changes permanent.

```
┌ Cluster 3 ════════════════════════════════════════ Directory format ═┐
│ Cluster 3, Sectors 14-15                              Offset 0, hex 0 │
│                                                          Attributes   │
│ Filename Ext    Size      Date      Time    Cluster  Arc R/O Sys Hid Dir Vol │
│ ═══════════════════════════════════════════════════════════════════ │
│ ▐▌▐▌▐▌▌            23-11-90   5:44 pm     3                      Dir  │
│ ..                 23-11-90   5:44 pm                            Dir  │
│              unused directory entry                                   │
│              unused directory entry                                   │
│              unused directory entry                                   │
│              unused directory entry                                   │
│              unused directory entry                                   │
│              unused directory entry                                   │
│              unused directory entry                                   │
│              unused directory entry                                   │
│              unused directory entry                                   │
│              unused directory entry                                   │
│              unused directory entry                                   │
│              unused directory entry                                   │
│              unused directory entry                                   │
│              unused directory entry                                   │
│ ═══════════════════════════════════════════════════════════════════ │
│       Filenames beginning with 'ɾ' indicate erased entries           │
│                    Press Enter to continue                           │
│ 1Help  2Hex  3Text  4Dir  5FAT  6Partn  7      8Choose 9Undo  10QuitNU │
└───────────────────────────────────────────────────────────────────┘
```

Figure 7.67   Listing of cluster 3 data

The next problem to rectify is the cross-referencing of the \WIDGET89\OTHER directory. This currently appears to reference WIDGET90, in the same way that JOHN90 referenced the root directory. Viewing the data in NU confirms this, as illustrated in Figure 7.68.

```
┌ WIDGET89 ════════════════════════════════════════ Directory format ═┐
│ Cluster 5, Sectors 18-19                          File offset 0, hex 0 │
│                                                          Attributes   │
│ Filename Ext    Size      Date      Time    Cluster  Arc R/O Sys Hid Dir Vol │
│ ═══════════════════════════════════════════════════════════════════ │
│ ▐▌▐▌▐▌▌            23-11-90   5:44 pm     5                      Dir  │
│ ..                 23-11-90   5:44 pm                            Dir  │
│ FORECAST           23-11-90   5:45 pm     8                      Dir  │
│ ACTUAL             23-11-90   5:45 pm     9                      Dir  │
│ OTHER              23-11-90   5:46 pm     5                      Dir  │
│              unused directory entry                                   │
│              unused directory entry                                   │
│              unused directory entry                                   │
│              unused directory entry                                   │
│              unused directory entry                                   │
│              unused directory entry                                   │
│              unused directory entry                                   │
│              unused directory entry                                   │
│              unused directory entry                                   │
│              unused directory entry                                   │
│              unused directory entry                                   │
│ ═══════════════════════════════════════════════════════════════════ │
│       Filenames beginning with 'ɾ' indicate erased entries           │
│                    Press Enter to continue                           │
│ 1Help  2Hex  3Text  4Dir  5FAT  6Partn  7      8Choose 9Undo  10QuitNU │
└───────────────────────────────────────────────────────────────────┘
```

Figure 7.68   Listing of WIDGET89 directory data

As before, the correct data for this directory entry needs to be found by examination. It is known that the parent directory will reference cluster 5, and that the two other subdirectories from WIDGET89 occupy clusters 8 and 9. This tends to indicate that cluster 10 is a likely location. However, on examination it is found that cluster 10 contains data, and is used by the WIDGET89.WK1 data file in the ACTUAL subdirectory. Therefore cluster 10 cannot be the correct one. Using NU to view the FAT displays the disk usage in a more easily readable form, as shown in Figure 7.69.

```
┌ FAT area ══════════════════════════════════ FAT format ┐
  Sector 1 in 1st copy of FAT                  Cluster 15, hex F

     <EOF> <EOF> <EOF> <EOF> <EOF> <EOF> <EOF> <EOF>    11    12    13    14
     <EOF> <EOF>    17    18 <EOF>    20    21    22    23    24    25    26
        27 <EOF>     0     0     0     0     0     0     0     0     0     0
         0     0     0     0     0     0     0     0     0     0     0     0
         0     0     0     0     0     0     0     0     0     0     0     0
         0     0     0     0     0     0     0     0     0     0     0     0
         0     0     0     0     0     0     0     0     0     0     0     0
         0     0     0     0     0     0     0     0     0     0     0     0
         0     0     0     0     0     0     0     0     0     0     0     0
         0     0     0     0     0     0     0     0     0     0     0     0
         0     0     0     0     0     0     0     0     0     0     0     0
         0     0     0     0     0     0     0     0     0     0     0     0
         0     0     0     0     0     0     0     0     0     0     0     0
         0     0     0     0     0     0     0     0     0     0     0     0
         0     0     0     0     0     0     0     0     0     0     0     0
         0     0     0     0     0     0     0     0     0     0     0     0
                        Press Enter to continue
 1Help  2Hex   3Text  4Dir   5Fat   6Partn 7       8Choose 9Undo  10QuitNU
```

Figure 7.69   Display of FAT data

It can be seen from this display that cluster 10 is actually the first in a chain of 5, occupying clusters 10 to 14. The next cluster, number 15, is shown as <EOF>, meaning that it is either at the end of a chain or that it is a single cluster chain. Examination of the FAT shows there to be no other references to cluster 15, so it can be assumed to be a single cluster chain, and hence possibly the directory data that is required.

Viewing the cluster in NU produces the display shown in Figure 7.70. it can be seen from this listing that it is very likely to be the missing data, as the parent is specified as cluster 5. Furthermore, the directory contains a worksheet file called STAFF.WK1. If the disk was organised sensibly, then such a file may well be placed in a subdirectory of its own within an overall company subdirectory.

To make the relevant change, the WIDGET89 subdirectory is made current, and the directory entry for OTHER is altered to reference cluster 15. Once the data has been written to disk, NU can be exited and the directory structure can be tested using either CHKDSK, FindFile or multiple DIR commands.

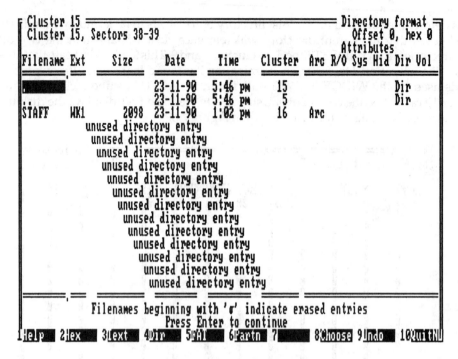

Figure 7.70   Listing of cluster 15 data

7.3.6.3   Summary

Whilst recursive subdirectories occur only infrequently, they do pose a considerable problem in terms of data loss. This is primarily due to fact that many users remain unaware that they have such a problem, and continue to use the disk in question. This can cause the original data to be overwritten, and therefore makes data recovery more difficult.

Corruptions of the directory structure are most often caused by mis-use of utilities, and by the use of utilities that contain programming errors. Many such products attempt to assist the user in maintaining the directory structure, by moving, create, and deleting subdirectories. If these programs fail to operate correctly, for example if they are not compatible with the version of DOS in use, then the results can be entirely unpredictable.

The best technique for solving this form of fault is to approach the situation in a very methodical manner, keeping notes of the directory structure and disk usage as it is examined. This will allow cross-linked directories to be more easily identified and remedied. There are unfortunately very few utilities which successfully tackle these problems on an automatic basis.

7.4   SUMMARY

The scenarios discussed in this chapter have illustrated six problems that may be encountered in data recovery. It should be noted that only in a select few cases will there be as little data to recover as used in these examples. However, the principles behind the data recovery process are exactly the same, and once the cause of the problem has been correctly diagnosed, the actual process of recovering the data will often be to repeat a particular routine again and again until all of the data has been located and corrected.

The most important point to remember is to keep a broad outlook on the problem, and not too channel too much commitment into a single solution at an early stage. In most situations there are several different solutions, and often several possible causes. The advantages and disadvantages of each one should be carefully considered and compared before a decision is taken.

8 Maximising System Usage

8.1 THE NEED FOR OPTIMISATION

Many problems are encountered when users attempt to exceed the limits of their system, either by attempting to run memory-hungry programs, or by filling the hard disk to capacity. Conversely, many computer systems are vastly under-used in comparison to their full potential. Many such problem situations can be overcome by ensuring maximum use is made of both memory and disk storage.

8.2 MEMORY

The MS-DOS restriction of 640K accessible memory continues to frustrate the PC user. It is, however, worth remembering that when the IBM-PC was first released in 1980, the onboard RAM capacity was 16K. The fact that this could, through the use of expansion boards, theoretically be expanded to 640K was considered irrelevant, as the maximum motherboard expansion was 64K. It is appropriate to note that at the time RAM chips were not cheap.

With the 640K RAM as standard in many PC clones, and configurations increasingly being supplied with 1MB, 2MB or 4MB, the 640K DOS restriction is a real one. However, the various ways of bypassing or evading this barrier and the related issue of memory speed is not necessarily straightforward.

The 640K barrier was primarily due to the design of the 8088 processor. This chip has 20 pins on the address bus which is only capable of addressing 1MB of memory directly. This must include BIOS, any other ROM installed on peripherals such as hard disk controllers etc, and the memory required for the screen mapping. As a result 384K is allocated to the system. This area is known as the *system memory*, leaving 640K available for applications and data, which is known as the *real* or *base memory*.

The situation was further complicated in 1984 when the 80286 processor arrived in the form of the IBM-AT. This processor can address up to 16MB of memory, using 24 address lines. However, to ensure compatibility Intel restricted the performance of the chip, causing it to be run in a mode compatible with an 8088. At power on, the 80286 is in *real mode*, with 1MB of addressable memory and all the other limitations of the 8088. It is possible, by changing a signal on a single pin at power up to put the 80286 processor into *protected mode*, giving access to the full 16MB. This is not, however, accessible through MS-DOS.

It was at the time of the AT launch that IBM introduced the term *extended memory* which refers to memory between 1MB and 16MB on an 80286 based PC. Extended memory was initially only available when working in protected mode and thus not directly accessible through MS-DOS. Therefore protected mode is accessed through software such as VDISK and RAMdisk as well as various disk caching packages, to give access to the additional memory. Other operating systems Unix, Xenix and OS/2 take advantage of extended memory in order to perform multi-tasking and multi-user operations.

The important point about extended memory is that the term refers to memory between 1024KB and 16MB. Therefore an AT compatible computer with 1MB of accessible memory uses the basic 640K and the addresses between 1024KB and 1408KB. The 384KB between 640KB and 1024KB is the restricted area required by the system for ROM and Video RAM (VRAM), as shown in Figure 8.1.

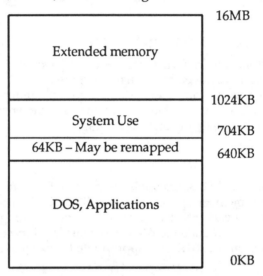

Figure 8.1   Memory usage for an 80286 processor

8.2.1   BREAKING THE BARRIER

There are three primary ways of overcoming the 640K DOS limitation:

– Remap a portion of the system area

– Use expanded memory

– Use extended memory directly

8.2.1.1   Remapping the System Area

There are a number of products available that will remap the memory usage so that some of the memory in the addresses 640KB-1024KB can be accessed. This is based on the fact that IBM originally reserved 384KB for system use in the PC design, but not all of this space is actually required. Therefore by remapping some physical RAM into the spare space an additional 64K can be released for programs and data, giving a total of 704KB to the user. This facility is available to both 8088 and 80286 machines, whereas extended memory is only available to 80286 systems.

8.2.1.2 Expanded memory

Due primarily to the growth in spreadsheet usage, it became necessary to overcome the 640KB barrier more effectively, and the result of the research and development performed was known as expanded memory specification (EMS). The first EMS was produced jointly by Lotus and Intel in 1985 and was soon followed by the Lotus-Intel-MicroSoft EMS referred to as LIM EMS 3.2.

This software controlled facility originally allowed MS-DOS programs to access up to 8MB of RAM using a technique called bank switching. The principle behind the technique is to set up a page frame of 64KB in the area between 640KB and 1024KB into which up to four 16KB pages of data from the Expanded RAM area can be mapped.

There were limitations to LIM EMS 3.2 and the latest offering is LIM EMS 4.0 which provides up to 32MB of expanded memory and can be successfully used by multi-tasking products such as Windows and DESQview, as well as many applications programs.

The main disadvantage of using this method is speed, as the relevant area of extra memory has to be transferred to the 64K page frame before the data can be accessed. This may seem to be a small overhead, but when the operation has to be repeated hundreds or thousands of times it can be very noticeable. A second disadvantage is that a special software driver is required, which uses a small amount of the base memory of the computer, thus reducing the amount available for the applications software.

8.2.1.3 Extended Memory

Some modern software products can directly access extended memory, thus giving access to the full 16MB on-board capacity. This technique means that data can be stored and retrieved at the same speed as if real or base memory were being used, without the need for the special software driver.

Examples of these products are Lotus 1-2-3 Release 3, AutoCAD and DataEase, all of which require high-specification systems before they can be used to best advantage. As this technique offers the fastest and simplest methods of data storage, it is likely that more and more products will be developed to take advantage of this feature.

8.2.1.4 Practical Systems

The division of PC memory into real, extended and expanded memory has caused much confusion, particularly with regard to where one finishes and the other begins. A typical configuration that is advertised in the computer press is an AT compatible with 640K of real memory, 384KB of Extended memory which is used for disk caching or RAMdisk, and 2MB or more of LIM EMS RAM which is used for applications that have been written to support it directly such as Lotus 1-2-3, SuperCalc, Symphony, Windows etc.

Other EMS products such as QEMM from Quarterdeck are available which handle the memory mapping, and with this software it is possible, using MS-DOS, to move RAM-resident software and software drivers into the area between 640KB and 1024KB and to then emulate LIM EMS 4.0 memory in Extended memory which negates the need for physical RAM mixtures.

The 80386 processor has removed many of the memory management problems as, for example, an 80386 system with 4MB of RAM and a copy of a suitable EMM driver can give any combination of real, extended or expanded RAM that users require. It does however bring new problems, not least of which are associated with speed as the 80386 processor can run at speeds of 16 to 33MHz, and most popular memory chips are too slow to cope with even the lowest processor clock speed.

8.3 DISKS

Unlike memory, the cost of disk storage is falling at a much slower rate. This means that it is still not cost effective for the majority of PC users to upgrade their hard disk storage on a regular basis. As a result, many hard disks are filled to capacity with a collection of data and application programs.

The situation is made even worse as modern releases of applications are tending to require more and more space for disk storage. For example, WordStar currently requires over 3MB if it is to be used to its full potential, Lotus 123 Release 3 requires a similar amount, and programs such as PageMaker and Ventura publisher require around 5MB.

With hard disk sizes becoming standardised at around 40MB, over 25% of the capacity is used by these three applications alone. A further facet of modern hard disks is the use of Large Logical Sectors (LLS). Whilst the use of this technique allows logical drives of greater than 32MB to be referenced, it also means that cluster sizes are 4 or 8K. Hence even the smallest batch file or memo uses 8K of disk storage.

Another disk-related problem that users complain of is performance loss due to disk fragmentation. As discussed earlier, this is not a particularly serious problem and any remedies that are found are usually only temporary.

8.3.1 IMPROVING DISK PERFORMANCE

There are several techniques that can be used to gain space, or can be used to reorganise the disk to improve performance. The most commonly encountered of these are:

- Purging
- File Compression
- Disk Optimisation

A variety of utilities and programs are available which perform one or more of these tasks, although the effectiveness and reliability of such systems is sometimes doubtful.

8.3.1.1 Purging

Purging is the act of removing from the computer system all unnecessary and unwanted data. The term is most often used in conjunction with databases and networks, although it can be applied equally well to other computer usage.

Before any data file is purged, it should be copied to a floppy so that there is a permanent record of the information. A second copy should of course be made as a backup if no other system is in use. The file can then be erased from the hard disk of the computer to free space.

There are certain files that will almost certainly be present on all hard disks, and which can almost certainly be purged every time. These include:

- Files with a .BAK extension, which are usually automatically created by applications programs when data is saved. These must be backed up in the same way as standard data files, as they may be required at a later date.

- Files with a $ as the first letter of the extension. These are often temporary files created by an application for its own use. One exception to this is Ventura Publisher, which uses extensions starting with a $ as its backups.

- Another Ventura peculiarity is the fact that it produces files with a .CIF extension. These are designed to allow Ventura to be interfaced with other applications. However, as there are very few applications which make use of the facility, the files are largely redundant. It is possible that other software packages generate a similar type of file, and manuals should be checked to see if they can be removed.

- Files with a .OLD extension are usually created by users for a specific purpose, and are almost certainly not required again.

- It is quite common to find two versions of an application on a single disk, as the user may have upgraded from one to the other. In most cases it will be possible to completely remove the older version, although the user must be consulted before this step is taken.

- Many applications automatically install a number of sample data files, which can be erased if they are encountered during the examination of the disk.

The savings in disk usage that can be made by purging are enormous. For example, consider the .CIF files produced by Ventura. Each is only 128 bytes long, but one is produced for every Ventura document. Thus, if 20 different brochures are created, 20 different CIF files are also created. On a hard disk using LLSs, each file occupies 8K. Thus 20 of them consume 160K of space which can be recovered for further use.

The one rule that must be followed when purging a disk is that *there must be a copy on floppy, and a backup, of every file that is purged*. There are many examples of files being purged from a hard disk, only to find that they are required a week or two later. Without a copy or a backup they will have to be recreated from scratch.

8.3.1.2 File Compression

File Compression is a technique whereby data in a file on disk is written in a slightly different format, so that it uses less physical storage space. A variety of compression techniques are available, although they all produce very similar results. Two of the most popular utilities are PKZIP and ARCX, both of which can be obtained as shareware.

Such file compression techniques can free between 5% and 75% of the disk space used by a file, depending on its contents. The actual process of compressing and uncompressing the data is very simple, usually consisting of issuing a command such as PKZIP MYFILE.WK1 to compress a file and PKUNZIP MYFILE.ZIP to uncompress it again.

However, there is a problem surrounding the use of such programs: what happens if there is a disk corruption of the compressed data? Although the data can usually be recovered using the techniques discussed in Chapters 4, 5 and 6, if a full recovery cannot be made for any reason then it may not be possible to subsequently uncompress the data.

Thus whilst the use of such compression utilities can save large amounts of disk space, they do so at the expense of reliability. Ultimately, it will be found that the only reliable way to use compression programs is to keep a floppy copy and a backup of the data file in its original form. For this reason file compression utilities are best restricted to producing copies of data to send to someone else, thus reducing the number of floppy disks required, or for maintaining an extra backup of a disk.

8.3.1.3 Disk Optimisation

The two sections above have dealt with the problem of disk space. Disk optimisation is concerned with the issues of disk performance, as no disk optimisation program can free any space whatsoever. The reasons that disks may require optimisation are as follows:

The more a disk drive is used the slower it will become. This is because DOS will always save data in the next location on the disk where it can find an empty space, and it is not concerned about keeping all the data together. A file stored in this way is said to be a single logical unit, although it could actually be stored in many different physical areas. This will inevitably lead to slower access times as files become fragmented all over the physical disk:

Files are generally stored in clusters of 2K, 4K or 8K, so a relatively small file of 40K could be spread over 20 different locations. When DOS needs to access data in such a file, it may have to reposition the disk head as many as 20 times at 20 different locations on the surface of the disk. Head positioning is the most time consuming element in retrieving data, and so this activity is the considered to be an overhead work-load which in turn causes a deterioration in access time. The more a file is changed the worse the problem can become. The problem is not restricted to data files, as program files may also be scattered over the disk.

This problem of fragmented data and programs may be solved by software such as Disk Optimizer, Norton's Speed Disk, and PCTools' Compress utility. These systems consolidate the various clusters and thus makes the physical data layouts correspond with the logical data file. The effect of this process is that the new data or programs will be rewritten into a contiguous area. Figure 8.2 shows how a disk could appear before and after optimising.

Before Optimisation

PRTN	BOOT	FAT	DIR	AA	AA	BB	CC	DD	DD
CC	CC	CC	EE	EE	EE	FF	EE	FF	GG
GG	GG		HH	HH	II	HH	HH	JJ	II
II	KK			KK	KK		KK		LL

After Optimisation

PRTN	BOOT	FAT	DIR	AA	AA	BB	CC	CC	CC
CC	DD	DD	EE	EE	EE	EE	FF	FF	GG
GG	GG	HH	HH	HH	HH	II	II	II	JJ
KK	KK	KK	KK	LL					

Figure 8.2   Disk usage before and after optimisation

The optimising procedure can take between 2 and 60 minutes to run, depending on the state, size, and speed of the disk. The increase in speed of the system after optimisation will be between 0 and 50 percent, also depending on the original condition of the system. Databases and accounting systems benefit most from the disk optimisation, and such systems should be run about twice per month.

8.3.1.4   Optimisation Problems

In some cases applications load data at the same speed after disk optimisation as they did beforehand. This is because some programs adopt special disk formats for their data, which means that every byte of data read from disk has to be processed before it can be used. Thus the fact that the data can be loaded from disk more quickly makes little or no difference to the overall performance of the system, as the majority of time is taken in performing the relevant calculations.

The extent to which any application is disk or processor dependent can be ascertained by looking at the disk drive light as a data file is retrieved. If the drive light is on constantly, and the data appears on screen as soon as the light goes out, then the application is dependent upon the disk. If, however, the light flickers irregularly and there is a delay before the data appears on screen, the application is processor dependent.

Degradation of performance for processor dependent tasks can only be resolved by increasing processing power, usually by moving to a higher specification computer system. Disk dependent applications will benefit to some extent from optimisation, although it is only likely to be a temporary measure, as the disk will soon become de-optimised if it is regularly used.

A more serious problem surrounds the disk optimisation process: what happens if there is a power cut, or the system hangs in the middle of the optimisation process? If either of these situations occur, then it is very likely that some data will be lost. If the program was attempting to write a FAT or directory entry at the time, then even greater amounts of data could be lost.

If an optimisation program contains bugs, it could conceivably cause absolute havoc by overwriting data in the system areas.

These last two points far outweigh the advantages offered by the programs. If such a disaster happens, the consequences could be catastrophic.

8.3.1.5   Alternative Optimisation Techniques

If optimisation is deemed essential, then there is a technique which does not expose the system to the risks outlined above. The procedure is very simple, and should be executed as follows:

-   Make a copy of all data and programs that are required. A tested and trusted backup utility, or the DOS COPY or XCOPY commands should be used for this, and the copies should be made to reliable media, such as floppy disks.
-   Make a backup copy of the each floppy disk, so that in the event of an accident all is not lost.
-   Re-format the hard disk (high-level format)
-   Reinstate all data from floppy, again using the copy command.

This process will ensure that the data files and programs are in contiguous clusters, and exposes the system to no risks, as there are always two copies of the data available at any one time.

However, this technique is only temporary for the same reasons that affect the disk optimisation programs; if the disk is in normal use, then it will soon become de-optimised due to the creation and deletion of files.

8.4 SUMMARY

The issues of memory management tend to baffle many users when they are first confronted. However, it has been shown that the memory in a PC can be divided into three groups:

- Real memory - ie the 640K directly accessed by DOS.

- Extended memory - used by some special software, and more recently by proprietary software such as Lotus 1-2-3 version 3.1. Other operating systems make better use of extended memory to provide multi-user and multi-tasking abilities. These include OS/2, Unix, and Xenix.

- Expanded memory - used in conjunction with a special software device driver to allow many software packages to access memory beyond the standard DOS barrier.

In the past these categorisations have lead to considerable confusion among users. These problems are being resolved in new releases of some software packages which are able to directly access extended memory, thus allowing easy manipulation of large amounts of data. These products will no doubt remove the need to use expanded memory, simplifying matters considerably.

The problems involved in managing disk usage are more subtle, and in general are much harder to circumvent. The only reliable way to maintain an acceptable level of performance and free space is to regularly purge the hard disk of unwanted programs and data. However, many organisations will find themselves unable to determine what is required and what is not, and so the purging process cannot be effectively followed.

The processes of file compression and disk optimisation have been shown to expose the personal computer to many risks, and offer little or no benefits in return. It is therefore recommended that these processes are never carried out, except in cases where the benefits clearly outweigh the disadvantages.

9   The Computer Virus

9.1 WHAT IS A COMPUTER VIRUS?

A computer virus may be defined as a piece of software which infects programs, data or disks and has the ability to reproduce itself in the same or in some other form. It is therefore a program and not a strain of biological bacteria.

The origin of the computer virus is said to have been the result of an experiment conducted by Dr. Fred Cohen. He presented the virus as a computer security threat at a conference in November 1983. Since then viral infection of computers, and PCs in particular, has continued to develop at an alarming rate, due largely to the interest the concept of a virus generates among computer hackers.

For a virus to exist and become infectious it needs three basic properties:

- **A person to design and code it.** A virus cannot create itself and must be originated by a computer programmer. Programmers of viruses have become known as *virus perpetrators* or *data invaders*.

- **A suitable environment to reproduce and spread.** The portability of data on personal computers provides ideal conditions for hosting and breeding viruses.

- **An opportunity of which it can take advantage.** A virus must be given the opportunity to run in order to reproduce and thus propagate. It must be able to spread in order to grow. It is for this reason that virus infections often come from tempting free software or from appealing games and pirated packages.

The main characteristics of a virus are:

- They are hidden so as to avoid detection and destruction, often sitting in a computer in a benign state for some time.

- They are self-replicating so as to ensure the continued and contagious infection of computer resources.

- They interfere with normal computer operations in a number of different ways, including deleting files, corrupting screen displays, corrupting data, slowing down the operation of a system, displaying messages and creating system and disk errors.

It has recently been suggested that the computer virus may be considered as a living entity, as it fulfils the four primary requirements of life, namely:

- It can reproduce itself
- It can move around within its environment

- It can affect and change its environment
- Separate virus programs will often group to form a population.

An additional requirement for a living entity that is sometimes stated is that it should be able to mutate, to alter itself to take advantage of changing circumstances. At present, this condition does not appear to have been met by the computer virus, although some mutated viruses have been produced by programmers. However, it is generally agreed that this phase is not far off.

9.2   TYPES OF VIRUS

Over the last few years, since the subject of computer viruses became popular interest, they have been divided into two main categories; parasitic viruses and boot sector viruses.

9.2.1   THE PARASITIC VIRUS

A parasitic virus is carried by an executable application program and is copied into other applications as they are run. The virus code attaches itself to the application's program code so that it is activated every time the program is loaded. A parasitic virus can be resident or non-resident. A resident virus makes itself memory resident and it is this copy which infects other program files. A non-resident parasitic virus will infect a program before it is made active.

9.2.2   THE BOOT SECTOR VIRUS

A boot sector virus is quite different in that it modifies the boot sector, or occasionally the partition record, of a floppy or hard disk and in effect becomes part of the computer's operating system. The most common methodology used is to copy the original boot sector or partition record to an unused sector on the disk and then to overwrite the original area with the virus code. Boot sector viruses are spread when the system is booted from the infected disk, as during this process the virus is read from the disk instead of the original data and becomes resident in the memory of the system. It then loads the original boot sector or partition record information from the new position on the disk, thus hiding the presence of the virus from the user. Whenever another disk is used by the system, even if a program or data file is simply copied to or from it, the virus will copy itself into the boot sector and infect that disk.

9.3   DESIGN ELEMENTS

There are a number of design elements that can go into the creation of a virus and some of the more common terms applied to such elements are described below.

9.3.1   TROJAN HORSE

The term Trojan Horse describes a program which pretends to be something harmless, and indeed often useful, such as a shareware utility, a program compiler, password checker etc, but which actually contains a hidden and harmful function. The program that carries the virus is sometimes known as a *dropper*. A Trojan Horse can only be transferred to another machine if the actual program it is carried with is copied to another system, but it cannot actually reproduce itself. A Trojan Horse is therefore not strictly a virus, but in fact most viruses masquerade as Trojan Horses, because the skill of producing a highly infectious virus is to hide and delay its action until the user least expects to be hit. Thus when a virus is being carried from one disk to another, the executable file it has attached itself to can be considered a Trojan Horse.

9.3.2 LOGIC BOMB

This is code within a program that is triggered by certain events. A program containing a logic bomb will appear to be completely normal until a set of conditions is met, at which point it will start to cause damage. Situations that may trigger the logic bomb include:

- Booting up the computer a set number of times
- number of users on a network exceeding a limit
- taking a certain path through the use of an application

9.3.3 TIME BOMB

This is actually a type of logic bomb which is triggered by time. Code within a program checks the system date and time, and when certain criteria are met performs unexpected and often damaging functions. For example Friday 13th and April Fools Day are suspected targets for time bomb programs. A time bomb can also be linked to a logic bomb to give greater sophistication.

9.3.4 TRAP DOOR

This is a legitimate term used to describe the ability to get into the code of a computer operating system or application program. Typically a trap door will be built into software to help developers modify the product without having to re-write it from scratch. Most trap doors are not included in the software's design specifications and consequently may be forgotten. The result is that commercial software could be inadvertently released with the trap door still present, or it could be left in deliberately by a potential data invader who will attack at a later date.

9.3.5 WORM

A worm is a single entity that burrows through a computer or computer network, but does not continually replicate to produce a mass of infected programs. The term should not be confused with the new type of storage media referred to as WORM, meaning Write Once Read Many times. For most practical purposes the effects of a worm and a virus are much the same in that they do damage. However, a virus replicates and typically causes widespread damage quickly whereas a worm slowly eats its way through the system causing chronic damage.

9.4 METHODS OF INFECTION

In the personal computer environment the most common, if somewhat crude, way a virus shows itself is by giving some kind of message or screen display, usually after infecting the users floppy disks so as to ensure the spread of the infection.

The degree of sophistication in the design of a virus is often evidenced by the sort of damage it does. Destroying an entire hard disk is not at all subtle and the effects will be noticed immediately by the user. After detection, destruction of a virus is considerably easier. Selective alteration of data may only be noticed periodically – at the time of an audit for example, and by then it may then be extremely difficult or even impossible to correct the situation. The effects of the cleverest viruses may be so well hidden in the normal day-to-day course of business that the virus may, even after months of damage, still not have come to light.

Before it can do damage a virus must be run. Typically infection to a program file will take place in advance and the damage will be done when the infected program is run. When a system disk is infected the virus will run the next time the computer system is restarted. When executed a virus may show itself immediately by displaying a message or by obviously damaging a file or the disk. Alternatively it may wait, using a logic and/or time bomb to trigger the action.

It is important to remember that the unexpected deletion and/or changing of data in a computer system is not always due to virus infection. Computer hackers and fraudsters have been invading data and program files for years. Examples of such crimes have been widely reported in the banking industry in particular. An example of such a program, which is sometimes referred to as a virus, but which is really just a defrauding technique, is the Salami Technique which slices off cents from an account and adds them to the account of the perpetrator; or the French Round-Off which takes fractions of cents less than 0.005 in interest computations and adds them to the account of the perpetrator.

9.5   PC INFECTION

Virus infection of a PC can take a number of different forms, some of which are not immediately obvious. Generally speaking, the targets selected by viruses for infection have to be executable, so that the virus code is itself executed. The most obvious targets are program files, although there are many other items stored on the computer disk that fall into the category. Some of the more common targets include the following:

–   The partition record, which stores the locations, types and sizes of the partitions on a hard disk. The partition record contains some machine code instructions that are executed when the machine is first booted up.

–   The boot sector, which contains various details about the disk, as well as executable code that is used when the system starts to load DOS. This code takes care of the tasks of loading the two hidden systems files (see below) and the command interpreter (COMMAND.COM).

–   The two boot files, often named IBMIO.COM and IBMDOS.COM or similar. These have the Hidden and System attributes set in their directory entries, so do not appear on ordinary DIR listings. However, they are normal program files and so can be attacked in the same way as any other application.

–   COMMAND.COM, the command processor, which is also just another program file, albeit a very important one.

–   All executable program files. Program files can be distinguished from data files by their file extensions. The following list shows some of the more common ones:

- EXE – Standard executable files
- COM – Standard executable files
- BIN – Machine code files
- SYS – Special system programs
- DRV – Device driver programs
- OVL/OVR – Program overlays

In addition the virus may store some of its own code in various other areas of the disk, including the following:

– Any unused sectors that follow the partition record

– The area of disk used by the FAT

– The area of disk used by the root directory

– Unused clusters in the data area, which are then marked as unusable to prevent the code from being destroyed.

– Clusters in the data area that are already in use by data or program files.

Obviously if the virus uses some of the above areas then data loss will result, and in the case of the FAT and directory areas this can be quite severe. However, in such cases the loss or corruption of data will alert the user to the fact that there is indeed a problem, and thus the virus has little chance to spread.

The first, simple parasitic viruses infected programs by overwriting the original contents of the files. However, this was reasonably easy to detect and so a more subtle approach is now taken by the majority of viruses. They use the spare space at the end of a file which is situated between the end-of-file marker and the end of the cluster. At the time of implanting itself on the disk the virus will modify the program by encoding a pointer to the appended virus code, thus ensuring that when the user executes the program, the virus code is also automatically executed. Once the virus code has completed executing, it returns control to the host program. Thus it appears as though the program executes correctly, when in fact the virus has actually become resident in memory. However, in order to ensure that the virus code is not destroyed if the program is moved or copied, it is necessary for the virus to amend the size of the file in the directory listing. This tell-tale sign is one of the most reliable ways of identifying and locating parasitic viruses. In fact many of the viruses are named according to the amount of bytes they increase the file size by. Thus the Israeli or Jerusalem virus is also known as 1813, as it increases the size of infected program files by 1813 bytes.

Another method that is often employed on PCs is for the virus to create and occupy false bad sectors. Bad sectors are areas on the disk which have been identified as unusable by the operating system and are thus bypassed by data when it is written to disk. A virus can be placed on the disk and then all but a small part of its code can be marked as bad sectors. A small controlling part of the virus will be located in a program or in the boot sector and then when executed it will invoke the code in the main body of the virus located on the so called bad sectors. This means that it is possible to hide all but a tiny portion of the virus code. However, few modern disks suffer from bad sectors, and so the unexpected appearance of them rarely goes unnoticed.

9.6 MEMORY RESIDENT VIRUSES

Many viruses that infect PCs become memory resident, which means that once loaded they remain in the memory of the computer, waiting to be triggered, until the system is reset, rebooted or switched off.

The key to memory resident viruses is the way in which interrupts are used. An interrupt is a mechanism whereby the computer's processor is interrupted from its normal course of action to perform a particular task. For example, when a key is typed at the keyboard, processing will temporarily stop while the key is stored in the keyboard buffer. Interrupts such as this are taking place all the time and in this way the processor performs to the greatest efficiency, processing the user program and data most of the time and only dealing with housekeeping tasks when required.

The system services the interrupts when they occur by looking at the appropriate interrupt vector. This is a memory location which stores the actual address of the interrupt routine to be executed. The system will then go to this routine and perform the required task before returning control to the application program. A virus may alter one or more of the interrupt vectors, causing the system to go to an address containing the virus code instead of the interrupt routine. For example, by changing the interrupt vector for disk accesses, a virus can take control of the system every time an attempt is made to perform a disk operation. This will allow it to corrupt or modify disk data without the user being aware of the fact. Figure 9.1 shows the way in which this can occur.

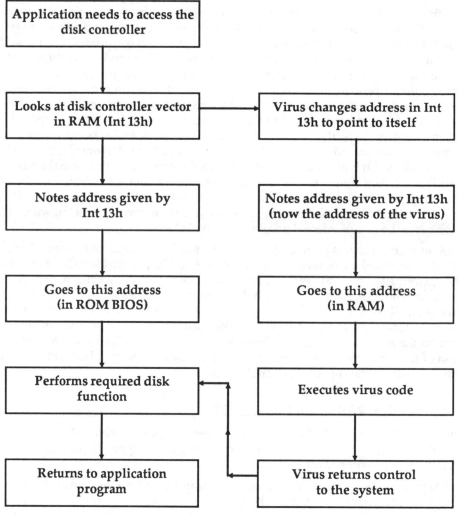

Figure 9.1   Flowchart showing how a virus uses interrupts

In order for the virus to remain active while other programs are run it may use the Terminate Stay Resident (TSR) interrupt. This interrupt is normally used by programs which remain active and available for use in RAM whilst another program is run, for example Sidekick. In a virus situation the virus program uses this interrupt to ensure that it remains in memory after the program it is attached to is exited. This means that the viral code will still be executed when another application program is running. Only when the computer is switched off, or in some cases when it is rebooted, will infection cease. However, the virus will probably have also written itself to each application program that was executed and so when the computer is next used and one of these applications executed, the virus will immediately be re-activated.

9.6.1 RECOGNISING A VIRUS

The symptoms of virus infection can take many different forms. Some symptoms are obvious whether the virus is active or not, particularly those relating to parasitic viruses. Other symptoms, notably those connected with boot sector viruses, are only obvious after the system has been infected. Figure 9.2 shows some of the tell tale signs that may appear if a DOS file becomes infected with a parasitic virus.

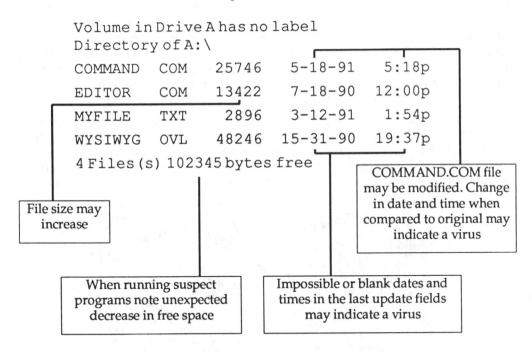

Figure 9.2   Tell-tale signs of viral infection

If it is suspected that the virus is located on the boot sector of the disk the DOS command INSTALL may be executed which will rewrite the boot sector on the infected disk. It should be noted that some game programs use the boot sector for copy protection code. Since many viruses in the boot sector will by default overwrite the copy protection, a games program that will not run may be an indication as to the presence of a virus which may have already infected the system.

9.7   SOME POPULAR VIRUS PROGRAMS AND THEIR EFFECTS

There are literally hundreds of documented viruses circulating around the world. There are however a core of more common ones, brief descriptions of which follow:

9.7.1   BRAIN

The Brain virus originated in Pakistan and affects the IBM PC/XT/AT/PS2 and compatible computers. It only affects floppy disks (both bootable and non-bootable) and is located on the boot sector which is, in effect, the first part of DOS to be loaded. It is about 4100 bytes in length, but only half the code as actually used. The effect of being infected with Brain is actually minimal, as existing data is not altered or deleted. However, it does slow down floppy disk operations, and also uses 3K of space on every infected disk, and 7K of memory in an infected computer.

The virus infects a system by creating three successive clusters of the virus code and flagging the six sectors that it has used as bad sectors. The virus code then makes a copy of the FAT, changes the FAT code numbers and destroys the original FAT and boot sectors. The virus alters the memory size by changing the address on interrupt vector A2h in order to disguise it's presence in memory. The virus then substitutes the floppy disk interrupt vector (13h) with its own address so that when the application program attempts to access the floppy disk the virus code is executed rather than the original interrupt routine. Therefore when new floppy disks are used in the same working session the virus copies itself onto spare space within the data area on the disk, and then modifies the boot sector and FAT for this disk. Thus the virus continues to replicate from the newly infected diskette. If the floppy disk has no volume label, the virus writes the word 'Brain'.

This virus is sometimes referred to as the Pakistan Brain as it originally spread to universities in the UK and USA from Pakistan. It was thought to have come from exchange students who bought pirated and infected software from Pakistan. As can be seen from Figure 9.3 the code contains the name, address and telephone number of the authors in Lahore who suggest that any victim of the virus contact them for the vaccine.

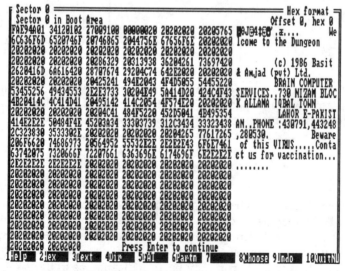

Figure 9.3   Listing of the Brain virus code

The Brain virus spread to the University of Delaware where employees of 480 of the Fortune 500 company headquarters attended computer classes. The students were allowed to do college homework on the company computers during lunch breaks and it is said to be as a result of this that the virus spread rapidly to various corporate computer systems. It has also been reported in a number of other US universities as well as in corporate computers in Australia, UK, Israel, West Germany and Switzerland.

Unfortunately the Brain virus has more recently been reported in several mutated forms, one of which being the introduction of random errors on hard disk files.

9.7.2 THE JERUSALEM VIRUS

Sometimes referred to as the Hebrew University or Friday 13th, this time bomb virus was originally set to activate on Friday 13 May 1988 which happens to be the 40th anniversary of the last free Palestinian entity before the creation of Israel on 14 May 1948!

The virus was written by a Palestinian student as an act of 'hi-tech sabotage' and was discovered because of a bug in the virus code itself. It began to treat previously infected programs as uninfected and copied itself twice onto the disks. This caused an obvious increase in the use of available memory and enabled the virus to be detected.

The virus operates in two stages. Firstly when an infected EXE or COM file is executed the first time after booting the virus copies itself into RAM as a TSR. Secondly once the memory is infected, any time an EXE file is run, the virus code is copied to the end of that file. When a COM file is run, the virus code is copied to the beginning of the file. The virus is also sometimes referred to as the 1808 or 1813 virus because of the lengths by which it increases the size of EXE and COM files respectively. As an indication of infection the virus writes the string MsDos to the end of a COM file.

Being a parasitic virus, this virus makes its presence known by increasing the size of program files. It also moves a small section of the display up, 30 minutes after infection and slows the operation of the machine down from this point until it is rendered virtually unusable. As soon as reinfection has taken place the previous host file is deleted from the disk.

Staff at the Hebrew University claim that this virus had been so virulent that several years of research, financial information and student files have been destroyed. They also think that thousands of files and years of research were wiped out before the virus was discovered.

The Hebrew University computers are networked to computer systems in the Israeli Military and Intelligence centres and it is possible that the virus could have spread to these systems, adversely affecting Israel's national security.

Having lain dormant for sometime after detection, the virus reappeared on Friday 13 January 1989, the first Friday 13th after 13 May 1988. In this version the bug that was present in the original had been removed.

9.7.3 THE ITALIAN VIRUS

This virus is sometimes referred to as the Ping Pong virus and only affects floppy disks working with 8086 and 8088 processors. It is a boot sector virus, and is triggered by the system clock. It can reside on any disk, whether it is bootable or not, bearing in mind that all disks have boot sectors. If an attempt is made to boot up with an infected non-bootable disk the usual error message will be displayed to request a bootable disk, but infection will already have taken place as the virus will have executed itself and therefore will be in RAM. It will then copy itself onto any unprotected floppy introduced into the system during that working session.

The virus uses the time of day register in the system clock. The computer clock ticks at a rate of 18.2 times per second or 65,200 times per hour. As part of the infection process when the register goes above 14 bits, an oval bouncing ball activates and bounces around the screen. When the ball encounters a character, it will deflect off it, but will also remove it in the process.

9.7.4   THE STONED VIRUS

The Stoned virus is one of the more virulent and widespread viruses that is encountered. It was devised and distributed in its original form at the start of the virus boom, but has since appeared in several mutated, more destructive forms.

Stoned is a boot sector/partition record virus. It attacks both floppy and hard disks, and is effective on any hardware configuration. The original form was not intentionally destructive, although it can cause data loss on some media due to the way in which it infects the disk:

–   On floppies, Stoned replaces the boot sector with its own code, and then moves the original boot sector data to side 0, cylinder 0, sector 11. On 360K floppies this is the last sector of the directory so will not cause data problems unless there are over 96 files on the disk. On 1.2MB floppies this is the third sector of the directory, and so will overwrite the directory entries for files 33 through 48.

–   On hard disks Stoned replaces the partition record with its own code, and then replaces the original code at side 0, cylinder 0, sector 7. For most disks this area is unused, as by default DOS assumes that the first partition should start at side 1, cylinder 0, sector 1. Unfortunately some licensed versions of DOS do not obey this ruling and start the partition immediately after the partition record. On such systems, the virus will overwrite a part of the FAT, leading to severe data loss.

The virus infects the computer when an infected disk is used to boot-up. Floppy disks can be infected whether they are bootable or not, just as with the Italian virus. As soon as the virus is executed it becomes memory resident, and immediately looks for the partition record on the hard disk. If it finds one it infects it straight away. From this point on, any write-enabled floppy that is used in the system will be infected, irrespective of whether it is read or written to. Thus all disks are immediate targets, regardless of whether they contain program files or data files.

The virus shows itself by producing a message saying *'Your computer is stoned – Legalise Marijuana'* on every 8th bootup. Other than this seemingly harmless message, and the corresponding loss in performance due to the memory resident nature of the virus, Stoned produces no other ill-effects. However, the variants of Stoned, of which there are many, tend to be much more destructive. Very few actually produce the original on-screen message, instead they tend to trash disks, destroy data files etc.

One of the reasons for the 'popularity' of stoned amongst virus writers is that it is extremely well written. The actual code is about 400 bytes which makes it very easy to interpret and modify as required.

9.8   MACINTOSH VIRUSES

Virus attacks are by no means restricted to the IBM-PC compatible market. For some time the Apple Macintosh has been a target for a number of destructive viruses. The following are some of the more common.

9.8.1   SCORES VIRUS

This parasitic virus increases application file size by 7000 bytes and is RAM based. It attacks only EDS application software which contains the unique programming signatures of ERIC or VULT. These are programs which control MAC word processors and spreadsheets. The virus is not difficult to detect as it changes the shape of the notepad and scrapbook icons displaying them as 'dog-eared'.

The Scores virus is thought to have attacked a number of US federal agencies, although some suspected victims have been reluctant to confirm the virus' presence.

9.8.2   FREEHAND VIRUS

This relatively harmless virus first appeared to Macintosh users in the US, Canada, Italy, Belgium and France on 2 March 1988 which was the first birthday of the Mac II computer. When users booted their systems the message in Figure 9.4 was displayed.

**Richard Brandow, Publisher of MacMag, and its entire staff
would like to take this opportunity to convey their
Universal Message of World Peace
to all Macintosh users around the world**

Figure 9.4   The message from the Freehand virus

The virus did not destroy data or programs, but some users complained that it caused the system to crash and that some programs would not run with the virus present in the computer.

Mr Brandow, referred to in the diagram above, said that he wrote the virus to show how easy it was to infect the Mac. He is said to belong to a religious group called the 'Church of the Sub-Genius' and wrote the virus to spread the message of good will.

Importation of the virus to the Macintosh was through an infected game supplied from a Compuserve network bulletin board and also through a training disk for the drawing application package Freehand supplied by the well known software house Aldus. The Freehand package was infected when Marc Canter, President of MacroMind Inc, was given a copy of an infected game program in Canada called Mr Potato Head. MacroMind make training diskettes for Aldus. Canter loaded the game program causing the computer to be infected and then went on to work with Freehand. As a result he infected a floppy disk containing Freehand that was delivered to Aldus and was subsequently distributed to customers.

9.8.3 NVIR

This virus places nVIR resources in the system file which contains all applications and the main operating system. The system file is mainly a series of initialising resources. As the virus is initiated a beep is heard when an application is opened and if using MacinTalk 'Don't Panic' is broadcast. Files then start to disappear. nVIR is very virulent and can infect all programs within an infected system in minutes. It was originally distributed at MACWORLD EXPO in San Francisco by two one-person companies on demo diskettes.

9.9 VIRUSES IN THE NETWORK ENVIRONMENT

There are many types and sizes of networks ranging from relatively small Local Area Networks (LANS) to large sophisticated configurations spanning long distances referred to as Wide Area Networks (WANs).

A typical LAN is an office based system serving a number of PCs, Macintoshes or stand-alone workstations. In addition to each user's machine there is usually a file server which may be a PC dedicated to providing information services on the network. It is clear therefore that a virus has the opportunity to attack a number of personal computers as well as the file server and so the LAN environment provides a free rein to attach all machines in the LAN community. How much damage a virus can ultimately do is largely a function of the controls applied to the LAN.

Whilst the general nature of LANs is one of open architecture which could be seen to encourage attack, network software such as Novell's NetWare and SFT NetWare has a good set of security features which can reduce the risk. When selecting the type of network to install in conjunction with virus attack, a hierarchical system provides more possibility for control. For example, a star network requires any two PCs that wish to transfer information to pass through the file server in the centre of the network. This means that virus controls only need to check between the file server and one PC and there is no immediate way to spread to other PCs on the network. On a bus or ring network it can be the responsibility of each node of the network to establish the bona fides of the other nodes with which it wishes to transfer information and thus there is greater scope for a virus attack.

In addition to password and login controls, the file server should have a good set of file access controls, giving access only to limited, defined sets of data. By reducing the scope for data access means that a virus has to do more work in order to exploit any trap doors in order to be effective.

9.9.1 ELECTRONIC MAIL SYSTEMS

Both dedicated electronic mail systems and applications available on networks are particularly susceptible to virus attack, due primarily to the free and open environment which support them. Electronic mail may sometimes come from any source worldwide and it is unreasonable to expect users to necessarily know the source of a message. Therefore protection is generally provided by placing the electronic mail system in an entirely separate environment to all other applications. When mail arrives for a user it will be written to his/her mail folder, thus restricting the possibility of a virus attaching itself to the electronic mail sub-system and the mail folder. This does, however still leave two areas of weakness. Firstly a user must get into the mail system and so it cannot be entirely isolated within the computer, thus exposing the user/mail interface to possible attack. For example, a virus program may be copied into a user's mail folder without him/her knowing, and on opening the file to discover the contents, damage can be done and infection can be spread. Secondly there could be a flaw in the mail system itself which allows a virus writer to break out of the restrictions applied to the system and wreak havoc on the rest of the system.

9.9.2 THE CHRISTMAS VIRUS

This is a popular example of a network virus that hit IBM's worldwide MVS computer network on 11 December 1987. The virus was in the electronic mail system as a Christmas card and as can be seen in Figure 9.5 contained a picture of a Christmas tree composed of rows of asterisks.

Figure 9.5   The Christmas virus message screen

When a user typed 'Christmas' the virus code was triggered and copies of the virus program were sent to every name and address on the user's mail directory file. The recipients, when they read the message and typed "Christmas" caused the virus to duplicate and be sent to all the names and addresses on their respective distribution lists. This resulted in a worldwide network lock up and affected IBM offices across the US and around the world. The virus affected 250,000 users and resulted in 2 hours of E-Mail down time. It was eventually traced to a West German law student at the University of Clausthal-Zellerfield who had created it as a seasonal prank. He had wanted to send Christmas greetings to his friends within the University, but did not realise that the University E-Mail system was part of EARN - the European Academic Research Network - which in turn connects with BITNET in North America, which is the gateway to the

IBM E-Mail network, VNet. Fortunately for IBM the Christmas virus did not destroy any programs or data. However it is on record as having replicated one million times in a few days. If the downtime per user was 2 hours and there were initially 50,000 users, and the cost of downtime was $20 per hour, the damage in financial terms would be $2 million. Assuming the same figures for EARN and BITNET, the total loss could be around $6 million which goes to prove just how costly a virus attack can be.

9.10   PREVENTING AND CURING A VIRUS ATTACK

Prevention is better than cure with electronic diseases in the same way as with biological ones, so it is wise to take steps to safeguard computers from infection in the first place.

The most fundamental precaution is to limit physical access to a machine so that unauthorised users cannot tamper with the system. In the case of floppy disks the simplest form of protection is to place write protect tabs on all program disks so that any attempt by a virus to write to the disk would result in an error message. It should be remembered, however, that even the simple act of inserting a floppy disk and getting a directory listing can be enough to infect a machine. Whilst write-protect facilities are generally not available for hard disks, hardware products have started to appear on the market offering users the ability to write-protect hard disks, but as they are expensive they are not likely to become widely used. Software products to write-protect hard disks are also available, but these of course can be circumvented by the virus. In the network arena, the popularity of diskless workstations is increasing. By their very nature, these devices make virus infection of the system more difficult, thereby enhancing security.

Programs that prevent virus attack are usually TSR programs that monitor systems activity and watch out for characteristic viral replication activities. They check all disk reads and writes and generate a warning message when potential viral activities are attempted. This includes actions such as writes to executable programs, systems device drivers and the boot sector. The problem with these programs is that they are generally not able to distinguish between valid write requests and an invalid request. The result can be a large number of messages leading users to eventually ignore the warnings, with the risk that a genuine virus attempt to overwrite a disk file would also be ignored. This type of protection has the advantage of stopping viruses before they get the chance to enter a system, but as time goes on and virus programs become more sophisticated, new versions are written to overcome the protection programs.

Another approach are anti-viral programs that help identify already infected systems. These must first be installed on a clean system and they work by periodically checking key information such as date stamps, file sizes and check-sums on the system disks, looking for changes that would indicate a virus has infected the system.

Both the above types of program are generically referred to as vaccines. Suppliers of vaccine software admit that their products are only effective against known viruses and will most likely lag one step behind the most recent virus strains. Not only are newer versions of a virus likely to be more resistant to existing vaccines, they are also likely to be more difficult to trace due to increased complexity.

Although names have been given to some of the more popular viruses, it is certain that different program structures exist for different versions of a virus. For example anyone with the appropriate technical expertise could take a copy of the Brain virus and modify the code so that existing anti-Brain virus software would be useless.

The results of an evaluation show that very few anti-viral products on the market actually offer a comprehensive level of protection. About 40% will only report on virus damage to programs or data files after the event. Furthermore, those viruses that do not create detectable files such as the Pakistan Brain, are only detected by a few.

The following are examples of some of the anti-viral products currently available.

9.11   DR SOLOMON'S ANTI-VIRUS TOOLKIT

This high quality anti-virus product accurately identifies whether a virus is present, and in the majority of cases will report which one is the culprit. It then allows the user to vaccinate the computer against the virus, either by obliterating the code or immunising the data and programs against infection.

Early versions of the package contained a number of different programs to deal with different aspects of viruses. For example FINDVIRU located the common viruses by identifying the viral signatures in programs, SHERLOCK, HOLMES and WATSON identified changes made to software and the operating system etc.

The more recent versions have improved upon this situation by controlling the entire operation through menus. All programs and tasks can be executed through the menu structure, which allows inexperienced users to make the most of this sophisticated product.

Version 3.5 of the toolkit was very widely distributed, and can be executed from either hard or floppy disk. Once running, it produces the display shown in Figure 9.6.

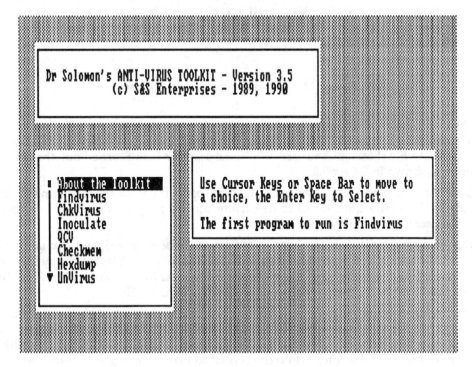

Figure 9.6   Anti-Virus Toolkit opening menu

The required command is highlighted and the Enter key pressed to activate the appropriate program. Note that the window to the right of the menu options gives further information on the currently selected command.

The option most often used is FindVirus. This is a general program that attempts to detect the presence of over 140 different viruses, by looking for signatures etc. Figure 9.7 shows the opening display for FindVirus.

```
Integrity checking A:\FINDVIRU.EXE ... is ok.
Findvirus version 6.21 - locates computer viruses.
Copyright (c) 1988 to 1990 S & S Enterprises.
Includes Boot Sector Viruses: 2730,  Ashar, Brain (7), Ogre(2), EDV,
Den Zuk (6), Den Zuk I, Italian (3), Nichols, Pentagon, AJH
Stoned (5), Big Italian, Typo, Yale (8), Print Screen and Twelve Tricks.


and file viruses Lehigh (2), 405, Vienna (8), Icelandic (4), 1260,
Suriv1, Suriv2, Suriv3, Datacrime (2), Cascade (6), June 16th, AIDS,
Jerusalem (12), Fu Manchu, Traceback (2), Datacrime II, VP, 4096, V2000,
Virus-B (2), Syslock (2), Mix (2), Vacsina (7), Dark Avenger, Virus-90,
Virdem, Fumble, Alabama, Ghostballs, Yankee Doodle (9), Halochen, Dbase,
W13 (2), Lisbon, Oropax, Perfume, Sylvia, Zero Bug, Saturday 14th, Taiwan,
Tenbytes, Sunday, Stupid, Vcomm, Eddie 2, Twelve Tricks, Devil's Dance,
Number Of The Beast, December 24th, Pixel (3), Eight Tunes, Yankee(2)


Including all variants of these (Radai list), a total of 142 viruses.
To keep this list up-to-date, be sure to send off the registration card.
Which drive to examine?
```

Figure 9.7   FindVirus opening display

The user is prompted to specify where to search, what to search for etc, and then the actual searching is started. This can take a considerable time, as the program actually searches each file chosen by the user. Whilst the search is being carried out, the display appears as shown in Figure 9.8.

Once the search has been completed, a short report is displayed to summarise the results, as shown in Figure 9.9. Of course, if any infected programs or files are detected, then the user is immediately alerted.

The remaining options in the menu allow viruses to be removed, and also allow the system to be immunised against future attack. The Toolkit also offers a memory checker, that shows how the memory of the system is being used by various applications. The report produced by the memory checker is shown in Figure 9.10.

Later releases of the Anti-Virus Toolkit incorporate even more sophisticated search techniques to detect the most recent viruses. An innovative method of producing updates is used, in which the user is faxed with the signature data for any new viruses which appear. This data can be entered into the Toolkit so that it can deal with even the most recently discovered viruses.

```
Den Zuk (6), Den Zuk I, Italian (3), Nichols, Pentagon, NJH
Stoned (5), Big Italian, Typo, Yale (8), Print Screen and Twelve Tricks.


and file viruses Lehigh (2), 405, Vienna (8), Icelandic (4), 1260,
Suriv1, Suriv2, Suriv3, Datacrime (2), Cascade (6), June 16th, AIDS,
Jerusalem (12), Fu Manchu, Traceback (2), Datacrime II, VP, 4096, V2000,
Virus-B (2), Syslock (2), Mix (2), Vacsina (7), Dark Avenger, Virus-90,
Virdem, Fumble, Alabama, Ghostballs, Yankee Doodle (9), Halochen, Dbase,
W13 (2), Lisbon, Oropax, Perfume, Sylvia, Zero Bug, Saturday 14th, Taiwan,
Tenbytes, Sunday, Stupid, Vcomm, Eddie 2, Twelve Tricks, Devil's Dance,
Number Of The Beast, December 24th, Pixel (3), Eight Tunes, Yankee(2)


Including all variants of these (Radai list), a total of 142 viruses.
To keep this list up-to-date, be sure to send off the registration card.
Which drive to examine?  c
Output to printer? (Y/N)   n
Do you have a virus, and a string to search for,
that is not in the above list? (Y/N)   n
Check for boot sector viruses? (Y/N)   y
Check for file viruses? (Y/N)   y
Just check executable files? (Y for executables, N for all files)   n
C:\COMMAND.COM ...
```

Figure 9.8   FindVirus search in progress

```
Jerusalem (12), Fu Manchu, Traceback (2), Datacrime II, VP, 4096, V2000,
Virus-B (2), Syslock (2), Mix (2), Vacsina (7), Dark Avenger, Virus-90,
Virdem, Fumble, Alabama, Ghostballs, Yankee Doodle (9), Halochen, Dbase,
W13 (2), Lisbon, Oropax, Perfume, Sylvia, Zero Bug, Saturday 14th, Taiwan,
Tenbytes, Sunday, Stupid, Vcomm, Eddie 2, Twelve Tricks, Devil's Dance,
Number Of The Beast, December 24th, Pixel (3), Eight Tunes, Yankee(2)


Including all variants of these (Radai list), a total of 142 viruses.
To keep this list up-to-date, be sure to send off the registration card.
Which drive to examine?  c
Output to printer? (Y/N)   n
Do you have a virus, and a string to search for,
that is not in the above list? (Y/N)   n
Check for boot sector viruses? (Y/N)   y
Check for file viruses? (Y/N)   y
Just check executable files? (Y for executables, N for all files)   n
3382 files were on the disk.
0 files were not checked.
3382 files were checked and are clean.
0 files appear to have a virus.
No boot sector viruses were found.           ┌─────────────────────┐
No partition sector viruses were found.      │  Press Any Key ...  │
                                             └─────────────────────┘
```

Figure 9.9   FindVirus report produced on completion

```
Copyright (c) 1989 S & S Enterprises.
Integrity checking A:\CHECKMEM.EXE ... is ok.
The BIOS reports that the computer has 640 kb

Memory allocation :
Start   End  Owner    Length  Owner
address addr  ID      bytes

0A32  114A  0008       29056  DOS Kernel
Interrupts controlled: 02 08 0E 1B 29 70 76
114B  121E  114B        3376  COMMAND.COM
Interrupts controlled: 2E
121F  1222  0000          48  Free memory
1223  122E  114B         176  Environment
122F  123A  123B         176  C:\KEYB.COM prefix
123B  13C9  123B        6368  C:\KEYB.COM
Interrupts controlled: 09 2F
13CA  13D6  13D7         192  C:\MOUSE.COM prefix
13D7  15AA  13D7        7472  C:\MOUSE.COM prefix
Interrupts controlled: 0B 10 33
15AB  15B7  15B8         192  C:\PZP\PZP.COM prefix
15B8  2068  15B8       43776  0 prefix
Interrupts controlled: 05 1C 21
2069  2075  2076         192  A:\TOOLKIT.EXE prefix
Press a key to continue.
```

Figure 9.10   Toolkit memory checking utility

A number of utility programs are included in the package including a low level disk read routine, an undelete program, and a hard disk write-protect program, all of which can be used in the detection, analysis, immunisation and prevention of virus attack.

9.12 NORTON UTILITIES

The Norton Utilities package has included an elementary virus detector since version 4.5. It is provided in the form of a batch file that uses the TextSearch utility to look for the characteristic signature of the Vienna virus.

The signature of a virus is the special piece of text, or the collection of numeric values, that the virus looks for to determine whether or not a file has been infected. For Vienna, the signature is the following sequence of hexadecimal values:

CD 21 EB 65 90 B4 3F

A batch file then uses the TextSearch utility to locate any infected files. For Vienna, the infected files can be recognised as they also contain a signature, although the values are different:

EA F0 FF 00 F0

The batch file does not attempt to delete or inoculate the infected files, but just returns the file names that are suspect. It is then up to the user to take the appropriate action to remove the threat.

This technique can be used for any virus that has a signature, which currently means most viruses that have been detected. The only part of the file that needs to be changed is the actual text of the signature, which can be entered in ASCII, or in hexadecimal using NU.

Figure 9.11 below shows the display when the virus checker is operating.

WARNING !!!

VIRUS DETECTION IN PROGRESS

UNEP has been badly infected with what is known as the "Vienna" virus. All MS-DOS computers are susceptible. A search is now being conducted for any instances of carrier or injured files. All carrier or injured files should be deleted and replaced with new versions.

Searching for Carrier Files

TS-Text Search, Advanced Edition 4.50, (C) Copr 1987-88, Peter Norton

Searching contents of files

Searching C:\DOS\chkdsk.com

Figure 9.11   NU virus detection utility

9.13   ASP

This is a menu driven program that uses checksums to detect the spread of viruses and restricts access to the machine by fencing it off with a password and pass number. A simple install command copies ASP to the hard disk. A checksum for the ASP disk is also transferred as part of this process, to check that the act of installation has not infected the ASP program itself. After installation it is necessary to delete the ASP checksum in order that all the COM and EXE files on the hard disk can be registered. The system works by presenting a menu of all the programs in the current directory. The user runs a program by selecting from the directory at which point ASP checks the program checksum with the one stored and if it has altered a prompt will be displayed requesting whether the program should be run, whether the checksum table should be updated or whether the operation should be rejected.

After running the program a further test can be performed so that if a TSR virus has been installed, the amount of free memory will have been reduced and ASP notes and reports such a change. A further check looks at the table of interrupt vectors. If the vectors have changed they can be corrected at this stage, but otherwise ASP will report that the system is still suspect. It will also check the boot sector.

9.14   VIRUSEEK

Viruseek is one of many third-party virus detectors available from smaller companies. Viruseek is very quick in operation, and checks as many executable files as it can find for the presence of a few virus signatures. The display produced by Viruseek is shown in Figure 9.12.

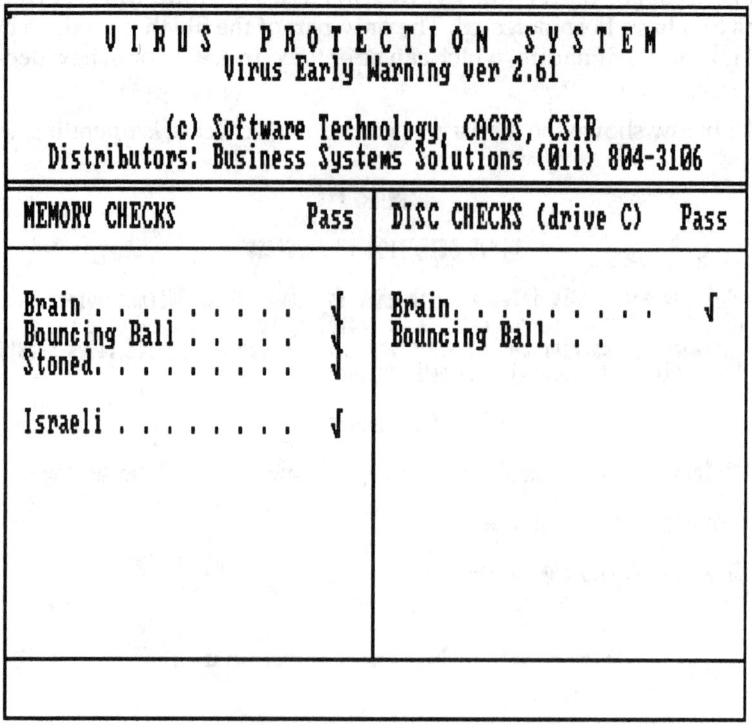

```
┌─────────────────────────────────────────────────────┐
│        V I R U S   P R O T E C T I O N   S Y S T E M  │
│            Virus Early Warning ver 2.61               │
│                                                       │
│            (c) Software Technology, CACDS, CSIR       │
│        Distributors: Business Systems Solutions (011) 804-3106 │
├─────────────────────────────┬───────────────────────┤
│ MEMORY CHECKS        Pass   │ DISC CHECKS (drive C)  Pass │
├─────────────────────────────┼───────────────────────┤
│                             │                        │
│ Brain . . . . . . . . :   √ │ Brain. . . . . . . .   √ │
│ Bouncing Ball : : : : :   √ │ Bouncing Ball. . .     │
│ Stoned. . . . . . . . .   √ │                        │
│                             │                        │
│ Israeli . . . . . . . .   √ │                        │
│                             │                        │
│                             │                        │
│                             │                        │
└─────────────────────────────┴───────────────────────┘
```

Figure 9.12   Viruseek display

9.15   PACKAGE COMPARISONS

The packages cited here are only three examples of the hundreds of anti-virus programs that have now invaded the market. The fact that there are so many packages available means that the task of choosing the most appropriate product for a particular situation can be very long-winded. However, it is worth bearing in mind that products such as *Dr Solomon's Anti-Virus Toolkit* and *Symantec/Norton Anti-Virus* are generally considered to be the most reliable and easiest to use for every day virus checking and removal. Other products are not without their benefits though; many of them concentrate of particular operating environments, or specialise on certain aspects of virus prevention.

The following list outlines some of the key features that are found in many of the anti-virus products that are available.

– Many anti-virus products have built in self-checks that are performed every time the user attempts to run the program. These self checks attempt to determine whether the anti-virus program itself has been infected by a virus, as such a situation could lead to serious problems. If the program has been infected then a warning will be displayed on screen, and the program will terminate. Various techniques are used for this purpose, including mathematical checksums and CRCs and encrypted textual signatures.

– Some systems require the user to supply a list of filenames, sizes and types when they are first installed. This is then used to monitor any changes that may be made.

The production of such a list is time consuming, and is therefore not performed in many cases. The majority of packages will produce the list automatically, although they will still offer the user the chance to edit or modify it as required.

– Some of the more advanced systems will maintain a complete log showing exactly what changes were made to the data, what programs made those changes and what the changes involved. Obviously such a log can grow to an immense size, but it is of great value if the system is later found to be infected as it can be used to identify the location of any corrupted data.

– Almost every package uses virus signatures in an attempt to identify an infected system. Some packages limit themselves in terms of which signatures they look for, which means that some modern viruses may be missed. It is worth noting that there are in excess of 600 individual viruses that have been found to attack systems, each of which may have its own unique signature!

– Checksums can be maintained for program and data files on the disk, and these can be periodically checked to see if the data has been altered in any way. However, this will alert the user to the presence of a virus only after it has infected the system, possibly damaging a significant amount of data.

– Many packages monitor the system interrupts. As explained previously, it is through the use of interrupts that the virus gains control of the system. However, to do this it must modify the interrupt vectors, and these changes can be noted by special software.

– Most packages allow certain areas of the disk to be write-protected. If an attempt is made to write to one of these areas, a warning is displayed on screen and the user prompted to decide whether or not the change should be allowed. However, as with all software write-protect schemes, they can be circumvented by the virus.

– Some systems are extremely limited. Thus it is important to ascertain the limitations of each system under consideration to determine if it is suitable for the desired situation. Limitations may be in the form of disk drive numbers, disk drive types or sizes, processor speeds, DOS versions, applications software etc.

– The way in which detection is performed can also vary substantially. Some systems only perform test routines when the system is first booted, whilst others become memory resident and check the system constantly. Others check the system at irregular intervals so as not to degrade system performance excessively. Almost all can be invoked on demand by the user.

9.16 PC VIRUS COUNTERMEASURES

The following recommendations will, if followed, minimise the risk of becoming a victim of a virus attack. Of course, in a realistic situation it is not always possible, or indeed practical, to follow all these steps to the letter. They do however draw attention to the danger areas.

– **Use standalone PCs**
  As mentioned previously networks, if not properly controlled, leave themselves open to easier infection than a standalone PC, the security for which can be more easily monitored.

- **Avoid the use of modems**
  As viruses can be passed through electronic mail, bulletin boards and other communications software, the avoidance of modems will make this sort of infection more difficult.

- **Ensure that your computer and software are only used by you**
  This is often a very hard condition to meet and the term 'you' will invariably mean you and your secretary/partner/clerk etc. However, try to minimise the number of people using a particular computer. If the system becomes infected with a virus it is then easier to determine the original source, and hence which other systems may be affected.

- **Prevent others from accessing your computer and software**
  The use of passwords and user identification can make it more difficult for unauthorised personnel to access a computer. Although these steps are commonplace in the networking environment they can be applied to standalone systems as well.

- **Avoid sharing programs or files with others**
  There is a tendency, particularly if a new software package is being evaluated, to install a system on one machine and then to make a copy and pass onto another machine which can give a free ride to a virus. It can be even more difficult where data in concerned as many firms depend on the regular movement of data on floppy disks from office to office. However, as long as there is no possibility of booting from data diskettes then there is little chance of infection through this media.

- **Avoid using unauthorised copies of proprietary software**
  Many viruses are carried on pirated versions of well-known software products and so users should always ensure that they are using a genuine copy of all packages on the PC. Of course the use of pirated software is strictly illegal, and will put the organisation into a very awkward position should the use of such products be discovered.

- **Exercise care in the use of public domain or shareware software**
  As public domain software is so easily copied and sent from user to user it provides a good vehicle for the transportation of viruses. This is a pity as the shareware market has grown a lot over the past few years offering a wide range of good quality utilities and software packages at very low prices. However, if these programs are obtained from reputable sources who guarantee the software has been checked for viruses with a proprietary product, then the chance of receiving a virus through this route is no greater than with any commercial product.

- **If infected with a virus ensure all infected software, including back-up copies are purged of the virus**
  All to often a virus is eradicated from a system, only to mysteriously return some time later because the user reinstated their system from backups that were already infected. This is one of the key reasons for write-protecting original disks and keeping them in locked storage. If a system becomes infected, the software can then safely be reinstalled. It is also important to inform any other users who could possibly have become infected as a result of using disks or software from an infected machine.

– **Ensure employees use only designated standalone PCs for homework**
  With all the controls possible applied to in-company machines it is equally important to control home computers that personnel might be using which could be infected without their knowing. As games software is a common carrier of viruses the home computer can be a major threat.

– **Avoid using non-certified vaccine software**
  As mentioned above there are now hundreds of anti-virus software packages and some of these are not as reputable as they might be, containing lethal viruses themselves. Beware particularly of free software offered in the classified ads section of magazines or distributed as free gifts.

– **Write protect critical or sensitive files**
  The simplest form of virus protection on floppy disks is to place a write protect tab on the disk. As any virus has to get onto a disk in order to do damage, this simple precaution is almost failsafe. It is more difficult to write-protect hard disks, although this can be done through software (a suitable program is included in recent versions of Norton Utilities and Dr Solomon's Anti Virus Toolkit), or through hardware.

Up-to-date program and file information (Date, Size) should be maintained for master, working and backup copies. This becomes extremely difficult to do manually when working with more than a few files, so an automated system may be more appropriate. As many viruses display themselves by incrementing the size of program files, precautions such as this can help in the detection process if infection is suspected.

9.17 HOW MUCH SHOULD YOU WORRY?

Donn Parker of the Stanford Research Institute in California says that computer viruses are the current crimoid. They have, without doubt, captured the imagination of the press and the resulting myriad of articles have brought the problem to the attention of many computer users.

It does, however, appear that the publicity exaggerates the problem to quite a high degree in that the incidence of virus infection is actually quite low, and for most organisations is far from being a day-to-day occurrence. The problem does seem to be largely confined to the PC environment and as a result users en masse are taking precautions to avoid exposure to viruses.

The inconvenience and indirect cost factors of a virus attack should not be underestimated. Even if a relatively harmless virus invades an organisation the time involved in clearing all affected disks, performing low level formats on hard disks and then reinstating clean versions of all software packages can be considerable. The resulting downtime and loss of productivity to users can add up to a substantial bill.

9.18 SUMMARY

Computer viruses have caught the attention of the media, both at a local level in the computer press, and on a broader level, with many virus occurrences being reported in regional or national television bulletins and newspapers. This has brought the problem to the attention of almost all PC users.

However, in reality, and taking into consideration the number of PCs worldwide, virus attacks are fairly infrequent and can be prevented altogether if a few basic precautions are taken. If such preventative measures are not taken then there is a possibility of serious data loss or corruption from a malicious virus.

It should always be borne in mind that the corruption caused by a virus is much more serious than that caused accidentally. The virus is malicious, and is designed to cause damage, annoyance and inconvenience. For this reason, it is essential to take appropriate steps to ensure that virus attacks never occur.

10 Hardware, Software and Data Security

10.1 INTRODUCTION

The issues of hardware, software and data security are often not considered as an issue that is separate from the security of the main office premises. However, the problems that affect computer systems tend to be very different from those encountered in ordinary security operations. In fact the measures that are required to protect each of these three areas are very different even from one another. Thus it is necessary to separately consider how the hardware can be protected, how the software can be protected and how the data can be protected.

10.1.1 HARDWARE SECURITY

The value and portability of computer systems and peripherals means that they are very attractive for the common thief. Offices in which previously the most valuable item was a typewriter are now having to face the fact that their computer systems are of great value, both financially and in terms of the amount of work that would be required to reinstate them. With computers becoming ever smaller, it is apparent that it is now easier than ever for thieves to steal valuable equipment.

10.1.2 SOFTWARE SECURITY

Software is open to even more threats. It is normally supplied on floppy disks, which are small and easily concealable, thus increasing the chances of their being stolen. Additionally, software can often be copied onto other diskettes which may then be removed. Although this does not prevent the company from using the product, their name can be displayed every time the illegal copy is used, thus creating a possibility of prosecution under the Copyright Act.

10.1.3 DATA SECURITY

Most corporate computer systems, whether they are WANs, LANs or standalone PCs, will contain data vital to the ongoing business of the company. It may be of particular importance to the company itself, such as order processing information, or it may be of interest to other companies, such as design data. In either case, it is important that no unauthorised personnel gain access to the information, as this will allow them to read, copy, modify or destroy it.

Despite the value of hardware, software, and the information held on computer systems, many companies have no formal procedures or safeguards to ensure the security of their systems. This means that hardware and software may be stolen, and data misused, a situation that may produce many undesirable consequences for the organisation concerned.

10.2 PROTECTING THE HARDWARE

Hardware must be protected against theft, either by securing the devices so that they cannot be removed, or by making them unattractive to the thief. To ensure these measures are effective, it is necessary to introduce policies and procedures into the firm which must be followed by all staff. This will reduce the risks and also enable an up-to-date register to be kept of all devices.

The measures that may need to be taken include the following:

– Prominently mark all system boxes, so that they cannot be sold by the thief without considerable effort to disguise their origins. This may be done in two ways:

  • Brand boxes with identification marks, preferably several, including the full name and postcode of the company. These marks should not be easily removable. Soldering irons are effective for marking plastic parts.

  • Spray boxes with permanent paint. Paint is available which is 'graffiti-proof', meaning that it cannot easily be removed or sprayed over. Either the entire system box can be sprayed a particular colour (bright red is popular) or appropriate stencil images can be sprayed to indicate ownership.

– If there is no need to move systems on a regular basis, they can be bolted to the desk on which they are situated. The bolts should go through the case of the computer and through the desk. Thus to remove a PC it will be necessary to dismantle it to a considerable degree, a task which only a dedicated thief is likely to undertake.

– Appoint a PC security supervisor to be responsible for the overall security of hardware and software. They should be vetted to ensure that they are reliable and honest, and should be empowered to have overall control over the placement and usage of all computer systems. Before any system may be altered or moved, express permission must be obtained from the supervisor.

– Each departmental head should be made responsible for the equipment used within their department. They should report directly to the PC security supervisor. This policy will have the effect of making management take an interest in what equipment is in use, where it is and who is using it. This may produce additional benefits in that these observations will reveal if any systems are extraneous, or if further systems are required.

– Create an asset register, detailing each machine, its location, its most regular users and any other appropriate details. If any changes are made to the machine specification, or if a machine is moved to a new location, the new details should be recorded immediately in the register.

– Laptop computers and portables should be treated with special care. Their use should be limited to senior management, or if necessary, a few individuals whose work requires them. The user of each system should be responsible for its security.

If these measures are implemented, then there should be a minimal risk of computer systems being misplaced or stolen. It should be remembered that these procedures should be followed in addition to the standard security techniques that should be implemented in any modern organisation.

10.3 PROTECTING THE SOFTWARE

As stated before, the threats to software are considerably more complex than those facing the hardware. The two most common problems are that the original disks for a software product are stolen or misplaced, or that the software is illegally copied.

The initial problem of software being stolen can be overcome by ensuring that the original disks are locked in a strongroom after the product has been installed onto the hard disk of the appropriate machine. The PC security supervisor should be responsible for the safe keeping of these disks, and should be the only person to handle them from the time they are purchased. This ensures that the location of the software is known at all times. However, further measures can be taken to minimise the risks:

- Disks can be tagged with special labels, similar to those used within clothing in department stores. These labels are used in conjunction with detectors at all exits to the building. If one of the disks with a special label is carried through a detector, an alarm is triggered. As these labels are quite small, they can be hidden under a standard disk label.

- An asset register should be kept to detail all software owned by the company. This is treated in the same way as the hardware register. This is also of use in determining whether the company is using any unauthorised copies of software.

- The problem of preventing unauthorised duplication can become very complex, and the effective solutions vary between organisations, depending largely on the usage of the computer systems.

- Some security products offer a facility to prevent programs from being copied (see later section), but this can often be overcome by a determined programmer.

- If original system disks are kept in a safe place then the only way that software can be duplicated is by copying it from the hard disk of a system to a floppy. An obvious way of preventing this is to make all systems into hard-disk only installations. This is particularly easy where a network is involved, as new software can be loaded onto the server which can be situated in a secure room. However, with standalone PCs, it will be necessary to plug in a floppy disk drive to load new software or data.

Note that once programs have been copied onto floppies that are not tagged, it is impossible to detect their removal from the premises. Thus in the case of preventing software theft, prevention is not just better than cure, it is the only effective measure that can be taken.

A UK based organisation offering advice and help in preventing the unauthorised duplication of software is FAST, the Federation Against Software Theft. They can be contacted at 2 Lake End Court, Taplow, Maidenhead, Berskshire SL6 0JQ, and are pleased to send information packs to any interested party.

10.4 PROTECTING THE DATA

Data is more valuable to an organisation's competitors than either the hardware or software involved. Data is also essential to the organisation itself, as it ensures the continued success of the business operation. However, computer data is open to misuse, perhaps even more so than hardware and software, due to the fact that it must be made available to the legitimate users of the computer systems.

It sometimes happens that the threat to the computer data comes from an employee, either by accident or maliciously. A solution adopted by many organisations is to include in the employees contract of employment a statement to the effect that all data used in the employees everyday work, and all data produced in conjunction with that work is owned by the company, and that the employee has no legal right to distribute, modify or destroy that data. This does not however prevent the data from harm, it merely seeks to deter the vandal from committing the act. If data is destroyed, then it may be no consolation to the company to know that it can sack the person concerned, it is probably more interested in retrieving the lost information.

To counter these risks, many suppliers have produced devices and programs to improve the security of a computer installation. These range from simple, inexpensive programs requiring the user to enter an identification code and a password before they can use the computer, to sophisticated hardware devices that require a special key to be inserted before the computer will boot up. The latest devices use *biometric* techniques, ie the measurement of biological data. These systems use a variety of methods for identification of the user, including fingerprints, signatures, hand geometry and voice recognition. There are even some highly advanced systems that scan the vein pattern on the retina. Some systems do not restrict access to the machine, but rather restrict access to the data. This is most commonly achieved by *encrypting, encoding,* or *scrambling* the data before it is written to the disk. All of these terms have the same basic meaning – that the information is re-written in a different form so that it would appear meaningless to the casual reader. The data can only be translated back to a usable form by supplying the program with the same code with which it was originally encrypted.

10.5 ANALYSING REQUIREMENTS

Before selecting a security product it is important to determine a variety of factors relating to the use of the system concerned:

- How safe should the system be?
- Is it to be protected against unauthorised access, malicious damage or accidental data corruption or loss?
- How computer literate are the users of the system?
- How many users are likely to require access? Is it just one, or are there several people sharing the same computer?

10.5.1 HOW SAFE SHOULD THE SYSTEM BE?

Initially most organisations feel their systems should be as safe as possible, within a limited budget. This approach can pose problems as there are some products available on the market which not only prevent unauthorised access, but also in some cases prevent legitimate users from gaining access. Therefore it is necessary to determine how important the data is, and just how secure it needs to be made.

Generally speaking, the more sensitive the data, the more secure it needs to be. For example, banks and financial institutions with electronic funds transfer capabilities will require a greater level of security than a word processing department. Similarly, military and government systems will require better security procedures and safeguards than most other systems.

As the system is protected more and more, there will be a greater number of checks and keystrokes required to gain access. All of the correct routines, identification codes and passwords have to be learnt by all users, so implementing a system that is too secure for the chosen application may have the effect of reducing productivity.

It is also important to realise the possibility of data loss due to forgotten passwords. In many cases the systems are so secure that neither the system administrator nor the products supplier will be able to retrieve it if the relevant password or key is lost.

10.5.2   WHAT IS THE SYSTEM TO BE PROTECTED AGAINST?

There are three possible threats to data held on a computer system:

- Unauthorised access
- Malicious damage
- Accidental damage

The majority of security systems protect against unauthorised access, by using a combination of passwords, identification codes, hardware keys, or biometric techniques. Many also protect against malicious damage, by allowing only selected users to write or modify data in a file.

However, few security systems address the problem of accidental damage. One of the more recent additions to this category is the Opus Datasafe. This is a computer system designed with security in mind:

- It has an integral high-security lock, the keys for which are unique to each machine. This lock keeps intruders out of the system box (so it cannot be bypassed) and prevents booting from the A: drive or the hard disk.
- There are sophisticated log-on procedures and password protection facilities supplied with the machine. These cannot be bypassed as the break key is disabled until they have been correctly executed.
- It has two hard disk drives. They are mechanically separate from each other, and one is kept as an exact copy of the other. Thus if one crashes, no data is lost as it can be retrieved from the other.

The Datasafe has very high performance figures for disk-intensive applications, as Opus have rewritten the disk I/O routines. All disk read operations now look at whichever disk has the information most readily available.

10.5.3   HOW COMPUTER LITERATE ARE THE USERS?

The experience of the regular computer users is an important factor when considering security systems. Some offer a menu-type front end from which applications can be selected. These systems are generally much easier to use, prompting for passwords and identification codes etc, before access is permitted. Other systems act only as a shell around DOS, allowing all DOS operations to be carried out as normal once the initial security procedures have been performed. These systems require the user to be more experienced with DOS commands, and may not prompt for passwords and codes, but rather expect the user to enter them automatically. Inexperienced PC users will almost certainly encounter problems when using such systems, problems that may become very serious indeed if file encryption is involved.

The exact choice of system thus depends on how experienced the users are. If they are not familiar with DOS, it may be better to consider a menu based system. If however they are regular computer users with a good knowledge of DOS then a DOS based system may be more suitable.

10.5.4   HOW MANY USERS REQUIRE ACCESS?

Different systems cater for different numbers of users. Some systems allow only a single user to access the data, whilst others can keep passwords and identification codes for unlimited numbers.

If data is being shared among several users, a single user system cannot be implemented, and a more sophisticated multi-user system must be used. However, if the computer is to be used by only one person, then the increased complexity of the multi-user system will be an unnecessary waste of time.

For a single user system, there is a very simple form of security; lock the computer in a strong room when it is not in use. This is particularly relevant to laptops and luggables which can be easily transported, although ordinary PCs can be placed on a movable trolley to make transport easier.

10.6   LEGAL REQUIREMENTS

Data held on a computer system is subject to the Data Protection Act (1987). This states that companies are required to take steps to prevent information held on a computer from falling into the wrong hands. Individuals can claim compensation from companies who allow leaks to occur.

The Act states that *'Appropriate security measures shall be taken against unauthorised access to, or alteration, disclosure or destruction of personal data, and against accidental loss or destruction of personal data.'* The company holding the data is solely responsible for taking appropriate steps to prevent unauthorised access. In the event of a leak, the company must be able to show that it took reasonable measures to prevent a breach of security. Furthermore, security should be at a level appropriate to the information. For example, details of bank accounts should be more secure than details of magazine subscriptions.

The Act also says that it is not sufficient to have password protection on its own. Rather, it is necessary to have different levels of access for different staff. Companies must also take suitable backup measures to ensure that data is not lost. Any data that is no longer required should be disposed of properly, so that it cannot be retrieved.

Although the above statements tend to indicate that software and hardware are of fundamental importance, it is also necessary to protect the area in which the data is located. This may be achieved with entry restrictions to the computer room, and by taking steps to minimise the risk of burglary. Employees using the data should be vetted to ensure that they are reliable and honest. All data processing personnel should be properly trained to know their responsibilities and the procedures that they must follow.

If the above measures are not taken, then the company may be considered to be in breach of the Data Protection Act. Any loss, distress or embarrassment caused to an individual by a data leak from the company will render them liable for compensation, as well as open to prosecution. Note that none of these restrictions currently apply to information held on paper.

10.7   SECURITY METHODS

Security systems can be software or hardware based.

10.7.1   SOFTWARE SYSTEMS

Original security products simply prevented the user from gaining direct access to DOS by routing all commands through their own programs. These could be circumvented by interrupting installation at boot-up time, booting from the A: drive or otherwise escaping from the program shell.

More recent products attack the problem in a different way, by re-writing sections of the system area on the hard disk. Thus it is no longer possible to bypass the system as all requests to access the disk must be routed through these areas. This form of control is offered in several forms, either as standalone software security systems, or as a built in part of an operating system. For example, DR-DOS allows passwords to be set for individual files and directories to prevent unauthorised access. However, even these methods can be bypassed by using absolute disk control routines from the A: drive.

The most secure form of software protection is to encrypt the entire contents of the hard disk. Thus although information can be read from the disk, it is meaningless unless it is first decoded. This of course requires the user to know the appropriate encryption key. Software systems lose out in this area as the routines used for the encryption of data can be extremely long-winded and time consuming, which means that system performance for all disk accesses is extremely poor, irrespective of the speed of the disk drive.

10.7.2   HARDWARE SYSTEMS

Hardware systems are not necessarily more expensive than software systems, and generally offer greater protection. They often take the form of plug-in boards that occupy a standard expansion slot or ROM chips that fit directly into sockets on the motherboard. These systems intervene as soon as the system is powered up, before DOS can boot.

The normal form of protection is for the system to ask for a user name and password before allowing access. Hardware systems are obviously only effective if access to the system box is restricted, to prevent removal of the board or chips.

Hardware systems that scramble the hard disk offer the greatest protection. The encryption routines are often stored in the form of ROM chips, which allow them to be executed at great speed. These systems ensure that the computer remains secure even if the board or chips are removed as the data cannot be unscrambled.

Many hardware devices support the use of *tokens* or *keys* as identification. The system cannot be accessed until the correct token or key is inserted into a special device.

Therefore users must have their own key or token to gain access to the computer. These keys and tokens take many forms, including credit-card style items, small plastic keys and electronic devices that supply a special code sequence. Most token based systems will also require the user to enter a password, to guarantee that the user is genuine.

It is important to consider how easily additional keys can be obtained, and how much they will cost. If the keys are unique to each client then the supplier may charge a high price for replacements. if not, then users of similar systems may be able to gain access by using their own keys.

10.8 SELECTING A SYSTEM

Once the requirements have been analysed, the security system can be chosen. There are many different systems on the market, of which 7 are examined below. When approaching each system, the following features should considered:

10.8.1 AUDIT LOG AND FILTER

Some products can be configured to collect information about usage or attempted usage of the PC. The Audit facility provides statistics on each user or on the PC as a whole. It can also highlight attempted security violations. This information is stored in the audit log, normally in the form of a file on disk. This can quickly grow very large, meaning that the task of examining the log becomes extremely time consuming. The Filter is designed to extract certain information matching chosen criteria, so that it is much easier to examine the log. These criteria may include specified time periods, user names or event types.

10.8.2 ENCRYPTION

Data can be encrypted either to a known and officially sanctioned standard, such as DES, or by a proprietary algorithm. The first method is generally much more secure, and is guaranteed to be recoverable. The latter method relies heavily on the quality of the product, as the data is at the mercy of the supplier. If something goes wrong with the program then it may not be possible to decode the information.

It should be remembered that a standard such as DES has no known general decryption solution. Thus if a password is forgotten then there is absolutely no way that the data can be recovered.

10.8.3 TIME-SLOTTING

It is often useful to be able to limit access for some users to particular times of the day, such as when supervision is available. Some packages allow several different time-slots to be created for each user, possibly with different times for different days of the week.

10.8.4 MAXIMUM ACCESS ATTEMPTS

Attempted security violations often show themselves in the form of a number of tries at logging on under the same identification code. Some packages allow the maximum number of tries to be limited, and access denied when this limit is exceeded. The identification code cannot then be used until it is reset by the system administrator.

This effectively thwarts one of the most common techniques for breaching security, in which a computer is used to generate every possible password combination for a given account. To do this manually would take years, but a computer could produce all possible combinations in hours. However, the computer would need to attempt to login many thousands of times to be successful, and so can be prevented by the above technique.

10.8.5 TIMEOUT

Users who forget to log out or who leave their machines unattended while they go for a cup of coffee provide the perfect opportunity for unauthorised access. Therefore, many programs automatically lock the keyboard after a specified period of inactivity. The system is reset normally by entering the user's password.

10.8.6 MAXIMUM USERS

As discussed above, different products allow different numbers of users. Always choose the product allowing the maximum number of users that is likely to occur in the future.

10.8.7 GROUPS

Users can be categorised into groups or project teams to allow access rights to be quickly assigned. This also helps with analysing system usage or collating billing information.

10.8.8 SECURE DELETION

The DOS DELETE command simply marks the space used by a file as re-usable, it does not overwrite the data. When the legal obligations of the company are remembered, it will be realised that this is not satisfactory as the data can be retrieved with any good utility program. Therefore several programs offer a secure delete facility, whereby the data is overwritten so that it cannot be retrieved.

10.8.9 EXECUTE PROTECTION

All versions of DOS prior to 3.0 required program files to have read access before they could be executed. However, since DOS 3.0 was introduced, programs can be executed without this, and some products exploit this to prevent illegal copies of the software to be made. This allows users to run the programs, but not copy them.

Unfortunately there are many applications which need to have read access to their own program files, so that they can perform the appropriate copy-protection routines for example. Programs such as these cannot be protected using this technique as they will fail to operate.

10.8.10 OTHER FACTORS TO CONSIDER

There are a great number of security systems currently available, the majority of which offer many of the above features. Figure 10.1 indicates the facilities offered by some of the more popular security products. Unfortunately there seems to be little or no correlation between price and quality, so opting for the most expensive system will not necessarily provide the best protection. The situation is made even more difficult by the fact that most users will be unable to determine whether or not a system is actually secure, as the process of circumventing these products requires great technical knowledge and often an even greater amount of time and effort. Thus the task of choosing between the most appropriate systems is not an easy one.

	Kinetic Access II	PC Boot	PC-Guard	Protec	Stoplock IV	Trispan	Triumph
Software	Y	Y	Y	Y	N	Y	Y
Hardware	N	Y	N	N	Y	Y	Y
Number of users	16	10	U/L	52	33	64	8
User ID	Y	Y	Y	Y	Y	Y	Y
Password	Y	Y	Y	Y	Y	Y	Y
Minimum length	5	1	1	1	1	1	1
Case sensitive	N	Y	Y	Y	Y	Y	Y
Number of access attempts allowed	3	V	V	V	V	3	3
Token	N	Y	N	N	N	Y	Y
Boot protect	Y	Y	Y	Y	Y	Y	Y
Independent clock	N	Y	N	N	Y	Y	N
Peripheral control	Y	Y	Y	N	Y	Y	N
Time-slotting	N	Y	N	N	Y	Y	N
Timeout	Y	Y	Y	N	N	Y	Y
DES Encryption	N	N	N	Y	Y	N	N
Proprietary encryption	N	Y	Y	Y	N	Y	Y
Execute protect	Y	Y	Y	Y	Y	Y	Y
Secure delete	N	N	Y	N	Y	Y	Y
Group permissions	N	Y	Y	N	Y	Y	N
Audit trail	Y	Y	Y	Y	Y	Y	Y
Audit filter	Y	N	Y	Y	N	Opt	Opt
Variable lockout time after failed access	Y	Y	Y	Y	Y	Y	Y
PRICE (UK)	£295	£295	£195	£195	£500	£695	£145

U/L – Unlimited
V – May be varied by system administrator

N/A – Not applicable
Opt – Optional

Figure 10.1   Summary of features of 7 security products

Useful advice and reviews can often be found in computer magazines. The articles often determine the overall effectiveness of each system by comparing it directly against its competitors, and subjecting all of the products to rigorous tests. For many organisations this will be the only realistic set of guidelines available.

Once a system has been purchased it should be used on a trial basis first, preferably limited to one or two machines. If problems do occur then the effects will be limited, and can perhaps more easily be reversed. Once the system has proven itself in everyday use on the trial machines then it can be installed onto the remainder of the required systems.

10.9   POLICEMAN

One product not listed in the table is Policeman, from Plus5 products. Policeman is a hardware based security system that offers many of the features considered to be essential in such a product. Policeman is marketed in the UK at around £200, so is priced very competitively.

The Policeman package consists of the following:

- A plug-in option board, containing special security software on ROM
- A special tag reader, which connects to the option board
- 2 special security tags
- System software in 5.25 and 3.5 inch disk formats
- A comprehensive manual

The most astonishing fact that is noticed almost immediately is that Policeman can be installed on almost any personal computer system in under 5 minutes, which includes the time taken to install both hardware and software.

In fact it is not necessary to install the disk software to have the system operational, as all of the necessary access-control routines are written into the ROM on the option board. The disk software simply allows the system to be configured for more users, and provides the other security controls provided by the system.

Once the option board is installed correctly, and the tag reader plugged in, the system can be powered up. Rather than boot up in the traditional way, the option board intercepts the boot process and executes the access control routines. Policeman firstly checks for the presence of a tag in the reader. If it cannot detect one it asks the user to insert a tag and press any key. The user is then prompted for a PIN and a password, which are checked against the valid entries stored in battery-backed up RAM on the option board. Note that each tag is unique, and has a set of unique passwords and PINs associated with it. This means that many users can use the same tag, but have different PINs and passwords to control their use of the system once they have access to it.

The first time the system is used, the PIN 9999 can be used with the password Plus5 to gain access. Needless to say these entries should be deleted (see below) as soon as possible as they work with all tags.

Once the access criteria have been satisfied DOS boots in the normal way, and the presence of Policeman is transparent to the user. In fact the tag can be removed without affecting the system.

However, Policeman is much more than just a rudimentary access control system; this is only its first line of defence. The disk software contains a utility called 999, which can be used to invoke the other features of the product. 999 is menu driven, and produces an opening display as shown in Figure 10.1.

As this utility controls the operation of the system, the user is again prompted for a valid PIN and password. Once these criteria have been satisfied, the menu options are displayed. Selections are made from the menu by highlighting the required option and pressing Enter.

Figure 10.2 shows the selections available under the first menu option, PASSWORD.

These commands control the allocation of passwords for the current tag. Each tag can have up to 13 PINs and passwords associated with it, each of which must be unique. The Delete command should be immediately used to remove the default 9999 PIN and Plus5 password, and the Change command used to add a new PIN/password combination.

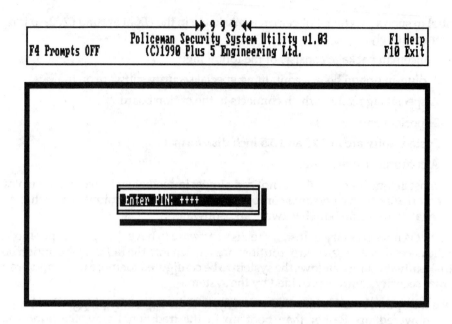

Figure 10.1   Opening display for the 999 utility

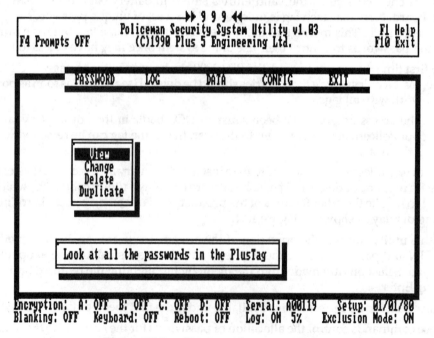

Figure 10.2   Password menu options

The next menu option is Log, and controls the handling of the in-built audit log. The log is held in battery backed up RAM on the option card, although only 128 entries can be contained in this area at once. It is therefore necessary to flush the log to the disk at regular intervals. The commands available for controlling the use of the log are View, Write and Clear.

- View allows the audit log entries to be viewed on screen. These are the entries currently stored in RAM, rather than those previously flushed to disk

- Write causes the entries in the log to be written to a file on disk, so that it can be viewed with a text editor or word processor. There is a utility supplied on disk to do this automatically, and this can be run from AUTOEXEC.BAT if required.

- Clear deletes all memory-resident audit log entries.

Figure 10.3 shows the display produced when the view command is selected.

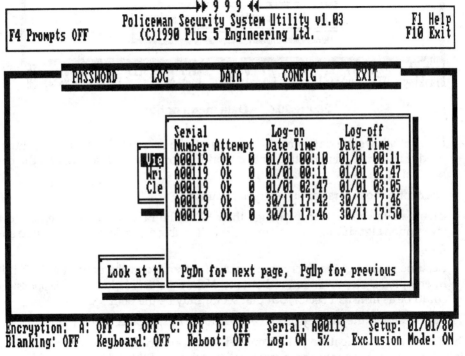

Figure 10.3   Audit Log entries

The next option, Data, controls whether or not the data encryption techniques supplied with Policeman are implemented. The encryption can be limited to any combination of drives A: to D:, and files can be manually encrypted or decrypted at will. The commands available are shown in Figure 10.4, as Drives, Encrypt, Decrypt, Change and Resume.

- Drives is used to specify which drives are to be encrypted. All data that is written to the specified drives will be automatically encrypted, and all data that is read will be decrypted.

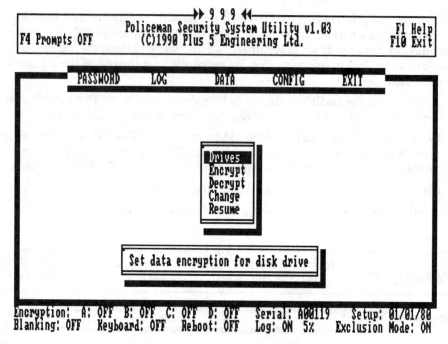

Figure 10.4   Data menu options

- Encrypt allows the data already on a disk to be encrypted. This option must be used if the system is installed onto a working computer, as the data on the drive will not be encrypted to start with.

- Decrypt is the reverse of the encrypt command.

- Change allows the user to change their PIN. The PIN is used as the key to the encryption algorithm, hence changing it will enable some data to be read and some not.

- Resume continues the Encrypt or Decrypt command at the point it left off if it is interrupted by a power cut, re-boot etc. *Note: Data may be lost if this happens.* This could be as little as 1 sector, but that sector may be the boot sector.

Figure 10.5 shows the display produced when the Drives selection is made.

The data encryption feature of Policeman is very powerful, and means that even if a PC is stolen, the data cannot be recovered without the tag, PIN and password. However, it also means that corrupt data cannot be recovered if these are lost or forgotten.

The Config option controls the operation of the system, including how the system reacts when the tag is removed from the reader. As standard, the system is unaffected if this occurs. However, the options in the menu, shown in Figure 10.6 can be used to alter this.

- Screen Blanking causes the screen to be blanked immediately when the tag is removed. This ensures that no information can be read from the display whilst the user is away from the system, but does not affect system operation in any other way. On re-inserting the tag the display will reappear.

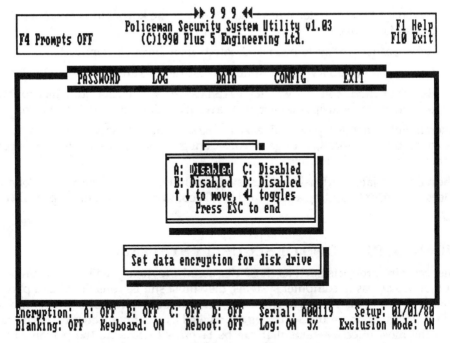

Figure 10.5   Effect of choosing the Drives command

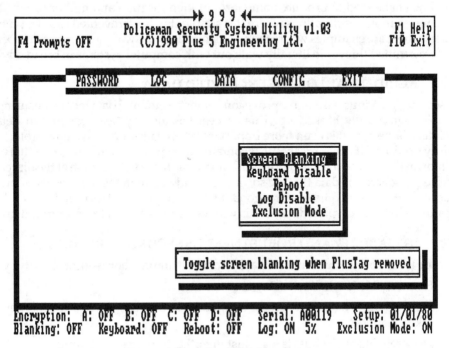

Figure 10.6   Config menu options

- Keyboard Disable determines whether or not the keyboard is operational when the tag is removed.
- Reboot causes the system to be rebooted when the tag is removed.
- Log disable controls whether or not access attempts are recorded in the log.
- Exclusion mode controls which tags can use the system. Selecting this option will prevent all tags except the current one from gaining access to the system.

Overall, Policeman is a powerful, easy to use and effective security system. It is also very competitively priced, especially considering it uses a hardware access control system as well as a software one.

The risks associated with using such systems are however also applicable to Policeman, and loss of a tag, or forgetting a password or PIN could be catastrophic, especially if data encryption is employed.

10.10   RESTRICTIONS OF SECURITY SYSTEMS

Whilst security products such as those discussed previously will help in preventing unauthorised access to computer systems, they must still be considered as a part of an overall security plan. This plan must take into account physical security, including adequate locks on doors and windows etc, as well as computer security. Furthermore, one of the most effective steps that can be taken is to educate the personnel in the organisation on the issues of security.

For example, if an unfamiliar person is seen removing a computer system then they should be challenged to produce some form of identification and authorisation. There are many examples of situations where this simple step has prevented catastrophic loss; similarly there are examples where the astonishing lack of awareness from office personnel has permitted thieves to literally walk out with computer systems in broad daylight.

10.10.1   ACCIDENTAL LOSS OF ENCRYPTED DATA

The security plan must also make provision against accidental data loss by ensuring that valuable data is fully backed up. This process has already been covered in detail in previous chapters, and is even more important when considering systems protected by security products. If a disk crashes that contains encrypted data, it is unlikely that any of the information can be retrieved in a usable format as there will be none of the discernible patterns present in the data that are so valuable and useful in the data recovery process. In fact one of the prerequisites for a good quality encryption algorithm is that it leaves no patterns in the encrypted data, as this will help an attacker in the decryption process.

10.10.2   RELIABILITY AND ROBUSTNESS OF SECURITY PRODUCTS

There are three points which must always be borne in mind when using a security system:

- How reliable is it in day-to-day use?
- How robust is it against natural wear and tear on items such as tokens, keys and token readers?
- How reliable and robust is it against unauthorised access attempts?

The answer to the first two questions is ultimately dependent on the environment in which the product is used. If it is harsh, then it is likely that the life of the product will be severely reduced. In this case it is important to ascertain whether there will be any problems involved in replacing or upgrading the system at a later date. Typical problems may relate to the uniqueness of particular tokens, on-board ROM chips, board serial numbers etc. It may not be possible to easily change to a new device.

The third question is generally of greater importance. If the security controls implemented by the system can be overcome by an intruder then the system is of little use. In actual fact any system which only provides access controls to the data stored on a computer system falls into this category. If it is a hardware system then the boards or chips can be removed. Software measures can be counteracted by rewriting the appropriate system areas on the disk. Thus any security system that works in this way is open to attack.

For this reason, the only secure way to protect data is to encrypt it using an irreversible encryption technique such as DES. This standard was developed for use by the American Military and so is deemed suitable for securing even the most important data.

10.11 SUMMARY

The issues of computer security must be addressed in every organisation, whether the data is essential to the ongoing success of the enterprise or not. Legal requirements alone mean that firms must take appropriate steps to ensure that data is not disclosed to unauthorised personnel.

There are a wide variety of security products available to aid in this task, each offering different levels of facilities. However, even the best of these will not solve the problem on its own. The solution also involves training the users, and adopting security policies within the organisation. A badly installed or misused security system is probably more dangerous than none at all, as there is a distinct possibility that important data will be irretrievably lost.

To ensure that there is as little chance of this as possible, it is important to make regular backups of the information held on hard disks. Even with the best security procedures available, it is of little comfort when the hard disk crashes to know that the data was secured by encryption.

11 Setting Up a Software and Data Safety & Recovery Centre

11.1 ESTABLISHING A DATA RECOVERY CENTRE

The issues of software and data safety are usually beyond the experience of most end-users. Thus to introduce the concepts and techniques from previous chapters into an organisation it will be necessary to set up a centre to deal with such problems. In a large organisation, this can be formed as a part of the existing ISD, adapting the current structure of the department to encompass the new issues. However, smaller organisations may not have a formal ISD, and so the task of setting up a new department is much more challenging.

The following seven step approach provides a comprehensive series of guidelines for not only the creation of a software and data security/recovery centre, but also a more general PC support centre. Any organisation that makes use of personal computers should contain an information centre, even if it only consists of a single member of staff.

11.1.1 CREATE A PC SUPPORT ORGANISATION

The main form of PC support organisation is the information centre. Information centres are set up for the purposes of assisting users obtain the best value from their systems. In larger firms the information centre will include a help desk which will act as a front line troubleshooter. Help desks will often give advice on the phone and thus help individual users find faults and make minor repairs. Similarly help desk staff will often assist users install hardware or software. The duties of data recovery will of course fall to the staff of the information centre. Therefore such personnel will need to be properly trained in appropriate techniques and methods, and will ideally be experienced in solving data recovery problems. In small firms an individual may be designated to be both the information centre and the help desk.

11.1.2 USER TRAINING

In an attempt to minimise the number of calls which the help desk will receive appropriate training should be given to users. Users should attend a training course in hardware and software configuration as well as basic troubleshooting techniques. In addition users may be given checklists which they can use to do preliminary diagnostic work to see if they are experiencing very trivial faults before they call for assistance from the help desk.

11.1.3 DEPARTMENTAL GURUS

In larger firms a technique that is frequently used is the appointment of departmental gurus. A departmental guru is an individual who has a particular interest and aptitude in personal computing and who is prepared to assist his/her colleagues with minor problems as they arrive. Departmental gurus take some of the pressure off the help desk.

11.1.4 PC REGISTERS

In order to assist users, gurus and help desk staff, it is important that the exact nature of each system configuration be known. Therefore PC hardware and software asset registers must be established and continually updated by the support centre. In addition to the asset register, information on who has access to each machine should be held.

11.1.5 TOOLS AND EQUIPMENT

As previously discussed, very few problems can be solved through the use of a single tool. Therefore it is necessary for the information centre to purchase a range of appropriate software tools, including the following:

- A general utilities package such as Norton Utilities, PCTools etc.
- An image copier for floppy disks such as COPYIIPC, CopyWrite etc.
- A virus diagnosis and immunisation package such as Dr Solomon's Toolkit
- A copy of each version of DOS that is in use within the organisation
- A word processor or text editor
- Manufacturers diagnostics software for each computer system.

In addition to these essentials, there are a number of applications which will prove beneficial. The most important of these is a programming language such as Pascal or Basic. There are many good quality programming languages available, the most popular being supplied by Borland and MicroSoft. Communications software may also be useful, as many good shareware programs can be obtained from bulletin boards. Specialised programs such a TestDrive, Disk Explorer will also be beneficial, allowing the information centre staff to tackle advanced problems.

The information centre should also hold the original copies of all software in use throughout the organisation. Thus if an application needs to be reinstalled, it can be done quickly and easily by a member of staff who knows what they are doing.

11.1.6 INSURANCE AND WARRANTY

It is possible that the firm's insurance may not cover accidents to either staff, equipment, and especially data when users attempt to make repairs.

- Personal injuries are very rare when dealing with personal computers, and usually only occur when inexperienced personnel try to repair hardware. However, the inside of a computer system is hazardous, and even the process of installing an option board can prove dangerous.
- Equipment can be damaged more easily; wiring a mains plug the wrong way can prove disastrous, as will dropping hardware while it is being moved. Damage can also be caused when installing devices, especially option cards.

- Data damage is almost certainly excluded from insurance; it is down to the information centre to ensure that no losses occur by maintaining an up to date, effective backup system for all computer in use.

With these points in mind, it is important to ensure that the firm's insurance covers both staff and equipment adequately.

Similar to the issue of insurance is the question of hardware and software warranties which may be nullified if equipment is not handled in the correct manner. Therefore if the equipment is under warranty ensure that nothing is done to put this is jeopardy.

11.1.7   COMMITMENT FROM MANAGEMENT

In order for the previous six issues to be fully addressed as well as funded it is important to obtain the commitment of senior management to the use of personal computers in the firm. Without this the PC support function will not be properly staffed or funded.

11.2   INFORMATION CENTRE SIZE

The number of staff employed in the information centre is always a point of contention. Management generally see the information centre as non-profit making, and so are unwilling to supply any great degree of funding. However, recent research has shown that many information centres are understaffed, with ratios of one support person for every 100 users, or worse. Ideally the ratio should be in the region of 1:50, or better, depending on the experience and ability of the end-users.

Information centre personnel will need to be highly skilled in a wide variety of computer-related applications and topics. Within the department, there should be at least one member of staff who has a detailed knowledge of each application in use within the organisation. As new systems are acquired, relevant members of the information centre should be trained in their use, so that they can immediately offer support to end-users.

Situations will almost certainly be encountered which exceed the abilities of the information centre staff. These are often complex data recovery problems in which a number of factors have contributed to produce a seemingly unsolvable mess. Cases such as this will never be fully resolved, so it is essential to realise that it is necessary to bring in outside help. Consultants from specialised data recovery organisations will have experience of many different situations, and will have a broad knowledge base of possible causes and solutions. Additionally they will have tailor made data recovery tools, and will more than likely be proficient programmers. Thus they are almost guaranteed to succeed in solving the majority of data recovery problems, even those where others have tried and failed.

11.3   SUMMARY

The philosophy that has underpinned all the discussion in this book is that users and internal support staff can save the firm considerable time and cost in undertaking routine data recovery exercises, advising on preventative measures, and providing general support and maintenance. To enable this, they must be backed up by management through the formation of a support centre. Such a department must be provided with appropriate software tools, hardware and training to allow the wide variety of problems to be dealt with effectively and efficiently.

Appendix 1
Glossary

Access control   A routine that is executed when a user attempts to gain access to a computer system, in order to determine whether the user has any right to access the system.

Algorithm   A structured procedure that provides a solution to a problem in a finite number of steps. Algorithms are often the first stage in the design of a computer program.

Application   The system or problem to which a computer can be devoted. It may be of a computational type, in which case it requires mainly arithmetic operations, or of a processing type, in which case data-handling operations predominate.

Application program   An ordered set of computer instructions which allow the computer to carry out its specified tasks.

Assembly language   A hardware dependent, low-level source language for computer programming.

Attribute   A special value that is associated with every file stored on the computer which determines how it should be treated. The attribute may indicate whether the file should be treated as a subdirectory, a volume label, a data file or a system file, and whether it is hidden, backed-up and changeable.

BASIC   Acronym for Beginner's All-purpose Symbolic Instruction Code. It is a high-level programming language using English-like statements. It is one of the simpler programming languages to learn.

Binary   Numeric system implying counting and arithmetic performed in base 2. Binary numbers consist of a stream of 0s and 1s. As 0 and 1 can be easily represented by distinct voltage levels, the vast majority of computers use binary for internal storage, arithmetic and processing.

Bit	Acronym for Binary Digit. A bit can have a value of 0 or 1. Bits are grouped into 4s to form Nybbles, 8s to form Bytes and 16s to form Words.
Boot Sector	A special area of disk that contains assembly language instructions that tell the system how it should operate when it first starts up. The boot sector transfers control to DOS when the code has executed. It also contains information on disk usage.
Bug	An error in a computer program. Most bugs are fixed before the program is released for sale, but there are normally some that elude all attempts to find them. So named after a small insect caused untold havoc when it crept into one of the very early computers developed by Countess Ada Lovelace, one of the computer pioneers.
Byte	A group of 8 bits. The byte is the standard unit of computer storage, and has the ability to represent any decimal value from 0 to 255, or 00h to FFh in hexadecimal.
C	A high-level programming language used extensively for developing commercial application programs and utilities. It is so named because it was the third generation of computer language produced by the designers, the first two being named A and B.
Cluster	The unit of disk storage used by DOS when allocating space to files. All clusters in a given partition are the same size, which will be 1, 2, 4, 8 or 16 logical sectors.
Contiguous	If two or more entities are said to be contiguous then they are adjacent. Thus clusters 1, 2, 3 and 4 are contiguous as there are no gaps, but clusters 5 and 7 are non-contiguous.
Cylinder	A term referring to hard disks, denoting the tracks on each platter that can be accessed by the read/write heads without requiring any movement. Now used interchangeably with the term Track.
Data	A graphic, textual or numeric representation of facts, concepts, numbers, letters or symbols suitable for communication, interpretation and processing by computer.
Decimal	Numeric system implying counting and arithmetic performed in base 10. Decimal numbers consist of digits with values 0 through 9. Decimal is the standard method used by humans when counting and performing arithmetic. However there is no suitable representation that can easily be used by computers.
Decryption	The process of decoding data after it has been encrypted.

	Decryption usually requires the same key or password that was used to encrypt the data originally.
Directory	A list of files, their attributes, sizes and locations on the disk. Directories may also contain subdirectories.
Disk	A circular plate coated with magnetic media on one or both sides. The plate usually rotates around a spindle, and is divided into sectors and tracks to simplify usage.
Disk Sector	A radial division of a disk. On a PC Disk sectors are numbered sequentially from 1 upwards, starting at an arbitrary point.
Diskette	Magnetic storage media comprising a disk of mylar coated on both sides with ferric oxide. The disk is housed in a flexible plastic envelope. Diskettes store upwards of 360K of data.
Encryption	A process used to secure data by transforming it into a sequence of seemingly random characters using a special algorithm. The algorithm relies on a special password or key which must also be used to reverse the procedure.
Extension	A three character suffix applied to filenames. The extension is used by DOS to differentiate between file types.
FAT	File allocation table. A special area of data on a disk defining how the remainder of the storage area is used.
File	A collection of data used as a unit. A file may contain data representing any type of information, from stock lists to correspondence to financial plans. Files may also contain executable program instructions.
Firmware	A piece of software that cannot easily be changed once it is implemented. ROMs and EPROMs are examples of firmware, as once the code has been written to the device it requires hardware techniques to change it.
Floppy Disk	See diskette
Fragmentation	Situation whereby the clusters allocated to files are non-contiguous.
Gulp	A term that has only recently come into use, used to describe a collection of 4 or more bytes (ie two or more words). Not yet common.
Hard disk	Term applied to non-removable storage media commonly encountered in PCs. The device consists of one or more disks made of metal, coated with ferric oxide. The disks revolve around a central spindle.

Hardware	The physical components of a computer system, including all electronic and electromechanical devices as well as the connections between them.
Hex	Abbreviation for hexadecimal
Hexadecimal	Numeric system implying counting and arithmetic performed in base 16. Hexadecimal numbers consist of the digits 0 to 9, and the letters A through F. Hexadecimal provides a happy medium between the computer oriented Binary counting system and the human oriented Decimal counting system.
High-level language	A computer programming language that uses English-like statements for instructions.
Index hole	A small circular hole punched in the surface of a floppy disk denoting the position of the first sector on the disk.
Interrupt	A special signal generated by a program or component of the computer when it requires attention from the CPU.
Logical Sector	The unit of disk storage seen by the operating system. A logical sector may consist of 1, 2, 4 or 8 physical sectors.
Low-level language	Term used to describe primitive computer programming languages, often which have a 1-to-1 relationship with machine code.
Machine code	A set of computer programming instructions that the computer is capable of recognising directly, without any translation or interpretation. The lowest level language available.
Machine language	A programming language that can be used directly by a microprocessor. Often used interchangeably with the terms machine code or assembly language.
Memory-resident	A program which remains in the memory of the computer even after it appears to have finished executing. Device drivers, operating systems, pop-up utilities and many viruses are all examples of memory resident programs.
Nybble	A term applied to a collection of 4 bits. Two Nybbles make a byte.
Octal	Numeric system implying counting and arithmetic performed in base 8. Octal numbers consist of the digits 0 through 7. Once common when dealing with computers, but has now been superseded by hexadecimal.
Partition	A subsection of the disk storage area, set aside for the express use of a single operating system.

Partition record   A special area of the disk that denotes the locations, sizes and usage of the different partitions on a disk.

Pascal   A high-level programming language. Pascal is said to be one of the most structured programming languages available. Can be obtained from several different vendors in forms suitable for the PC.

Physical Sector   The area of disk storage that occurs at the intersection of a track and a disk sector. Physical sectors on PC disks usually contain 512 bytes of data.

Platter   A term used to mean a single disk in a disk drive unit that rotates around a central spindle. A hard disk unit may consist of 2 or more individual platters.

Program   A set of ordered computer instructions that direct the computer to perform a specified task, such as finding the solution to a mathematical problem, or sorting a set of data.

Program file   A disk file that contains a program. In DOS, program files usually have extensions of COM, EXE, BIN, SYS, DRV, OVR, OVL, APP etc.

Programming language   A language used for the preparation and production of computer programs. Pascal, BASIC and C are examples of programming languages.

Register   A simple storage device, built into the CPU, which allows one or two words of data (ie 8 or 16 bits) to be stored and manipulated using machine code instructions.

Root Directory   A special instance of a directory. The root directory forms the base of the hierarchical tree structure that is applied to the directories used on any PC disk. The root directory information is always situated at a known position, and is created when the disk is formatted.

Sector   A term used in conjunction with disk storage. There are three types of sector, Disk sectors, Physical sectors and Logical sectors.

Software   The applications, utilities, routines, procedures and languages that are used in a computer system.

Spindle   The central part of a disk drive that actually rotates the disk. Spindle speed (ie the speed of rotation) of floppy disk drives must lie within specified limits if operation is to be trouble- free.

Stiffy   Jocular term applied to 3.5 inch floppy disks, due to their rigid outer casing.

Subdirectory   Any directory contained within a root directory or another subdirectory. The subdirectory on the level immediately above (ie towards the root) is the Parent, and those subdirectories stemming from the current one are the child directories.

System files   Special instances of program and data files that are placed on the disk by DOS when it is installed. System files contain the majority of the DOS programs, allowing commands to be issued by the user, and implementing the appropriate disk and memory management routines.

Track   The path along which information is stored on a disk. A track is actually a concentric division of the disk surface, and is further divided into sectors.

Utility   A special program that assists in the operation of the computer, often by performing routine tasks.

Vaccine   A special program designed to prevent a virus from operating on a computer. When applied to a disk, the vaccine will search out and attempt to destroy any viruses that it can find.

Virus   A special type of computer program that is designed to attack computer systems. Viruses typically attach themselves to a computer disk or program file and then replicate whenever they are execute. Most viruses are malicious, in that they cause damage to the data stored on the computer. A few are benign, only producing messages on the screen etc.

Winchester   A term used interchangeably with hard disk.

Word   A term used to describe two bytes.

Appendix 2
Acronyms

ALU
Arithmetic and Logic Unit

Part of the CPU that controls simple arithmetic procedures.

ASCII
American Standard Code
for Information
Interchange

Standard text format through which data can be read and transferred from one system to another. Also term used to define the character set.

BIOS
Basic Input Output
System

Program material stored in ROM used to organise the logic of the computer when it is switched on or rebooted.

BIT
Binary digIT

Smallest unit of computer storage. Can have a value of zero or one.

BPB
BIOS Parameter Block

An area of the disk that stores technical information relating to the logical dimensions of the media and its method of storage allocation.

CAD
Computer Aided Design

A generic term applied to computer systems that assist designers, engineers and developers in the planning, design and development on new products. CAD systems are most often orientated towards engineering, mechanical, electrical, electronic, or architectural design applications.

CHKDSK
Check Disk

A DOS utility that reports on the amount of disk and memory usage and performs simple data recovery.

CP/M
Control Program for Micros

An operating system developed around the same time as the original MS-DOS.

CRC
Cyclic Redundancy Check

Check performed on a storage device or communication circuit to detect errors.

CUI
Character User Interface

Method using the keyboard and characters to enter information into a computer (see GUI).

DAM
Data Address Mark

Number written to disk at the start of every sector to record various location information such as the sector ID.

DD
Double Density

Term to describe the amount of data that can be stored on a floppy disk.

DDD
Dysan Diagnostic Disk

Special disk supplied by disk manufacturer Dysan which is capable of performing a range of specialist diagnostic routines on floppy disks.

DMA
Direct Memory Access

Part of the motherboard that allows data to be transferred from the disk to RAM without having to pass through the CPU.

DOS
Disk Operating System

Term to describe programs that maintain overall control of the operation of the computer system, and in particular all operations associated with the disk drives. The term DOS is also used to refer specifically to Microsoft's disk operating system (MS-DOS) or its derivatives.

DTP
DeskTop Publishing

Systems that provide a typesetting ability for personal computers. DTP systems are able to produce very high quality output, but generally require very high specification systems.

EBCDIC
Extended Binary Coded
Decimal Interchange Code

IBM standard for data storage on disk. Not directly compatible with ASCII.

EEMS
Enhanced Expanded
Memory System

Later versions of expanded memory management utilities such as LIM Spec 4.0 and later.

EMM
Expanded Memory
Manager

General term to describe expanded memory management utilities.

EMS
Expanded Memory
System

Alternative term to describe expanded memory management utilities.

EOF
End Of File

Most files have and end of file marker or flag and this will often be seen in the program or on the disk as EOF.

ESDI
Enhanced Small Device
Interface

A modern disk drive technology popular with large capacity drives. Competes with SCSI.

FAT
File Allocation Table

Area of disk which retains information as to where different clusters of a file are located.

FM
Frequency Modulation

Refers to the way in which information is physically stored on the surface of a disk. FM refers to single density disks - usually floppy and not seen much today..

GB
Gigabyte

One thousand megabytes.

GUI
Graphical User Interface

The use of windows and mice to control the use of information on the screen. Much more graphically oriented than character oriented.

LLS
Large Logical Sectors

Facility supplied by some versions of DOS whereby a logical sector can be several time larger than the physical sector. This primarily allows disks in excess of 32Mbytes to be addressed.

LSD
Least Significant Digit

Right most digit when counting in binary, hexadecimal or decimal.

LSN
Logical Sector Number

Each logical sector is numbered, commencing at the beginning of the partition with LSN 0 and increasing thereafter.

MB
Megabyte

One million bytes.

Mb
Megabit

One million bits.

MBR
Master Boot Record

Another name for the partition record.

MFM
Modified Frequency
Modulation

Improved method of storing data on a disk from FM. Refers to double density disks - may be floppy or hard.

MHz
Megahertz

One million cycles per second

ms
Milliseconds

Millionth of a second

MSD
Most Significant Digit

Left most digit when counting in binary, hexadecimal or decimal.

ns
nanosecond

One billionth of a second

PSN
Physical Sector Number

Value referring to the number of each physical sector. Numbering begins at 0 on head 0, cylinder 0, disk sector 1 and continues for all the physical sectors on the disk.

QIC
Quarter Inch Cartridge

Form of backup media, a little larger than music cassette tape.

RLL
Run Length Limited

Type of disk drive interface technology. Competes with MFM.

SCSI
Small Computer Systems
Interface

Modern type of disk drive interface technology, popular with large capacity disk drives. Competes with ESDI. Recently adopted by IBM for the PS/2 range.

TPI
Tracks Per Inch

Number of tracks that will fit onto a disk in one inch of radius. Normally only used with reference to floppy disks.

WIMPS
Windows Icons Mice and
Pull-down Screens

Term used to describe the GUI working environment.

WORM
Write Once Read Many

Term used to describe laser disk technology which allows data to be written to disk once only, but it may be read many times.

Appendix 3
Bibliography and Reading List

Angermeyer J, Fahringer R, Jaeger K, Shafer D, *The Waite Group's Tricks of the MS-DOS Masters*, Howard W Sams, 1988

Brenner R C, *IBM PC Advanced Troubleshooting and Repair*, Howard W Sams, 1988

Cloke B, Run-Length-Limited Coding Increases Disk-Drive Capacity, *EDN*, Cahners Publishing, March 1987

Goldthorpe P, Disk Access, *PC Plus*, June/July 1990

Hordeski, M F, *The Illustrated Dictionary of Microcomputers, 3rd Edition*, TAB Books, 1990

Norton P, *The Peter Norton Programmers Guide to the IBM PC*, Microsoft Press, 1985

Nugus S, Harris S, Remenyi D, *Frontline Troubleshooting for PC Users*, NCC-Blackwell, July 1991

Penfold R A, *How to Expand, Modernise and Repair PCs and Compatibles*, Bernard Babani, April 1990

Simrin S, *The Waite Group's MS-DOS Bible, 3rd Edition*, Howard W Sams, 1989

Sheperd S, Digging Deep into Disks!, *.EXE Magazine*, Process Communications, June 1991

Solomon A, A 1600bpi Tape Drive for the PC, *.EXE Magazine*, Process Communications, December 1988

Solomon A, The Lotus Worksheet Format, *.EXE Magazine*, Process Communications, January 1988

Somerson P, *PC Magazine DOS Power Tools, 2nd Edition*, Bantam Books, June 1990

Personal Computer XT System Technical Reference, IBM, 1983

Appendix 4
Interrupt Calls

This appendix details the values and parameters that are specified for interrupt calls dealing with appropriate features. Whilst many of these interrupts can be called directly from programming languages such as Pascal and C, some are more restrictive and must be called only from a machine language program. Many advanced DOS manuals and programmers reference guides provide further information on the interrupts that can be used. It is essential to ensure that the syntax and operation of the interrupt is fully understood before it is called, as they provide a very low level access to the PC facilities, bypassing the safety net DOS offers.

INTERRUPT 13H - BIOS DISK ACCESS CALLS

Function 00h: Reset Disk System

To Call:

AH= 00h

AL= drive number
    00-7Fh Floppy disk
    80-FFh Fixed disk

Returns

CF= 0 no error
    1 error

AH= error code (see Interrupt 13h Function 01h below)

Function 01h: Get Disk Status

To call:

AH= 01h

Returns:

AL= Disk status:
    00h no error
    01h invalid command
    02h address mark not found

03h write attempt on write protected disk (F)
04h sector not found
05h reset failed (H)
06h floppy disk removed (F)
07h bad parameter table (H)
08h DMA overflow (F)
09h DMA crossed 64KB boundary
0Ah Bad sector flag (H)
10h data error
11h ECC data error (H)
20h controller failed
40h seek failed
80h time out
AAh drive not ready (H)
CCh write fault (H)
E0h status error (H)
Note: H=fixed disk only, F=floppy disk only

Function 02h: Read Disk Sectors
Function 03h: Write Disk Sectors
Function 04h: Verify Disk Sectors
Function 05h: Format Disk Track

To call:

AH=02h read disk sectors
03h write disk sectors
04h verify disk sectors
05h format disk track

AL= number of sectors
CH= cylinder number
CL= sector number (unused if AH=05h)
DH= head number
DL= drive number
ES:BX= buffer address (unused if AH=04h)

Returns:

CF= 0 no error
1 error

AH= error code (see Interrupt 13h Function 01h)

If AH was 05h on call then
ES:BX= 4-byte address field entries, 1 per sector
byte 0 cylinder number
byte 1 head number
byte 2 sector number
byte 3 sector size code: 00h 128 bytes per sector
01h 256 bytes per sector
02h 512 bytes per sector (standard)
03h 1024 bytes per sector

Function 08h: Get Current Drive Parameters

To call:

AH= 08h

DL= drive number

Returns:

AX= 00h

BH= 00h

BL= drive type

CH= low order 8 bits of 10-bit maximum number of cylinders

CL= bits 7 & 6: high order 2 bits of 10-bit maximum number of cylinders
bits 5 - 0: maximum number of sectors/track

DH= maximum head number

DL= number of drives installed

ES:DI= address of floppy disk drive parameter table

Function 09h: Initialise Hard Disk Parameter Table

To call:

AH= 09h

Returns:

Nothing

Function 0Ah: Read Long

Reads 512-byte sector plus 4 byte ECC code

To call:

See Interrupt 13h Function 02h

Returns:

See Interrupt 13h Function 02h

Function 0Bh: Write Long

Writes 512-byte sector plus 4 byte ECC code

To call:

See Interrupt 13h Function 03h

Returns:

See Interrupt 13h Function 03h

Function 0Ch: Seek to Head

Positions head buts does not transfer data

To call:

See Interrupt 13h Function 02h and 03h

Returns:

See Interrupt 13h Function 02h and 03h

Function 0Dh: Alternate Disk Reset

To call:

AH= 0Dh

DL= drive number

Returns:

Nothing

Function 10h: Test for Drive Ready

To call:

AH= 10h

DL= drive number

Returns:

AH= status

Function 11h: Recalibrate Drive

To call:

AH= 11h

DL= drive number

Returns:

AH= status

Function 14h: Controller Diagnostic

To call:

AH= 14h

Returns:

AH= status

Function 15h: Get Disk Type

To call:

AH= 15h

DL= drive number

Returns:

AH= drive type code:
    00h No drive present
    01h cannot sense when floppy disk is changed
    02h can sense when floppy disk is changed
    03h fixed disk

If AH=03h
    CX:DX= number of sectors

Function 16h: Check for Change of Floppy Disk Status

To call:

AH= 16h
DL= drive number to check

Returns:

AH=00h no change
    06h floppy disk change

Function 17h: Set Disk Type

To call:

AH= 17h

DL= drive number

AL= floppy disk type code

Returns:

Nothing

USING THE INTERRUPT ROUTINES

The above listings of interrupts and parameters may seem confusing to many users, even those who are familiar with other programming terms. Therefore a simple Turbo Pascal routine has been listed below to illustrate how easily the interrupts can be used in any program.

The routine illustrates the use of the BIOS Int 13h interrupt, using function 02h, *read a sector*. Note that this returns a true disk sector of 512 bytes, and does not necessarily work for system using LLSs. The routine has been implemented as a function, and will return a value of true if it is successful, or false if it fails.

```pascal
program READ_SECTOR;

{first of all some global definitions}
type  Registers = record
                    case integer of
                        0: (AX,BX,CX,DX,BP,SI,DI,DS,ES,FLAGS:word);
                        1: (AL,AH,BL,BH,CL,CH,DL,DH:byte);
                    end;

var BIOS_ERROR:byte;
    DATA:array[0..511] of byte; {This is a buffer to hold a sector}
    COUNTER:integer;

function BIOS_READ_SECTOR(DRIVE:byte;CY,HD,SE:integer):boolean;
var REG:registers;
begin {BIOS_READ_SECTOR}
   {Load parameters into registers}
   { specify op code for Read operation                        }
   REG.AH:=$02;
   { specify BIOS drive address                                }
   REG.DL:=DRIVE;

   {Specify physical disk address}
   REG.DH:=HD;
   { If the cylinder value exceeds 255, the extra two bits are }
   { combined with sector value and loaded to REG.CL           }
   { Overall cylinder number cannot exceed 1023                }
   REG.CH:=lo(CY);
   REG.CL:=SE+(hi(CY) shl 6);

   {Specify amount to read, in this case 1 sector}
   REG.AL:=1;
   {Specify where it is to be sent to}
   REG.ES:=seg(DATA);
   REG.DI:=ofs(DATA);

   {Call the Interrupt}
   intr($13,REG);

   {Get the error code, if there is one}
   BIOS_ERROR:=REG.AH;
   {Set the function value}
   BIOS_READ_SECTOR:=((REG.FLAGS and 1)=0);
end; {BIOS_READ_SECTOR}
```

```
begin {READ_SECTOR}

    {Can then use the function to read a disk sector}
    {For example, to read the partition record at PSN 0}
    {Choose Drive=80, Cylinder=0, Head=0, Sector=1)

    if BIOS_READ_SECTOR(80,0,0,1) then
        for COUNTER:=0 to 511 do
            write(DATA[COUNTER]:4);

end. {READ_SECTOR}
```

Appendix 5
File Formats

In many data recovery situations it is useful to know the format in which a data file has been saved to disk. This is especially so with packages such as spreadsheets, databases and accounting systems that do not necessarily follow any defined standards.

However, there are many different file formats, as almost every application package uses its own unique style, and so it is impossible to give a comprehensive list in these appendices. Therefore an overview of some of the most common file formats is provided, together with a detailed listing of the format employed by Lotus 1-2-3 worksheets, one of the most common victims of data loss.

Readers who require further listings of this form should examine two textbooks, both by Geoff Waldren, which are available:

File Formats for Popular PC Programs

More File Formats for Popular Programs

Whilst in the majority of cases these books are accurate, there are some instances in which the file formats have been found to be wrong, mainly due to the application having been upgraded since the book was published.

WORDSTAR

WordStar files are primarily ASCII in appearance, although it is often found that the last character of every word is garbled. This is due to the fact that WordStar will set the high bit of the last character of every word, primarily for its own use in justifying text etc.

The first 128 bytes of the WordStar file contain a variety of special information, including all of the defaults, the printer name etc. Much of this area will often be unused, and so will consist of 00h entries.

The remainder of the file consists of the actual document entered by the user, together with any special codes and controls that were entered. Line ends are specified by an 0Dh code, whilst hard returns (Line breaks) will be noted with an 0Ah 0Dh sequence.

At the end of the document WordStar pads the file to the nearest 256 byte division with end-of-file markers, for which it uses a value of 1Ah.

WordStar files are among the easiest of all to decode as they apply little or not formatting control to the actual text when it is stored on disk. This makes the task of recovering a damaged WordStar file much simpler, as it is usually possible to read to the end of a sector and then attempt to find the next piece of matching text by examination.

Some other word processors are not as simple as this, and one in particular, DisplayWrite 4, makes it virtually impossible for satisfactory recovery of damaged information to be achieved.

DBASE

dBase files store collections of database records, and are actually very simple to interpret.

The first 32 bytes of data contain various pieces of information such as defaults, sizes, number of fields etc.

Following this is a series of 32 byte records detailing the structure of the database. The first section indicates the name of the field, with subsequent values indicating field size, type, decimal points etc. Any unused bytes in these records are padded with 00h values.

After all of the fields have been defined there is a special byte inserted to denote that the actual data is about to start. This value is 0Dh.

The data records then follow, each being of exactly the same length. This length is determined by adding the lengths of each individual field in the database. Each record is preceded by a value of 20h, and thus the records are spaced at intervals of (LENGTH+1). It can be seen that this spacing is the same as the overall size of each record, as indicated by dBase when the structure is examined. Any unused bytes within a record are padded with values of 20h.

After the last record has been stored a value of 1Ah is written to denote the end of the file. There may be one or more blank records after the 1Ah value, depending on how the database has been handled and managed. These blank records are of no significance and can be safely discarded.

USING THIS KNOWLEDGE

Whilst the above information is insufficient to allow a user to create a data file from scratch, it is enough to allow parts of a data file to be recognised and, if necessary, reconstructed.

In some cases it will be found that the header or system information has been destroyed, and that even after the remainder of the file has been reconstructed the application will not recognise the data. In such situations the best approach is to convert as much of the actual data as possible into a common format such as ASCII. This can then be imported or translated so that the application can access the data. In the very worst case it will be necessary to re-enter the data manually, but even then the provision of an ASCII listing of the original values will be a great help.

THE LOTUS WORKSHEET FORMAT

The format employed by Lotus for storing worksheet data on disk is one of the more sophisticated schemes used by an application program. However, due to the number of Lotus users it is inevitable that there will at times be data disasters in which knowledge of the worksheet format is of great assistance. Unfortunately Lotus refused to issue this information for a long time, and even now there are only relatively few programmers, consultants and users who have a good knowledge of the format used.

The data format used by Lotus has remained fundamentally the same since the very first release. However, more recent versions have enhanced the flexibility of the format in order to handle the more advanced features that are provided. As most of these features deal with such non-critical things as printer settings, graph settings etc, they are not expressly documented below. If required, Lotus should be able to provide fuller details of each individual format.

One exception to this is the format employed by 1-2-3 Release 3. As the data is multi-dimensional, the standard file format is not suitable. However, the basic structure of the scheme is still the same, although obviously cell addresses etc will be quite different.

RECORDS

1-2-3 and Symphony use essentially the same format, in which a data file consists of a stream of individual records. Each of these records is of variable length, and so must be read sequentially.

Each record starts with a two byte integer, known as RTYPE, which determines what the record represents. The next value specifies how many bytes follow, and thus effectively denotes the length of the remainder of the record. This second value is known as RBYTES. Note that each of these values is stored in little endian format, to make things simpler for the program to interpret.

The first record is a special one, known as the start of worksheet record. It appears as

002044

RTYPE is zero, RBYTES is 2, and the 4 4 represents the version number of the spreadsheet that created the file. 4 4 represents 1-2-3 version 1A, which can be interpreted by any other release of 1-2-3 or Symphony. 1-2-3 version 2 is noted as 6 4 and Symphony is 5 4.

The last record in the file is the end of worksheet record, and contains the values

1000

ie RTYPE is 1 and RBYTES is 0 as there are no further values. Some versions of 1-2-3 and Symphony also place a 1Ah value after this record for good luck, although it is not really necessary.

Between these two special records are all of the data records that are used to store the information contained in the spreadsheet. This can be divided into two main areas:

Firstly there is a lengthy prologue detailing things such as cursor position, column widths, graph settings, named graphs, print settings etc. Whilst these records may be interesting to some, they are not really important from a data recovery point of view.

After the prologue comes the rest of the data, notably the cell contents. They are most often stored in a natural order with cell A1 first then B1, C1, D1 ...A2, B2, C2 etc. However this needn't be the case as Lotus does not rely on any order when interpreting the data.

The most commonly encountered records are listed below. These are the records that are of most interest from a data recovery point of view as they contain the important data entered by the user.

All of these records include some reference to column and row addresses, and it is important to consider how these are encoded before proceeding.

- Column addresses are encoded as a value one less than the column letter of the cell. Thus A is coded as 0, B as 1, Z as 25, AA as 26 and IV as 255.
- Row addresses are encoded as a value one less than the row number of the cell. Thus row 1 is coded as 0, row 2 is coded as 1, row 3 as 2, and row 8192 as 8191.
- Both the row and column addresses are encoded into 16-bit values, using little endian format.

THE DATA RECORDS

RTYPE 11

This record represents a named range, and will appear as

11 0 24 0 ASCIIZ STARTCOL STARTROW ENDCOL ENDROW

ASCIIZ is a null-terminated ASCII string that is padded with nulls to 16 bytes.

STARTCOL, STARTROW, ENDCOL and ENDROW denote the starting and ending row and column addresses of the range, and are encoded as shown above

RTYPE 12

This record represents an empty cell, and is required in the case of cells that contain no data but which have been formatted in some way. The record will appear as:

12 0 5 0 COL ROW FORMAT

COL and ROW are the column and row addresses, and FORMAT is a single byte that denotes the format status of the cell. The coding for this cell is somewhat complex, but is of little interest in terms of data recovery.

RTYPE 13

This record represents an integer value. The record will appear as:

13 0 7 0 FORMAT COL ROW VALUE

FORMAT, COL and ROW are the same as for the previous records, and VALUE stores the value of the integer. VALUE is a two byte value, and so can store values between -32768 and +32767. Values outside of this range must be stored as reals.

RTYPE 14

This record represents a real value, ie one containing decimal places or one that exceeds the boundaries of the previously defined integer. The record will appear as:

14 0 13 0 FORMAT COL ROW REALVALUE

The only difference between the Real and Integer values is that REALVALUE is an 8-byte data structure, known as an IEEE real. The encoding of an IEEE real is quite sophisticated, and is unfortunately not supported by many programming languages.

There are two special values that can be specified for Reals. Values of 0 0 0 0 0 0 240 255 represents an NA entry, and 0 0 0 0 0 0 240 127 represents the code for ERR.

RTYPE 15

This record represents a label entry, and follows much the same format as for the other cell records:

15 0 LENGTH FORMAT COL ROW LABEL

LENGTH, FORMAT, COL and ROW are used in the same way as before, and LABEL holds the actual text of the data. The last byte of LABEL will always be a 00h to denote the end of the label, although this is actually redundant as the length of the label is given by the LENGTH value.

RTYPE 16

This represents a formula, the most sophisticated record structure that is used in the Lotus format. The length of a type 16 record can be absolutely anything, depending on the complexity of the formula.

The first five bytes of the record are the Format, Column and Row as before, and the next eight bytes show the value that the formula last evaluated to (note that this is not necessarily up to date). Next comes an integer which gives the length of the formula, and then the actual formula follows. The formula is written in a special mathematic form known as Reverse Polish Notation, and is notoriously difficult to decode.

OTHER CODES

There are a number of other RTYPE codes that deal with features such as graphs, default settings, windows, print settings etc, and indeed more are added with every new release of 1-2-3. From a data recovery point of view it is unnecessary to know the detail of these records as they contain non-critical data. What is important is to know the size of the record, and hence where the next one in the sequence begins. As all of the records follow a common format, with the length being specified as the third and fourth bytes, this is made very easy and hence most possible problems in this area can be overcome.

In situations in which a spreadsheet file has been seriously corrupted, it may be best to only extract those records containing valid data rather than attempt to reconstruct the entire file. If this approach is taken then it will be necessary to use a utility such as DEBUG to bring the separate sections of the worksheet file together. Once all of the data has been coagulated, remember to add start of worksheet and end of worksheet records if they are not already in place.

Appendix 6
Product Details

Throughout this book many products have been mentioned, discussed and illustrated. The following list provides details of the manufacturers of these systems, and it is suggested that users wishing to purchase any product contact the manufacturer to obtain details of local vendors/suppliers.

DATA RECOVERY SERVICE

TechTrans Data Recovery Service
General purpose data recovery service offered on a no-fix, no-fee basis.

> TechTrans Ltd
> Curtis Farm
> Kidmore End
> Nr Reading
> RG4 9AY
> UNITED KINGDOM
> Tel: (0734) 724148

DISK UTILITIES

The Norton Utilities
The standard by which all utility suites tend to be measured. Offers a very wide range of disk editing and data recovery facilities.

> Symantec Corporation
> 10201 Torre Avenue
> Cupertino
> CA 95014
> USA
> Tel: 1-800-441-7234

> Symantec (UK) Ltd
> MKA House
> 36 King Street
> Maidenhead
> Berkshire
> SL6 1EF
> United Kingdom
> Tel: (0628) 776343

PCTools

Similar in approach to the Norton Utilities, although it offers more in the way of disk management facilities. However, provides less flexibility for detailed, low level disk editing.

Central Point Software Inc   CPS Europe Ltd
15220 N.W. Greenbrier Pkwy #200   Cardinal Point
Beaverton   Newall Road
OR 97006   Heathrow
USA   TW6 2EX
Tel: (503) 690-8090   United Kingdom

HCS Utilities

Specialised utilities for low level disk manipulation and testing. HCS also offer custom utilities designed for particular requirements.

HCS
37 Challis Place
Bracknell
Berkshire
RG12 1FT
United Kingdom
Tel: (0344) 868167

Disk Explorer

Unique in its ability to correctly diagnose disk problems. Whilst it is somewhat limited in terms of compatibility with hardware, an updated version is promised for release in early 1992.

Quaid Software Ltd
45 Charles St East
Third Floor Dept 734
Toronto
Ontario
M4Y 1S2
Canada
Tel: (416) 961-8243

TestDrive

A unique product that can successfully diagnose problems with floppy disk drives. It is actually available as shareware from many different sources, and all registrations should be sent to:

MicroSystems Development
4100 Moorpark Avenue #104
San Jose
CA 95117
USA
Tel: (408) 296-4000

CopyIIPC

Probably the most versatile disk copying program available. It is updated on a quarterly basis.

Central Point Software Inc
15220 N.W. Greenbrier Pkwy #200
Beaverton
OR 97006
USA
Tel: (503) 690-8090

CPS Europe Ltd
Cardinal Point, Newall Road
Heathrow
TW6 2EX
United Kingdom
Tel: (081) 848 1414

CopyWrite

Very popular disk copying program from Quaid Software. It can copy some disks that CopyIIPC does not recognise.

Quaid Software Ltd
45 Charles St East
Third Floor Dept 734
Toronto
Ontario
M4Y 1S2
Canada
Tel: (416) 961-8243

OTHER UTILITIES/SOFTWARE

Shareware Marketing

High quality shareware distributors. Extremely varied catalogue of programs including many utilities, applications and programming languages.

Shareware Marketing
3A Queen Street
Seaton
Devon
EX12 2NY
United Kingdom
Tel: (0297) 24088

DOS

Every machine should have its own copy of DOS, which may be MS-DOS from Microsoft, PC-DOS from IBM, or a licensed version of DOS from the manufacturer of the system. Microsoft now offer a full upgrade for DOS version 5.

Microsoft Corporation
16011 NE 36th Way
Box 97017
Redmond
WA 98073-9717
USA
Tel: (206) 882-8080

Microsoft Ltd
Freepost
Reading
RG1 1BR
United Kingdom
Tel: (0734) 500741

Turbo Pascal

Turbo Pascal is provided by Borland, and is available in DOS or Windows versions. Borland also provide other programming environments such as C and BASIC.

Borland International Inc.
1800 Green Hills Road
PO Box 660001
Scotts Valley
CA 95067-0001
USA
Tel: (408) 438-5300

Borland International (UK) Ltd
8 Pavilions
Ruscombe Business Park
Twyford
Berkshire
RG10 9NN
United Kingdom
Tel: (0734) 320022

Microsoft C

Microsoft produce programming environments for C, Pascal and Basic.

Microsoft Corporation
16011 NE 36th Way
Box 97017
Redmond
WA 98073-9717
USA
Tel: (206) 882-8080

Microsoft Ltd
Freepost
Reading
RG1 1BR
United Kingdom
Tel: (0734) 500741

Dr Solomon's Anti-Virus Toolkit

This has become one of the industry standards for anti-virus software. A comprehensive upgrade policy ensures that the product is kept up-to-date with virus developments.

S&S International Ltd
Weylands Court
Water Meadow
Chesham
Bucks.
HP5 1LP
United Kingdom
Tel: (0494) 791900

Norton Anti Virus

A comprehensive anti-virus package released by Symantec. Has proved to be extremely accurate in identifying and removing many viruses.

Symantec Corporation
10201 Torre Avenue
Cupertino
CA 95014
USA
Tel: 1-800-441-7234

Symantec (UK) Ltd
MKA House
36 King Street
Maidenhead
Berkshire
SL6 1EF
United Kingdom
Tel: (0628) 776343

SECURITY PRODUCTS/SERVICES

Policeman

Sophisticated hardware/software security systems for personal computers.

> Plus 5 Engineering Ltd
> April Court
> Millbrook
> Crowborough
> East Sussex
> TN6 3JZ
> Tel: (0892) 663211

FAST

Organisation offering help and advice to companies who wish to combat software theft, and ensure that they are meeting the licensing requirements of the software they use.

> FAST
> 2 Lake End Court
> Taplow
> Maidenhead
> Berkshire
> SL6 0JQ
> United Kingdom
> Tel: (0628) 660377

Index